*Writing Early American History*

ALSO BY ALAN TAYLOR

*Liberty Men and Great Proprietors: The Revolutionary Settlement on the Maine Frontier, 1760–1820* (1990)

*William Cooper's Town: Power and Persuasion on the Frontier of the Early American Republic* (1995)

*American Colonies: The Settling of North America* (2001)

# *Writing Early American History*

ALAN TAYLOR

PENN

University of Pennsylvania Press
Philadelphia

Printed in the United States of America on acid-free paper

10 9 8 7 6 5 4 3 2 1

Published by
University of Pennsylvania Press
Philadelphia, Pennsylvania 19104–4112

Library of Congress Cataloging-in-Publication Data

Taylor, Alan, 1955–
Writing early American history / Alan Taylor.
p. cm.
Includes bibliographical references and index.
ISBN 0-8122-3883-4 (cloth alk. paper)
1. United States—History—Colonial period, ca. 1600–1775—Historiography. 2. United States—History—Revolution, 1775–1783—Historiography. 3. Books—United States—Reviews. 4. Historians—United States. 5. Historiography—United States. I. Title.

E188.T357 2005
973.2'072—dc22

2004063818

*For Harold B. Raymond*
*and*
*in memory of*
*Marvin Meyers*

# Contents

## Part III. Empire



## Part IV. Founders



## Part V. Historians

# Foreword

Alan Taylor is one of today's leading historians of early America. In assembling this collection of essays, published since 1996 in *The New Republic,* the University of Pennsylvania Press is making accessible some of the best short writing available on the history of the United States and its antecedents up to 1840. Trained in the 1980s, just as Americanists had turned toward the "New Social History," Alan Taylor is among the first of his generation to achieve the kind of public recognition for writing in his field that has long been accorded to senior scholars such as Edmund Morgan, Gordon Wood, and Joyce Appleby. Taken separately, each essay in this volume offers a trenchant and entertaining insight into the ways historians work. Taken together, the essays provide readers with a lucid and informative commentary on early American history and on recent developments in the ways it can be interpreted.

Although Taylor by no means claims to have provided a thorough survey of recent works in the field, these essays add up to an enticing and insightful introduction to early American history for students, scholars, and general readers alike. From the first English efforts to settle on the eastern seaboard of North America in the late sixteenth century to the political career of DeWitt Clinton and the murder of the prostitute Helen Jewett in New York in the early nineteenth century, the topics covered here range from the conventional to the unfamiliar and from the first encounters of natives and colonizers to the social ills of "civilized" society. Alan Taylor writes about each of them with verve and purpose. Whoever reads these essays—whether he or she follows the book from cover to cover or dips into chapters at random—will find the rich abundance and variety of early American scholarship set out before him or her. Readers new to the field will grasp a sense of its expansiveness and possibilities, but seasoned scholars, too, will find a feast of insights and possibilities that will engage, provoke, and inspire.

Among his colleagues and students, Alan Taylor has earned a formidable reputation for his wide knowledge, lucid prose, adeptness at analytical explanation, and eye for a good story. All these talents are on display here. These essays are book reviews, and so belong to the most common, but also the most uneven, kind of writing in any scholarly field. From bookstore Web sites and short-paper assignments in courses to library journals and the slew of scholarly periodicals, book reviewing is the most routine and often the least regarded form of writing about history. Yet, at its best, reviewing has long enjoyed a high literary reputation, and the offerings here enable us to enjoy the commentaries of a gifted historian at the height of his powers. Although Alan Taylor is modest to a fault about what he brings to the task of reviewing, these essays mark a standard for literary commentary in American history. Both as exemplars of critical scholarly writing and as a showcase for attracting a wider readership, they provide a true service to the profession that the field of early American historians is fortunate to have.

Judging by these contributions, being reviewed by Alan Taylor must be an invigorating experience. His commentary is incisive, both about the topics covered and about individual historians' approaches. Yet whether he is bestowing praise or doling out criticism, he always provides a fair-minded and intellectually consistent rationale for his treatment. Among the virtues of his approach is that he is evidently prepared to offer either: if you are reviewed by Taylor, you know that your shortcomings will be exposed, but if you write a book that he thinks is good, he will say so. Part of the interest of this collection for the reader is that it is rarely predictable at the outset of any review what the verdict is going to be. The suspense commands engagement, but also reflects the fact that Taylor does not employ a standard formula for reviewing, and this helps give these essays their richness of style and tone.

If these essays are read as they are, in part, intended—as a commentary on the current state of early American history—they do, on the face of it, contain a big gap: Alan Taylor's own books are missing. His impact on the conduct of early American history over the past two decades has been considerable. Both from the examples of his writing and his inspiration of cohorts of undergraduate and graduate students, he has begun to have a measurable influence on the ways people look at the field. Few historians of his generation have matched the quality and quantity of writing that he has accomplished. In little more than a decade, he published three books of expanding range and scope, an impressive body of article-length works, and numerous essays, of which those published here are a sample.

One overarching theme in his writing has been Americans' encounters with their own continent and with the appropriation and settlement of what is still usually called the "frontier." Superficially, this would seem to be a hackneyed and overworked subject, and, indeed, many of the first cohort of "new" social historians of the 1960s and the 1970s did turn their backs on it to explore other themes. Characteristically, Alan Taylor embraced it, approached it from new directions, dug countless new insights out of the archives, and has done perhaps more than any other single early Americanist to revivify and redefine it. His three books reflect the unfolding of striking new perspectives on a familiar theme, perspectives that parallel many of those in the wider field reflected in this volume.

The first book, *Liberty Men and Great Proprietors*, published in 1990, concerns an "eastern" location for a settlement process always popularly associated with the "West." Maine in the eighteenth and early nineteenth centuries was a focus for land settlement and migration from southern New England that prefigured the better-known westward movement. In Taylor's adept hands, it also becomes the locus for a long, bitter, and almost-forgotten struggle between proprietors who claimed title to vast tracts of land and settlers who established farms and habitations on these lands. Drawing on a wealth of overlooked archival material, Taylor traces this struggle, with its political and sometimes violent ramifications, and sets it in the context of the broader accomplishments of the revolutionary era.

Turning from Maine to the Northeast's first "western" frontier, he brings us to the heart of developments underlying some of nineteenth-century America's most evocative writing. Using the papers of the Cooper family, especially those of William Cooper, father of James Fenimore and founder of Cooperstown, New York, Taylor skillfully constructs an account of the social and political developments that gave rise to the *Leatherstocking Tales*, to James Fenimore Cooper's most famous characters, and to the posturings and anxieties that his novels describe and evoke. For the power and richness of this, his second book, *William Cooper's Town* (1995), Taylor was showered with critical acclaim and awards, including the Pulitzer Prize in history.

Both books are marked by the liveliness of Alan Taylor's narratives of human endeavor and human folly, elements that are very much in evidence in the essays collected here. But they have other characteristics, too, that point the way to the further development of his distinctive perspectives on early American history. Each book is firmly rooted in a locality—central Maine, in the one case, Otsego County, New York, in the other—which enables him to use records of specific events and processes to illustrate broader historical themes. In the best tradition of the new social history, he uses such instances to explore big problems. He also breaches the too-common distinction between social and political history: among Taylor's noteworthy contributions to his field has been his success at casting conventional political history in a wider social context and, by the same token, demonstrating the political dimensions of social processes and conflicts. So in no respect are these locally based studies "local histories" in the narrow sense.

Taylor's growing understanding of the complex issues at work in early American development, however, led him toward an altogether wider canvas for his third book. Conceived as a synthetic account of the colonial period, *American Colonies* (2001) becomes in his hands the broadest discussion we have yet of early American history in its continent-wide context. Most conventional studies trace how thirteen colonies founded mainly by the English progressed toward a successful bid for independence as the new United States. Taylor provides a sweeping history of the North American continent; its adjacent oceans and islands; its arrays of indigenous, settler, and enslaved peoples; and its subjection between the fifteenth and the nineteenth centuries to a succession of imperial ventures—Spanish, Dutch, French, and Russian, as well as English and, ultimately, American, also. In this view, the American Revolution becomes not the inevitable culmination of political and social maturity, but a sharp breach in a pattern of empire building and international competition that set part of the North American continent on a distinctive new path.

Even though Alan Taylor's own books are absent from this collection of essays, we still benefit handsomely from the insights that his distinctive and broadening range of perspectives on the North American past has given him. Many of these reviews were written while *American Colonies* was in preparation, and we can detect the influence of that project and of its critical reception on the comments he makes about other historians' work. From this and his earlier research, several key themes stand out as hallmarks of Taylor's interpretations of early American history. His continent-wide approach informs his commentaries on environmental history and on the history of disease, as well as those on political decision-making. His alertness to the diversity and conflict-ridden nature of early American society provides fresh insights into conventional topics and also lends them a pronounced degree of humane sympathy with men and women caught up in circumstances not of their own making. And while he is aware of the singularity of particular stories and patterns, he has become a trenchant critic of the more provincial forms of American exceptionalism, insisting that the continent's story, and that of the United States that grew up on it, be understood in broader comparative and international perspectives.

Although the books reviewed in these essays tend to avoid some traditional subjects, such as high politics, constitutional law, or military history, in fact, politics, law, and war are very much part of Alan Taylor's understanding of early America. He is interested in how societies worked and how individuals, systems, or structures influenced or revealed each other. He is also very alert to the ways in which the passage of time and events helped generate perspectives on the more distant past, to create myths whose effects can so often do more to blur than to illuminate our understanding. Stripping away these myths and categories of thought to construct new ways of seeing early American history has been one of the hallmarks of Taylor's published writings, and his critical faculties in this regard are very much in evidence in the essays collected here. For example, the attention he gives to biographical works about some famous Americans and, in particular, to the recent revival of popular interest in the Founders, provides him with the opportunity to set these traditional subjects in the light generated by recent research. Readers will learn things from Taylor's remarks that are not readily available from the biographies themselves.

Together, these essays provide a fact-filled, lively, entertaining, and thought-provoking prelude to the vast array of riches now to be found in early American history. Alan Taylor offers sympathetic, but astutely critical, observations on the works of some of the best American historians now writing, and a few who are perhaps not so good. What we all have to learn as we read his essays are his own high standards in appraising works about the past. He is a keen observer of historical context and holds other historians to account for doing the same. He suggests that historical evidence, carefully and thoughtfully deployed, has an integrity that can be conveyed in historical writing. He is most admiring of other scholars who employ a range of sources, intelligently used, and who are frank about what those sources can and cannot tell us. He accepts speculative judgments, as long as they are presented honestly for what they are and do not get used as (spurious) foundations for further argument. He prefers writing that has a clear sense of direction or line of argument to works that, in conformity with some (post)modern fashions, eschew either. Yet he is clear-sighted about the limitations of such writing if it achieves its internal consistency by ignoring contexts or being overselective. Indeed, in judging the merits of an approach, context is everything: if other evidence exists, then relying on a single source or set of texts is not good enough. But drawing evidence in small chunks from a wide range of sources is also unsatisfactory if the pattern that results is wholly the historian's invention. Good history, in Taylor's book (as in Taylor's other books), must make room for the perspectives of the men and the women whose stories are being told: there must be some indication that the argument being advanced might have made sense to people in the past.

These essays do not chronicle the new early American history systematically, but they do reflect some of the extraordinary range and diversity of recent developments in the field. Both in his own archive-based research and writing and in these illuminating discussions, Alan Taylor has been in the thick of the effort to reshape and redefine a vital, and vitally exciting, historical field. Here, he shows us a good deal about how that has been done.

*Christopher Clark*

# Introduction

I vividly recall the comments written on my essays in graduate school by my professor and mentor Marvin Meyers. "Premature Ascent to Sagehood," he entered beside one of my especially naive attempts to criticize a book by an accomplished historian. Another time, I sloppily applied the adjective "Hobbesian" to damn another scholar's perspective. For this, I reaped from Meyers what I had sowed: "Perhaps you should read some Hobbes first." Like most graduate students, I took a premature pride in my ability to "take a book apart," to demolish its pretensions to quality. My method consisted primarily of applying slogans preached from the New Left as channeled through the so-called New Social History, then the fashion for young historians. In recovery from the Old Left, Meyers had a keen eye for, and a sharp impatience with, any hollow posturing. He expected a scholar to support every point with evidence and to sustain every argument with reasoning. That done, however, he could accept work of many types and politics. He never demanded adherence to his own political views or to his own topics—he just despised sloppy scholarship of any stripe.

In graduate school, it struck many of my peers odd that I gravitated to Meyers as my mentor. I hoped to write for a wider audience and to expose injustice in American history by exploring an agrarian resistance movement. Neither of these hopes matched well with Meyers, who nurtured a jaundiced opinion of mass movements and a deep suspicion of sentiment. Devoted to the intellectual history of powerful minds, particularly James Madison, Meyers did not practice anything like the social and political history of common people that I aspired to write. And yet he was endlessly generous with his time and with his attention, reading my drafts with a close, careful scrutiny that still astonishes me. Often, I would ask some simple question, but he would reply with a long, apparently convoluted, exploration of all the possible permutations, circling around an idea. At first, I wondered why he did not just get to the point, but, eventually, I saw the care with which he considered complexities that I had been oblivious to. In fact, I especially needed his close attention and sharp criticism. And as long as I could demonstrate my points thoroughly, he supported my work, although so very different from his own. Ultimately, his support was deep and unflagging, ensuring my completion of the dissertation that became my first book.

As a reviewer, I strive to apply Marvin Meyers's attention to irony and paradox, and his emphasis on inextricably linking evidence to argument. I have adopted his wariness of new and flashy approaches—unless they are backed up by the careful, patient examination of all the available and appropriate sources. New historical approaches, however, become compelling when accompanied by new evidence to provide fresh insights. But even when a book disappoints, I try to offer a fair and thorough summary before exploring the problems. And those problems require careful explication rather than categorical rejection. Criticism is worthless unless supported by examples carefully drawn and explained by the critic. Mere assertion without evidence is as bankrupt in a review as in a book of history. But such detailed reviews require far more space than most journals and magazines can afford.

Fortunately, *The New Republic* seeks sustained reviews of scholarly books which offer some reach beyond the academy into a broader audience. Publishing reviews of about five thousand words, *The New Republic* affords an author the luxury of carefully exploring a book. My opportunity to review for that magazine came by mail and by surprise as an invitation in the spring of 1996 from Leon Wieseltier, the literary editor. In almost all cases, he suggests and sends books that have caught his eye (or that of his fellow editor, Ruth Franklin). Almost never do I propose a book for review. In revising the pieces for this collection, I have tinkered with the wording but not with the substance of the evaluation. The changes seek merely to tighten and to improve the clarity of expression.

Almost all of the books are by accomplished and able scholars who warrant careful consideration—even and especially when my final assessment is mixed. Most of the reviewed books address topics of timely interest, giving historical depth to contemporary concerns. And many of the authors adopt narrative strategies meant to appeal to a relatively broad readership—a goal that I share. Consequently the reviews treat history books as a literary genre where authors make creative (and debateable) choices in plot and characterization.

Although academics certainly read *The New Republic*, most of its readers pursue other careers. Primarily addressing them, no review assumes special insider knowledge of academic jargon or of historical facts. Indeed, each review places a particular book in a wider context by exploring a particular approach to history. For example, a review of Laurel Thatcher Ulrich's *The Age of Homespun: Objects and Stories in the Creation of an American Myth* considers the dilemmas faced by historians of material culture. And Elizabeth Fenn's *Pox Americana: The Great Smallpox Epidemic of 1775–1782* invites consideration of history written on a North American scale—ranging beyond the bounds of the United States. In addition to reviewing a particular book, each piece pursues a central theme or problem.

Each essay offers a critical dialogue with the book's argument and its links to the evidence. People who like the reviews generally praise their candor—particularly when I explore flaws overlooked by other reviewers. But I hope that a fair share of the reviews also identify careful and imaginative work that sets high standards and breaks new ground for historians. Examples include the books by Patricia Cline Cohen, Elizabeth Fenn, Jill Lepore, and Alfred Young. I like to think that all would have impressed Marvin Meyers.

# Part I
# Bodies and Minds

*1*

# The Voyage In

*December 9, 1996*

John and William Bartram, father and son, are timely subjects for a double biography: prescient men of the eighteenth century who speak to our own environmental dilemmas. John (1699–1777) and William (1739–1823) were Pennsylvania Quakers who achieved international renown as botanists, explorers, collectors, writers, and artists. The Bartrams detected a universal spirit and intellect in nature, uniting plants, animals, and humans into a divinely ordained whole. And they challenged the exaggerated sense of distinction and supremacy claimed by humanity as license to destroy. Consequently, they opposed hunting for sport and the relentless killing of snakes: the special passions of eighteenth-century Americans. Both men expressed a rapturous delight in the wild, where nature did not yet tamely bear the colonizers' transforming imprint. And although John never forgave all Indians for those who had killed his own father, William became a passionate advocate for the humanity and the culture of native peoples.

John Bartram lived a great American success story, akin to that of a contemporary, Benjamin Franklin. Orphaned by an Indian raid at the age of twelve, John inherited and steadily improved a substantial farm beside the Schuylkill River near Philadelphia. Developing a profitable nursery and garden, he became his township's leading taxpayer and an avid reader of books imported from London. Focusing on natural history and botany, he recognized his own special opportunity to find, identify, collect, and domesticate American species of plants unknown to European science.

As a self-taught botanist, Bartram was perceptive, industrious, resourceful, and tireless. Thomas Slaughter explains that Bartram was "personally responsible for one quarter of all the plants identified and sent to Europe during the colonial period." Through his London broker, a wealthy Quaker merchant named Peter Collinson, Bartram's letters and

*The Natures of John and William Bartram,* by Thomas P. Slaughter (Alfred A. Knopf, 1996); *William Bartram: Travels and Other Writings,* edited by Thomas P. Slaughter (Library of America, 1996)

samples reached scientific adepts among the English gentry and the Royal Society. These connections provided publicity, praise, and subsidies for his further travels—all very gratifying to a colonist of modest origins on the margins of the British Empire.

In 1765, with Collinson's help, Bartram obtained a coveted appointment as the royal botanist for North America. In addition to renown, the position brought a salary to finance his most ambitious and exotic journey: through the Carolinas, Georgia, and Florida in 1765–66. He took along his twenty-six-year-old son, William, who was at loose ends, having recently failed as a shopkeeper in North Carolina.

A precocious youth with a special talent for nature sketches, William shared his father's passion for travel and for the wild. Especially enamored of Florida, he lingered as a slaveholding rice planter, dreaming of much leisure for further botanical exploration. But within a year, his new plantation was a shambles, the slaves were mutinous, and he was gripped with despair. Returning home in defeat in 1767, William redeemed himself by developing his skill as a nature artist. Sketches sent to Collinson caught the eye of Dr. John Fothergill, a wealthy Quaker physician, who became William's patron. With money from Fothergill, William conducted an extended ramble through the Southeast to the Mississippi River during the mid-1770s. He returned enchanted by the landscape and impressed by the generous hospitality and rich cultures of the Cherokees, Creeks, and Seminoles.

Following John Bartram's death in the fall of 1777, William Bartram wrote a detailed account of his southeastern travels, which he published in 1791. Thereafter, he led a quiet and private life as the curator of his father's garden and memory. His book obtained scant attention in his own life, but subsequently inspired the Romantic poets in England and the Transcendentalists in America. Thomas P. Slaughter aptly characterizes *Travels* as "the most remarkable American nature and travel book of the eighteenth century."

In the southeastern forests, savannas, and swamps, William Bartram experienced a wild largely erased by our mechanized and urbanized world. Our sense of loss imparts an elegiac fascination to Bartram's evocative and rapturous descriptions. He encountered Creek council houses elaborately decorated with representations of human-headed animals and animal-headed people; extensive salt deposits, "which all kinds of cattle lick into great caves"; towering cypress, pine, and live oak forests; and blazing stands of wild azaleas and magnolias. In Florida, he marveled at the bubbling fountains of crystalline waters set in grottoes and surrounded by orange groves. With consummate skill and in vivid detail, William summons the mind's eye: "Behold, for instance, a vast circular expanse before you, the waters of which are so extremely clear as to be absolutely diaphanous or transparent as the ether; the margin of the basin ornamented with a great variety of fruitful and floriferous trees, shrubs, and plants, the pendant golden Orange dancing on the surface of the pellucid waters, the balmy air vibrating with the melody of the merry birds, tenants of the encircling aromatic grove." Offering more than static set pieces of natural beauty, Bartram invests his descriptions with motion and drama. He continues his description of the fountain: "But behold yet something far more admirable, see whole armies [of fish] descending into an abyss, into the mouth of the bubbling fountain: they disappear! are they gone for ever? is it real? I raise my eyes with terror and astonishment; I look down again to the fountain with anxiety, when behold them, as it were, emerging from the blue ether of another world, apparently at a vast distance; at their first appearance, no bigger than flies or minnows; now gradually enlarging, their brilliant colours begin to paint the fluid." Given this intense beauty and his vivid imagination, Bartram embraced the Creek tradition that the Okeefenokee Swamp contained an elusive paradise of incomparably lovely women, "whom they call the daughters of the sun."

Readers seeking his vision of that lost American world will be richly rewarded by an elegant new edition of his words, *William Bartram: Travels and Other Writings.* Published by the Library of America and ably edited by Slaughter, this edition features beautiful reproductions of William's remarkable drawings. Slaughter's full, precise, and helpful notes reveal the judicious care and attention to detail of a talented historian.

Those same qualities, however, are only intermittent in a companion biography by Slaughter entitled *The Natures of John and William Bartram.* Slaughter devotes most of this book to a problematic project in what he calls "emotional history." Rejecting with contempt any notion of objective detachment, he follows a recent trend among some historians to place the authorial self within the narrative, dissolving the distinction between the personal and the analytical, the historical and the fictional. Slaughter embraces the higher calling of emotive, imaginative art, which he pits against the supposedly cold, lifeless, and limiting rationality of social science. "Unlike the poetic view, the scientific shuns reverie; it attempts to elude idiosyncratic observation and tries to suppress the self." As the champion of reverie and self, Slaughter shares with William Bartram the higher calling of poetic art. Claiming an emotional courage beyond that of his scholarly peers, Slaughter insists that "no less than scientists, historians have feared emotions, both our own and those of our subjects, defining them as beyond our professional terrain."

Slaughter explains that his book "is more about interior than exterior exploration," more about his emotive bonds across time with the Bartrams than about their connection with their contemporaries in eighteenth-century America and England. In Slaughter's treatment, therefore, the Bartrams appear strangely detached from the social and political upheavals of a revolutionary century. In one intriguing sentence, Slaughter lets drop a bombshell: "William served, at least briefly, as a spy for Patriot forces in 1776 during his travels." But he offers no further discussion, although this episode would surely reveal much about William's life, as well as his times.

Preoccupied with interior exploration, Slaughter neglects the exterior. He treats "nature" as a construct within the minds of John and William rather than as the material and biological environment that just might exist beyond whatever humans think, say, and write about it. Noting that plants and animals dwarf the human figures in William's drawings of the Florida savannas, Slaughter concludes: "As always for William . . . dominance and control are deeply troubling prospects, implying responsibilities that he's not prepared to accept, a confidence that he doesn't really have, and a hierarchical configuration of nature to which he isn't emotionally attached." But an external explanation is more plausible. William's drawings convey the physical reality that in 1774 on the Florida savanna the human presence was minimal amid the exuberant proliferation of wild plants and animals.

Slaughter rarely proceeds beyond the Bartrams' minds to recover a material landscape that had at least as powerful an effect on their thoughts as did their receding childhoods. In particular, he neglects William Bartram's fascination with the abundant relics and the impressive ruins of ancient Indian towns in the Southeast. The extensive remnants of avenues, plazas, mounds, pyramids, terraces, council houses, orchards, and artificial lakes impressed William with the power of nature to overcome human artifice. Amid the ruins, he recognized a nature more powerful than human ambition and human conceit. But Slaughter's focus is so relentlessly psychological that it denies Bartram's depiction of an intoxicating natural and native world now lost.

Slaughter emphasizes his feelings of emotional kinship and spiritual immediacy with the Bartrams, as well as his sense of continuities between their experiences and his own. He explains that "all the things that I am and that have happened to me contribute to what this book became, what it is. In ways that I can only glimpse, this project is a chapter in my life, a connection to those long since and only recently dead, and to all those who, for me, continue to live. This includes John and William Bartram, both of whom live for me." Slaughter cites his own reveries as his ultimate source for interpreting the Bartrams. "The use of first-person paraphrasing throughout the book suggests how closely my life, consciousness and nature are entwined with my interpretation of the Bartrams. This method . . . exposes a belief that my experience provides an authority supplementing that of the sources mentioned in the Notes." Indeed, he explains, those sources "are filtered through my life; they have no independent standing as evidence apart from my understanding of them." The Bartrams function as symbolic material that Slaughter uses to explore his own fervid feelings about nature, fatherhood, death, and the Princeton faculty.

Because Slaughter places his own imagination at the center of his narrative, he feels compelled to provide more self-revelation than is customary for a historian: "I'm a Quaker. I'm a mix of Native-American, French-Canadian, and English heritages. I'm a father and, in common with all of my gender, I've been a son. This project crystallized in my consciousness during a year in which my father died and my son was born. Before I started writing, my maternal grandfather and my mother died, too. Halfway through a first draft, my daughter was born. Days after I completed the last chapter, before I wrote the conclusion, my good friend and dog, Willie, died ending a companionship of thirteen years." Exquisitely well read in the very best literature, Slaughter also shares with his readers his encounters with the poetry of Donald Hall; the novels of Cormac McCarthy, N. Scott Momaday, Wallace Stegner, Norman Maclean, and Joseph Conrad; the histories by Edmund S. Morgan, John Demos, Richard Price, and Simon Schama; and the biographies of Goethe, Bernard Shaw, and W. E. B. Du Bois. And he takes special pains to identify and applaud his patrons, cultivated "as a graduate student fifteen years ago" at Princeton. The education of Thomas P. Slaughter required a host of academic greats: John Murrin inspired his first book; Lawrence Stone passed on "his own storytelling talents"; "LeRoy Ladurie was a frequent visitor to Princeton during my four years there, Carlo Ginsburg a palpable presence in the books that I read, and Natalie Davis and Clifford Geertz were visible fixtures on the local landscape."

This exuberant name-dropping helps to establish one of Slaughter's emotive bonds to the Bartrams. Of himself, Slaughter shares: "Edmund Morgan's biography of Ezra Stiles . . . is my favorite among my favorite early American historian's books. Morgan once told me that it's his favorite, too. No one tells stories about the past better than Morgan and no one captures the humanity of historical figures better than he." Of John Bartram, Slaughter reveals: "his letters often drop famous names and an intimate detail about their lives for no reason but to establish the connections between great men and him." Erasing any boundary between his subjectivity and his subjects, Slaughter invests himself in characterizations of the Bartrams.

With imagination as his ultimate authority, Slaughter writes a history of the might-have-been. Always vivid, Slaughter's prose waxes enthusiastic whenever he can escape from drab documents and plunge into a gap in the record. The words "maybe," "perhaps," "if," and "seems" proliferate to introduce his fanciful reveries. Often, they cancel one another, denying the reader any conclusion. Reaching far beyond the evidence, Slaughter imagines that the renowned Swedish artist Gustavus Hesselius tutored the young William Bartram: "Maybe Billy watched the adult artist at work; perhaps the man gave some lessons, or at least pointers, to the promising boy. And, then again, perhaps not. Imagine John showing off his son's pictures to a famous artist with the boy in the room." Maybe. Maybe not. Imagine.

Slaughter treats the absence of documents as a variety of evidence—or he exploits explicitly irrelevant information. No letters from William to John survive for the years 1770–72, so Slaughter imagines that William destroyed them because they were despondent and self-damning. Completing the circle, Slaughter then concludes that their current nonexistence demonstrates that William was especially troubled during those years. He also devotes five pages to describing John Bartram's evolving personality as determined from an examination of two very different portraits, although he concedes that both probably represent other men. Of the second portrait, Slaughter concludes: "As he got older, John got simpler, too; but both men are John Bartram, even if neither of them really is."

Slaughter plays fast and loose with the evidence in pursuit of "emotional truth," which he considers vastly superior to the mere facts found in documents. He admires William Bartram's exaggerated stories because they "orchestrate facts and fancies into an emotional symphony that is William's Truth, his art, his gift to us." It is also Slaughter's gift to us. For example, he narrates the death and the burial in 1820 of Jack Snake, a Cherokee chief, during a visit to the Bartrams' famous garden. Slaughter observes: "Whether or not it's ironic, it's certainly poetically just that [Jack] Snake died on a farm purchased with money inherited from a man his ancestors had killed." This nicely dramatic line is historically disingenuous. As a Cherokee, Jack Snake descended from a people who had helped the North Carolina colonists to defeat their mutual enemies, the Tuscaroras, who had killed grandfather Bartram. But drama trumps history in Slaughter's emotional truth.

He asserts a prolonged psychological conflict between the Bartrams: a sensitive son's lifelong struggle to cope with an overpowering father, who was permanently scarred by his own traumatic youth. In Slaughter's telling, every twist of their fate flowed from two shocks, one experienced by each Bartram in adolescence. John's longing for control expressed a profound insecurity rooted in the pain of his father's murder. William's torment derived from being initially consigned to a detested career in commerce by his father's dictate.

Slaughter describes John Bartram as both a "daunting, craggy, immovable presence, a hard man to follow as a son" and consumed by "insecurity, fearfulness, and self-doubt." Slaughter attributes this painfully divided self to the early loss of Bartram's parents, although only another reverie can recover that undocumented trauma. As a father, John meant well, but his longing for control permanently damaged William's fragile psyche. Overriding his son's preference for art, John apprenticed the reluctant boy to a Philadelphia merchant. Thereafter, William nurtured a lifelong "sense of betrayal by a disloyal father." Noting that William never married, Slaughter concludes: "The patriarchal presence was too powerful, too intimidating in his life. He couldn't be the father, the husband, the lover, the provider that his father was." When William praised Indians, it was primarily "to compete with his father, to be a better, more tolerant, more Christian Quaker, thereby defining himself positively in contrast to John." And when William found typographical errors in his published book, "The rage must have returned, whether or not the depression again swept over him."

Slaughter detects psychological rage and familial conflict in almost every source, even the most apparently placid and innocuous. As a boy, William Bartram sketched the family farm beside the river, adding a small fisherman in the lower-right corner. Artistic convention suffices to explain the angler, but Slaughter imagines something more provocative: "a self-portrait of the artist enjoying nature at leisure and watching from the outside, judging and rejecting his father's role for himself." When John Bartram writes, "I was pleased with Billy's temperance and patience in his journey," Slaughter speculates: "Does that mean that John was pleasantly surprised; is it a comparison to past experience or what he had witnessed that summer in his home? Did William now drink, however little being too much in his father's eyes; did he often lose patience, perhaps with his father? Or maybe he had a temper that John found intemperate, too. Maybe this tells us something about how the summer had gone—badly, both cold and hot." Maybe. Maybe not. In fact, no one knows and no one can know. But Slaughter speculates freely, invariably finding a simmering resentment on the verge of eruption.

In fact, most of the Bartrams' writings reveal a deep mutual affection and a shared commitment to finding God in nature. In their spiritual and environmental convictions, they differed far more profoundly from almost all of their contemporaries than from one another. And by all contemporary accounts, they led lives of moderation, balance, patience, and dignity. But those virtues do not resonate with Slaughter's imagination, and so he treats them as superficial masks over a more perfervid reality found in his own reveries.

In *Travels*, William Bartram describes narrow escapes in Florida from hundreds of implausibly immense and vicious alligators billowing steam and bellowing their longing to eat him. Slaughter persuasively argues that Bartram exaggerated to more effectively convey the dread that the beasts produced in his mind. In Slaughter's biography, the psychological conflicts between John and William resemble those overblown alligators, as modest conflicts take on monstrous proportions in Slaughter's imagination. Rather than illuminating the Bartrams, his imaginary bond with them creates emotional caricatures of Freudian conflict.

Historians certainly need imagination to recover and to describe the past and its people. The problem is that Slaughter has trained his imagination so intensely and so narrowly on supposed commonalities between his emotions and experiences and those of the Bartrams. Indeed, he underestimates the power of imagination by confining it to a backward and anachronistic projection of his own feelings. A truly rich historical imagination takes us beyond the self, beyond personal and contemporary limits, into the lives of people who have been rendered alien by the passage of time. The potential fascination of the Bartrams, after all, is that they lived so fully in an America so very different from our own.

## 2

# Blood and Soil

*October 8, 2001*

Popular belief formerly credited superior technology for the colonial conquest of North America: European colonizers won because they had the guns that Indians lacked. In recent decades, we have grown more aware of the devastating impact of European diseases unwittingly introduced to the Indians by their colonizers. Lacking the partial immunities provided by prior experience with those pathogens, the natives died by the thousands. During the sixteenth and the seventeenth centuries, the native population probably collapsed to a tenth of its former numbers, weakening the Indians' capacity to resist invasion. In the current shorthand of colonial triumph, Europeans prevailed because they had long known smallpox, and the Indians had not. In a learned, wide-ranging, insightful, and provocative book, Joyce E. Chaplin gives the great wave of epidemic death a further credit: it empowered white colonizers to create their sense of racial supremacy and entitlement to the continent.

Working the creative intersection of gender, environmental, and cultural history, Chaplin contributes to a great, ongoing debate among colonial historians: how, why, and when did American racism originate? Most scholars focus on the emergence of slavery for Africans in the English-speaking colonies, especially Virginia. During the 1960s, Winthrop Jordan mustered evidence that the early modern (and highly xenophobic) English nurtured such negative stereotypes of foreigners, and especially of "black" Africans, that the early seventeenth-century colonists immediately invoked racial supremacy and rapidly adopted slavery. Other historians view the emergence of slavery in Virginia as more gradual and halting, becoming institutionalized only late in the seventeenth century. They also see slavery as preceding the development of strong racial categories. In this view, racism was a belated rationalization for a system of exploitation that was originally animated by greed and opportunism. Both views have an eye to the place of racism in our own society—the

*Subject Matter: Technology, the Body, and Science on the Anglo-American Frontier, 1500–1676,* by Joyce E. Chaplin (Harvard University Press, 2001)

one fearful that racial thinking is tragically fundamental to American culture, and the other hoping that racism is a mutable rationalization for inequalities that can be rapidly reformed.

Chaplin switches our focus from Africans to Indians, and from slavery to disease. She pitches her inquiry in the dramatic key of the currently fashionable "history of the body." First developed by historians of science who study medieval and early modern Europe, the history of the body dissolves the distinction that privileges the mind over the body in the writing of intellectual or cultural history. The new approach insists that ideas about mind and body constitute and reconstitute one another in a constant loop; or, to be more precise, thoughts about body and mind cannot be disentangled from one another. If anything, ideas about the body must take precedence; Chaplin regards the body as nothing less than "the site for the construction of identity." In this view, people first and fundamentally define their corporeal being before proceeding to make the rest of their culture. Chaplin argues that, in constructing race, "the English created difference by focusing on the body, then moved out from this site into the rest of culture." She defines race as "an understanding of the human body that posited heritable and meaningful corporeal differences."

During the late sixteenth and the early seventeenth centuries, there did not yet exist modern "science" as we understand it: the militantly rational, experimental, empirical, and instrumental pursuit of knowledge dissociated from the supernatural. The age's protoscientists were "natural philosophers" such as John Dee, who combined without difficulty his positions as Queen Elizabeth's astrologer and mathematician, alchemist, and metallurgist. Elizabethan natural philosophers conducted empirical experiments to confirm theories derived from Christian theology, occult texts, and ancient writers, especially Aristotle. In their view, the body was more than mere matter. "Nature was a concatenation of animating forces," Chaplin explains, "a web of analogies, sympathies, and antipathies. A *microcosm* (such as the human body) reflected the structure and meaning of the *macrocosm* or cosmos." Divinely designed combinations of earth, air, fire, and water made up the body, as they did the earth and the universe.

Advancing a variant of the racism-came-later interpretation, Chaplin maintains that, at first, the English colonizers of America emphasized their common humanity with the Indians. Asserting such a commonality initially served colonial goals. Promoters needed to calm the pervasive anxiety that the North American environment might be fatal to the English body. The prevailing beliefs insisted that bodies were so finely tuned to local climates that they needed a prolonged and often painful "seasoning" to adapt to new settings; and, frequently, bodies could not survive the regional diseases that represented the shock of a new continent or a new latitude. Therefore, potential colonists (and investors in colonies) sought reassurance that the Indians were both healthy and fundamentally similar to the English in body and mind. To that end, John Brereton praised the Indian as "a perfect constitution of body, active, strong, healthful, and very wittie." Chaplin explains that colonial promoters were primarily interested in Indians "as indicators of America's usefulness to them."

Similar Indians could also be more quickly assimilated into English ways and rules. If akin in body, they would readily accept new roles as guides for English explorers, producers for the English market, consumers of English goods, worshipers of the English God, and subjects of the English monarch. Rather than define the Indians as alien and intractable "others," the colonizers cast them as earlier drafts of contemporary Europeans—as the equivalent of the ancient Britons, who, through Roman and Christian tutelage, had ascended in civility to become the English. Chaplin notes that the colonizers initially "represented Indians nostalgically as versions of their ancient, savage, and valiant forbears."

During the mid-seventeenth century, the colonizers' superficially benign view of the Indians broke down as a consequence of accumulating experience. It became abundantly clear that the Indians would not abjectly surrender their autonomy and their culture to become English pupils, wards, and menial servants. At the same time, on thriving farms and in growing families, the colonizers found a new source of reassurance that their bodies could adapt and could remake the land into a new England. In 1624, Richard Eburne concluded: "It be the people that makes the land English, not the land the people." In 1643, Roger Williams asserted: "Nature knowes no difference between *Europe* and *Americans* in blood, birth, [and] bodies."

Indeed, some colonists began to boast that they were improved by their new setting. During the 1640s, a New England colonist asserted: "God hath so prospered the climate to us, that our bodies are hailer, and Children there born stronger, whereby our number is exceedingly increased." The colonists waxed more confident in their own numbers, prosperity, and power at the same time that they lost faith in the Indians as proto-English in body and mind. Taking possession of the land, the colonizers began to dismiss the Indians as disposable obstacles rather than celebrate them any longer as potential assets and kindred bodies.

Formerly impressed by Indian technology—by their pharmacopeia, canoes, fish weirs, bows, and maize—the colonists became dismissive by century's end. Chaplin explains: "The body was the springboard from which the English then launched arguments about Indians' technical inferiority." The colonists imagined and cast backward a technology gap that has, Chaplin insists, long distorted our understanding of the initial generation of contact. "The English had not begun to settle in the new world with the conviction that they had superior scientific and technological abilities, but they would later think this way *because* they colonized America and invaded a people whom they would, in the end, decide that they could not think of as similar to themselves."

Indeed, Chaplin discounts the notion that, during their early encounters, the English asserted, and the Indians accepted, the technological advantages of the Europeans. In 1588, the Roanoke explorer Thomas Harriot reported:

> Most things they saw with us, [such] as Mathematicall instruments, sea Compasses, the vertue of the load-stone in drawing iron, a perspective glasse whereby was shewed many strange sights, burning glasses, wilde fireworkes, gunnes, hookes, writing and reading, springclockes that seeme to goe of themselves and many other things that wee had were so strange unto them, and so farre exceeded their capacities to comprehend the reason and meanes how they should be made and done, that they thought they were rather the workes of gods than of men, or at the leastwise [that] they had bene given and taught us of the gods.

Chaplin dismisses such reports as the "ventriloquism" of Europeans planting their own praises to mask an insecurity about their true backwardness. She minimizes the technological gap between the newcomers and the natives, dwelling particularly on the presence of a few bows in the arsenals of some of the earliest English voyages and colonies. Chaplin concludes: "Everywhere, the English went, they saw weapons similar to their own."

But if the English possessed similar bows, they also had different and far superior arrowheads of steel and iron, which cut more deeply than did the flint and copper that the Indians possessed. With good reason, the natives craved European metals for kettles, hoes, knives, arrowheads, and hatchets. They scavenged shipwrecks and avidly traded furs for cherished bits of metal. Nor were guns as inconsequential and fleeting an advantage as Chaplin suggests. During the early seventeenth century, the governors of Virginia jealously guarded their guns and the men who could fire them, taking special pains to recover those that had been taken, with such singular determination, by the local paramount chieftain, Powhatan. Indian behavior in the contact generation made plain their recognition that technology mattered and that their technology and that of the colonists differed radically. So did colonial behavior, for colonists adopted elements of the natives' far more productive horticulture and admired their more advanced herbal medicines.

As the crux of her argument, Chaplin asserts that, during the mid-sixteenth century, the colonizers contrasted their own natural increase (at least in New England) with the surging death rate among the natives to justify dispossessing the latter. Rather than acknowledge their role in introducing epidemics, the colonists insisted that the diseases were native to North America. Therefore, the widespread deaths revealed that the Indians had "a fateful propensity within their bodies" that kept them from ever becoming seasoned to North America. Strays from Asia, they had never put down proper roots, in contrast to the English bodies which so smoothly adapted to North America. Asserting "a cosmic synchrony between the invaders and their new place of abode," the colonists believed "that they were better suited to America than Indians and could supplant them as natives of the new world." Chaplin concludes: "[The] colonists seemed to believe themselves more natural than the aborigines, as if English bodies had always been meant to be planted in Virginia and Plymouth."

What, then, are we to make of the persisting colonial recognition that Indians were taller, straighter, faster, stronger, and tougher? Colonial accounts concede that the Indians could traverse the woods, see long distances, endure torture, conduct battles, and bear children more stoically and skillfully than any colonist. With considerable ingenuity, Chaplin detects a colonial subtext that undercuts the overt praise of these native qualities. By disciplining their children's bodies with cradleboards, cold baths, initiation rites, and greasy ointment, Indian parents deadened feelings of pain. Far from being more natural, Indians were (in colonial eyes) more artificial. As Chaplin puts it: "Indians were unnatural beings, bodies for which artifice had created a kind of unfeeling inhumanity." Superficially tough, Indian bodies remained internally weak, unable to survive the critical tests posed by alcohol and infectious disease.

In sum: by imagining biology, rather than culture, as the central and polarizing difference between peoples, and by insisting on their innate superiority, the colonists used the Indians to construct a new concept of race. In Chaplin's words, the colonists "defined a new idiom, one which argued that the significant human variation in North America was not due to external environment but instead lay deeper within the bodies of its European and Indian peoples." Confident in their bodily superiority, colonists became white racial supremacists who proceeded to conquer the continent as, properly, their own. They cast themselves as destiny's true Americans, properly supplanting the unfit and unworthy Indians. That "they were the *natural* residents of America" is "the powerful racist fiction that remains the basis of creole identity in North America."

Chaplin offers an innovative and powerful interpretation of the first century of Anglo-American colonization. Her argument is clever and original, but I wish it was better grounded in the colonial evidence. Perhaps some seventeenth-century colonist did directly state that the selective epidemics proved the innate inferiority of Indian, and the superiority of English, bodies. But if so, his words do not appear in Chaplin's book. Instead, her argument pivots on her own assertions. Indeed, for an intellectual or cultural history, *Subject Matter* offers relatively limited access to words from the past. Most of the quotations are brief snippets framed by the author's words, which give the sentences their import. Conveying details, the quotations do not match the bold sweep of the argument. Chaplin almost never invites the reader to join her in examining a sustained piece of writing that reveals the connections drawn by the original writer. In more than three hundred pages of text, only three quotations are sufficiently long (more than about three lines) to justify blocking and indentation. Apparently, Chaplin feels no need for any colonial writer explicitly to draw any of the connections of her argument. Instead, she recovers a covert unity found in many bits and pieces throughout the culture. But this manipulative control of the past's words is jarring in a book that faults other scholars for taking quotations out of context.

In general, the colonists said little about their own bodies and much about divine providence to explain the epidemics that killed more natives than newcomers. No respecter of bodies, their God chose who should live and die throughout the world, including who should prevail in North America. The seventeenth-century epidemics proved to the colonists' satisfaction that God favored them as long as they honored his dictates and as long as the Indians clung to their own errant faiths. Rather than seeing the diseases as endemic to North America, colonial observers consistently noted that the epidemics dramatically reduced populations that had once been numerous. And the first colonists recognized that the epidemics coincided with the advent of Europeans among a native people—which again suggested to them a supernatural rather than a protobiological explanation for the Indians' demise.

The mechanical consistency of Chaplin's argument overrides considerable variations in colonial experience. Her interpretation works best for New England, where the seventeenth-century colonists did enjoy healthful conditions and a prolific natural increase. But the great majority of English immigrants went instead to Virginia and the West Indies, where harsh work regimens, a hot climate, and chronic disease (especially malaria and dysentery) killed the colonists faster than they could reproduce. Between 1607 and 1622, about ten thousand English people immigrated to Virginia, but only 20 percent of that population was still alive there in 1622. An English critic belatedly remarked: "Instead of a plantacion, Virginia will shortly get the name of a slaughterhouse."

During the seventeenth century, 190,000 British people emigrated to the West Indies (compared to the 21,000 who went to New England), but only 33,000 resided there at century's end. Outside of New England, the slow growth of the colonial population required continued, large-scale immigration. In 1638, Parliament proposed legislation to limit emigration to Virginia, alarming the planters, who complained that their colony would "in [a] short time melt to nothing for want of supplyes of people."

What cause, then, did a Virginian or a West Indian have to celebrate his or her bodily triumph over the new environment? Indeed, the southern colonists generally concluded that their bodies were inferior to those of Africans in coping with hard work and hot climes. In a perverse manner, this sense of bodily inferiority informed the southern colonists' insistence on their mental superiority, and their conviction that they should own the labor of imported Africans.

In invoking the esoteric writings of natural philosophers as fundamental to colonial thinking, Chaplin suggests little difference between the notions of elites and the thoughts of common people. In the 1970s and 1980s, the triumphant New Social Historians asserted a stark divide in the early modern era between the formal discourse of the learned few and the "mentalité" of the unlettered many. The newer history of the body blurs that line, accepting a more holistic view of culture, blending low and high, and enabling a few texts to speak for entire populations. In this way, reading John Dee suffices for understanding how everyone in early modern England thought about their bodies. In this view, we need take no special pains to demonstrate that laborers shared the bodily concepts of natural philosophers.

Chaplin's argument also homogenizes the considerable variation in colonial thinking about native bodies, which persisted long after the momentous transition she alleges for the mid-seventeenth century. In rhetoric and law, the racial divide between Indian and white bodies remained far less certain than that between blacks and whites. During the eighteenth century, leading Americans, including the southern planters William Byrd II and Thomas Jefferson, often urged a general miscegenation with Indians, which they found appalling in theory (if not in personal practice) with blacks. Where separation and subordination seemed the solution to controlling blacks, the eighteenth-century racial theorists favored intermarriage and cultural assimilation as the most benign mode of dissolving Indian difference and resistance. And some colonists continued to celebrate the beauty and strength of Indian bodies and the naturalness of their cultures—if only as tropes to criticize the artificiality of colonial bodies and society.

Among scholars, bold new approaches—such as "the history of the body"—inspire an assertive zeal short on credit for predecessors. Newly possessed of a master key to the past, the adepts keenly detect flaws in older approaches as they advance bold revisions of sources and explanations. Much of what we thought we knew, it seems, turns out to have been wrong. Such sweeping and partisan claims have accompanied every boomlet in historical scholarship: once the New Social History, then the new cultural history, and now the history of the body.

Chaplin primarily faults the "ethno-historians": those scholars who combine anthropology and history to study native peoples during the initial stages of colonization. Ethnohistorians, she asserts, fail to detect the "ventriloquism" practiced by their colonial sources, which planted self-serving ideas in remarks allegedly made by Indians. "We will never begin to comprehend what Indians may have been trying to say in the sixteenth and seventeenth centuries," Chaplin notes, "until we turn down the background noise, the static of cultural expectations and assumptions that the English put into their accounts about their early colonization." Colonial accounts "were dependent on contemporary debates over natural philosophy and too eager to ventriloquize native opinions within the forms of that debate." Alas, the credulous ethnohistorians "have done little to examine English patterns of thought about nature (especially about the body) which would allow better decoding of these texts."

Consider, for example, the intriguing and influential account written by Thomas Harriot, the natural philosopher who visited the Indian villages near Roanoke on the North Carolina coast in 1585. Although Harriot had learned some of the local language and culture, that does not impress Chaplin. Noting the Indian dread of new epidemics, Harriot reports that they credited the colonists with the power to shoot "invisible bullets" that "killed the people in any towne that had offended us, as wee listed, how farr distant from us soever they were." Chaplin distrusts Harriot's metaphor as covertly conveying his own views on atomism, then a controversial new doctrine smacking of atheism: "It is possible that he ventriloquized dangerous hypotheses about matter through informants who would appear exotic to his readers, and therefore appropriate bearers of heterodoxy."

But perhaps we should not so hastily dismiss Harriot's observation as no more than the covert exercise of his own atomism. After all, other colonists with no investment in radical science reported much the same thing: Indian fears that the English could employ disease over long distances as a weapon. In 1621, according to Edward Winslow, the New England Indians suspected that the colonists kept "the plague buried in our storehouse, which, at our pleasure, we could send forth to whate place or people we would, and destroy them therewith, though we stirred not from home." A devout Puritan, Winslow held no brief for atomism. To paraphrase Freud, sometimes an invisible bullet *is* an invisible bullet.

To score points against the ethnohistorians, Chaplin paints her book into a corner, adopting an extreme skepticism about the value of colonial sources for revealing anything about the Indians: "We can never know the actual content of whatever Roanok[e] statement Harriot was quoting." In principle, Chaplin overtly rejects Stephen Greenblatt's agnosticism about recovering Indian culture through the texts made by colonizers, but, in practice, she almost always finds illusions rather than insights in the sources. This Euroskepticism limits the range of her vision. A detailed examination of what the colonizers thought about themselves and natives, *Subject Matter* does not devote comparable space and energy to how the Indians conceived of their bodies and of those of the newcomers. Consistently treated as the objects of the colonial gaze, Chaplin's Indians do not receive equal time as actors in the making of their own corporeal and racial ideas.

How, for example, did Indian beliefs about the body shift as they experienced massive epidemics that spared most of the invaders? Chaplin declines to answer, out of her conviction that European ventriloquism has rendered Indians virtually unknowable. Of New England's missionized Indians, she asserts, it is "difficult to determine what Eliot's converts (or any other Indians) truly did believe." In Rhode Island, archaeologists recently excavated the intriguing grave of a seventeenth-century Indian child bearing a traditional "medicine bundle" of sacred objects rendered syncretic by the folded page from an English Bible. After advancing multiple interpretations for the mix of objects, Chaplin ultimately rejects all potential meaning: "And our inability to know what these things meant is a consequence of English ventriloquism of Indians in the seventeenth century."

In this certainty of doubt, Chaplin has plenty of company. Scholars have recently become so sophisticated at detecting hidden bias and covert messages that we risk writing only about the construction of illusions. By discounting colonial documents as fatally flawed by "Eurocentrism," we retreat to a history that writes only about the subjectivity of Europeans. By seeing nothing but "ventriloquism" in European accounts, we deny our own capacity to read against their grain to recover the thoughts of native peoples. We also deny the capacity of native peoples to rattle the complacency and the categories of the colonizers. If the Indians did not make our sources, they often catalyzed their creation, and by the shock of their difference, they forced compromises on colonial writers initially bent on confirming their preconceptions. So, too, can that evidence, in its rich contradictions, serve modern scholars.

*3*

# Germ Colonies

*November 19, 2001*

Inspired in part by the public awareness generated by AIDS, historians now pay closer attention to the power of past epidemics to shatter and reshape human societies. A century ago, American historians thought of their continent as a "virgin land," as a vast wilderness virtually untouched by humans until colonized by Europeans. The great nationalist historian of the nineteenth century, George Bancroft, insisted that in 1492 the future United States was "an unproductive waste . . . its only inhabitants a few scattered tribes of feeble barbarians." That view obscured the large Indian populations that greeted the first European explorers—populations soon decimated by the deadly new diseases introduced by the colonizers. Correcting the old view, historians now see North America as, in the words of the late Francis Jennings, a "widowed land," rendered so by the fatal microbes that accompanied the European invaders.

Almost everywhere, the first explorers and colonists reported horrifying and apparently unprecedented epidemics among the native peoples. During the 1580s, Thomas Harriot described the fate of the Indians near the new English colony at Roanoke Island (in present-day North Carolina): "[They] began to die very fast, and many in [a] short space; in some townes about twentie, in some fourtie, in some sixtie, & in one sixe score, which in trueth was very manie in respect to their numbers. . . . The disease also was so strange that they neither knew what it was, nor how to cure it; the like by report of the oldest men in the countrey never happened before, time out of mind." In 1633, a New England colonist reported: "It pleased God to visite these Indeans with a great sickness, and such a mortalitie that, of 1000, above 900 and a halfe of them dyed, and many of them did rott above ground for want of buriall."

After 1492, the Indians paid dearly for their former isolation from the larger and more virulent disease pool of Africa, Asia, and Europe.

*Pox Americana: The Great Smallpox Epidemic of 1775–1782,* by Elizabeth Anne Fenn (Hill & Wang, 2001)

The world's champion killers—including smallpox, typhus, diphtheria, bubonic plague, malaria, yellow fever, and cholera—developed in the Old World after the Indians emigrated to the Americas (approximately fifteen thousand years ago). From many generations of internal combat with these microscopic invaders, the Africans, Asians, and Europeans developed partial defenses—antibodies and immunoglobulins. Over time, Europeans and their micropredators tended to work out a rough and always provisional equilibrium. Most people survived their bouts with disease, enabling human reproduction to keep pace with mortality. Consequently, as colonizers the disease-toughened Europeans carried viruses of even greater danger to others than to themselves. Their breath, blood, sweat, and lice conveyed micropredators that consumed Indians, who lacked the immunological resistance provided by past experience.

Smallpox was the most terrifying and devastating of the diseases unwittingly introduced by the colonizers. A highly communicable virus, *Variola major* passes by victims' exhalations through the air, on moisture droplets, or on dust particles that enter the lungs of a new host. After an incubation period of twelve days, victims come down with a high fever and vomiting, followed three or four days later with gruesome sores over the entire body. Painful, incapacitating, and disfiguring, smallpox transformed people into hideous masses of pustulated flesh. In New England during the 1630s, a colonist described Indians with pustules "breaking and mattering and running one into another. . . . And then, being very sore, what with cold and other distempers, they die like rotten sheep."

Among Europeans and Africans in the early modern era, the fatality rate usually approximated one quarter to one third of the afflicted; infected Indians died at about twice that rate. Although scarred with pocks, and sometimes blinded, the survivors reaped a precious lifetime immunity to the disease. But they could not pass this complete immunity on to their progeny, so every North American generation accumulated the human fuel to feed a spectacular new epidemic.

Compared to the Indians, the British colonists got off lightly. In addition to their better resistance, the colonists benefited from two systematic measures that restricted the disease: quarantines and an early form of inoculation known as "variolation," the intentional implantation of live smallpox matter into an incision made in an arm or a hand. Enforced by town or city governments, quarantines confined suspected carriers to remote pesthouses for care by doctors and nurses with the immunity of previous exposure and for isolation from the rest of the community. During the early eighteenth century, the British and their colonists also began to practice variolation. Smallpox artificially taken through a cut proved less debilitating and less deadly than when contracted randomly and naturally through the lungs. Less than 5 percent of the variolated died, compared to the 25 percent to 33 percent ordinarily killed by natural exposure. And, like any bout with smallpox, variolation gave immunity to its survivors.

But both quarantine and variolation had problems. In an age of expanding maritime commerce, identifying and confining carriers overtaxed the minimal governments of eighteenth-century America. And even if effective in the short term, a quarantine imparted no immunity to the local people, leaving them vulnerable to the next diseased newcomer. Variolation was also risky, for some patients died, and all of them increased the dangers of exposure for their neighbors who were not taking the treatment. Because of its considerable expense, variolation benefited the prosperous, who could afford it, while threatening their poorer neighbors, who could not. In self-defense, rather than out of backward prejudice, mobs of common people often drove from their towns any doctors who introduced variolation. To preserve social harmony, some colonies, especially in New England, banned the practice, preferring quarantine as an alternative.

Especially deadly and specialized, *Variola* suffered from its own success. The disease either killed or afforded immunity, rendering victims unsuitable for the virus to linger in or to return to. Elizabeth Fenn observes: "For the parasite this presents a problem. *Variola* consumes its human hosts as a fire consumes its fuel, leaving spent bodies, dead or immune behind it." Possessing no carriers or victims other than humans, the virus needed to find new hosts quickly. It thrived in places crowded with people, and it benefited from diseased (but not yet symptomatic) travelers visiting new communities. Finally, *Variola* was deadliest where social chaos prevailed. Bad enough in the best of circumstances, smallpox fatalities soared when people lacked nurturing care. Indians died in especially large numbers, because almost everyone in a village became sick at the same time, leaving too few to provide food, water, firewood, and care for the afflicted. Malnourished, dehydrated, cold, and demoralized people rarely survived the virus.

War maximized the crowding, the movement, and the disruption that promoted smallpox. Wars cluster people in filthy military cantonments and refugee camps, send soldiers marching and civilians fleeing over long distances, and rupture communities with death and fire. Fellow horsemen of the apocalypse, war and pestilence have long collaborated in their deadly work. It was no accident that smallpox came into North America with the invading and rampaging Spanish *conquistadores* of the sixteenth century. *Variola* surged anew in proportion to the scale of every subsequent colonial war. As the most extensive and destructive conflict of the eighteenth century in North America, the War of the American Revolution stimulated the most far-ranging and deadly smallpox epidemic since the brutal era of the *conquistadores*. In addition to Indians, the revolutionary epidemic killed thousands of Americans of European or African descent, illuminating their shared contacts in misery.

By examining the massive smallpox epidemic that accompanied the American Revolution between 1775 and 1782, Elizabeth Fenn provides a dazzling new perspective that embraces an entire continent. We tend to think of eighteenth-century North America as a set of distinct regions—a mismatched set of Spanish, French, Dutch, British, and even Russian colonies. Clustered along distant coasts, these colonies have seemed isolated by a broad and vague interior then still possessed by diverse Indian peoples. Consequently, historians of the American Revolution rarely examine the cultures and places beyond the thirteen new states along the Atlantic seaboard. By tracking an epidemic across colonial boundaries throughout North America, Fenn recovers the larger picture that we have long missed.

Like a marker in the bloodstream, smallpox generated far-flung documents, exposing the networks of human contact and exchange that crisscrossed the continent, from Québec to New Orleans, from Mexico City to Hudson Bay, and from South Carolina to the Pacific Northwest. The spreading epidemic demonstrated that war and trade had already interlocked the lives and the fates of native and colonial peoples. Fenn overrides the confining and parochial boundaries of regional and national histories to reveal a North American continent surprisingly integrated by colonial war and long-distance trade. In recent years, some scholars have called for a more transnational approach to American history; Fenn demonstrates how it can be done, and the benefits of trying.

On the Atlantic seaboard at the start of the war, the rival British and American commanders had to decide how best to protect their troops from smallpox. The British rather easily opted for variolation. Because the disease was more endemic to the more urbanized homeland than to the predominantly rural colonies (where it came in infrequent but spectacular epidemics), most of the British troops had suffered and survived smallpox as children or adolescents. The few who needed variolation could be easily cared for and protected by the majority. The superior professionalism, organization, and discipline of the British regulars also rendered effective their quarantine while undergoing the treatment.

George Washington faced a much tougher call. Most of his troops were American by birth and lacked the immunities provided by past exposure. Variolating them all was an expensive and massive operation initially beyond the limited funds, the makeshift organization, and the faulty discipline of the new rebel army. To variolate part of the army would increase the exposure for the rest, and to inoculate the whole would render them defenseless against British attack for several weeks.

Consequently, Washington and his subordinate officers initially rejected variolation in favor of quarantine—which proved ineffective among raw troops, who believed that fighting for liberty meant obeying only the orders they liked.

Sensitive to their greater vulnerability to smallpox on an epidemic scale, the Americans suspected that the British practiced a crude form of biological warfare by sending infected civilians and clothing inside the American lines. Although useful as anti-British propaganda, such reports also produced panic in the American ranks. Fenn tends to credit these rumors, although in only one surviving document (from the end of the war) does a British general actually propose the practice; and we have no proof that his superior applied the grim proposal.

Fenn's fresh new angle clarifies major episodes in the war. In late 1775, in Virginia, the British royal governor, Lord Dunmore, invited black slaves to desert their planter masters and to join his army in suppressing the revolution. To the horror of the planter class—which dominated the Revolution in the southern colonies—about a thousand male slaves escaped to enlist in Dunmore's "Ethiopian Regiment." To the planters' relief, smallpox soon killed most of the black troops, whom the British had neglected to inoculate. Fenn observes: "The very act of assembling the Ethiopian Regiment had brought together in one place a large, vulnerable population." At a critical, early moment in the Revolution, the collapse of the Ethiopian Regiment rescued the slave system. The untimely epidemic preserved the paradoxical linkage of black slavery and white freedom in the revolutionary movement.

Partial to neither side, smallpox also assailed the Americans who invaded Canada in late 1775. Despite hundreds of sick, their generals clung to the ban on variolation. Desperate to improve their odds of survival, dozens of men defied orders and covertly inoculated themselves from the pustules of the sick. But this only compounded exposure for the troops who obeyed the order to avoid variolation. As hundreds died, the commanders begged for reinforcements, but their arrival only increased the number of victims. Fenn explains: "With *Variola* coursing through the army, the arrival of new troops was akin to throwing gasoline on a fire." During the spring of 1776, the northern American army collapsed as the weakened survivors fled back into New York. One shocked soldier reported: "My eyes never before beheld such a seen, nor do I ever desire to see such another—the Lice and Maggots [that] seme to vie with each other, were creeping in Millions over the Victims."

The northern debacle threatened to undo the remaining American armies led by Washington. The northern veterans brought home both smallpox and demoralizing stories, spreading the epidemic to civilians and discouraging recruiting for the army. Men who might risk British gunfire balked at the more terrifying miseries of smallpox in a military camp. Facing a chronic shortage of manpower, Washington recognized that the Revolution could not survive another outbreak in the army. Reversing his policy, in early 1777, Washington ordered a mass inoculation, which he managed to keep secret from British intelligence. "The army had pulled off the first large-scale, state-sponsored immunization campaign in American history," Fenn notes. Given the probable consequences of either inaction or failure, the successful inoculation marks one of Washington's greatest accomplishments: a critical contribution to the narrow American victory.

Meanwhile, smallpox was spreading into the villages of Britain's Indian allies deep within the continent. In the spring of 1776, Indians helped rout the Americans retreating from Canada—but by donning clothes plundered from the dying, many warriors contracted smallpox, which they carried home to their far-flung villages around the Great Lakes. Farther south, on the Carolina frontier, Cherokee warriors picked up smallpox by raiding infected American settlements. *Variola* then spread through the native world of the vast Mississippi River watershed, conveyed via "an unbroken chain of person-to-person connections." Apparently, that chain brought the virus into the Spanish colony of Louisiana, at the mouth of the Mississippi, where smallpox proliferated during the winter of 1778–79.

During the summer of 1779, the disease appeared in Mexico City, where at least 9,000 people died by year's end. North America's largest and most cosmopolitan center, Mexico City annually gathered and disgorged thousands of travelers, making it the perfect ground for breeding and spreading smallpox. By collecting and analyzing the mortality returns from Mexican parishes, Fenn painstakingly and insightfully reconstructs the disease's trajectory northward deep into the hinterland. At the end of 1780, the epidemic reached New Mexico, then the northern frontier of the vast Spanish Empire. In Santa Fe, mortality surged from only 6 deaths (from all causes) in December 1780 to 39 in January 1781 and to 181 in February.

Beyond New Mexico, European observers were few and transient: occasional sojourners in a vast geography possessed by Indian peoples. On the Great Plains, which stretched northward into Canada, tribes of hunting-and-gathering nomads swirled around the more permanent villages of horticultural Indians dwelling along the few major rivers, principally the long and muddy Missouri. For most of the eighteenth century, the villagers more than held their own in wars against the nomads. In addition to war, the various native peoples traded over vast distances. Native middlemen sent horses northward from New Mexico in exchange for Indian slaves taken by other natives in wars fueled by guns sold by British traders at forts along subarctic Hudson Bay for buffalo hides and beaver pelts. Mounted on newly acquired horses and newly armed with guns, the Great Plains Indians could conduct war and trade at unprecedented velocity and over far greater distances. "It was," Fenn notes, "an intricate web of connections that could carry pox as well as pelts far and wide."

During the summer of 1782, native informants alerted the Hudson Bay traders to the demographic catastrophe raging in the immense interior. Thousands of Indians were dead or dying of smallpox. Traveling traders saw plenty of confirmation; one reported that "hundreds lay expiring together without assistance, without courage, or the least glimmering hopes of recovery." Panic compounded the mortality as relatives abandoned the victims, convinced that none would recover. Denied care, few did.

Fenn persuasively links the northern reports of 1782 to the New Mexican evidence of 1781 and the Mexican parish returns of 1779–80 as parts of one big epidemic rather than several isolated episodes. She concludes: "The Mexico City outbreak generated a tidal wave of smallpox that reached as far north as Hudson Bay and as far west as Alaska." In the transmission northward beyond New Mexico, Fenn emphasizes the role of the Shoshone Indians, who lived in the Rocky Mountains and on the northwestern Great Plains. During the early eighteenth century, they became the preeminent middlemen in the north-south trade in New Mexican horses for Indian slaves. In 1781, their enemies, the Blackfeet, struck back by raiding Shoshone camps. The raiders won surprisingly easy victories, for most of the Shoshone were dying from smallpox. Unwittingly, the victors carried the grim disease homeward. A survivor told a trader: "We had no belief that one Man could give it to another, any more than a wounded Man could give his wound to another."

In tracking the disease, Fenn makes the most of the sparse and terse records made by the Indians, principally some "winter counts": buffalo hides spirally decorated with historical pictograms, one per winter. Each symbol represents the most conspicuous annual event in a tribe's experience, beginning in the late eighteenth century. At least thirteen of these survive to attest that smallpox dominated the native memory of the years 1781 and 1782. But, generally, Fenn must rely on the erratic accounts of Spanish officials and British traders perched at the southern and northern edges of the Great Plains, looking in, with vague apprehension, on the native world.

By necessity, Fenn speculates to fill in broad gaps between disparate clues. At one critical point in her story, she concedes that her interpretation "hangs upon a single shred of substantial evidence and the concurrence of a number of widely varying circumstances." Frank about her speculative methods and limited sources, she invites readers into the detective work of making the most of a few traces in the documentary record. Rather than curse and dismiss this native world as historical darkness, she finds and lights the only candles available to her.

Fenn must be especially resourceful in deciphering the disease's probable route into the Pacific Northwest. Lacking colonies or resident traders, the Pacific Northwest remained, to eighteenth-century Europeans, the most mysterious and remote corner of North America. And so it is also terra incognita to colonial historians. Not until the late 1780s did sojourning mariners become routine, annual visitors with a precise understanding of the coastline. Come to trade with the natives for sea otter pelts, these mariners found signs of a massive smallpox epidemic: abandoned villages; bleaching skeletons scattered on the beaches; and native survivors with grim stories and pocked faces. But when and how had *Variola* arrived?

Fenn thoroughly and shrewdly examines the various European suspects. During the 1770s, Russian fur traders and Spanish explorers had probed the coastline, visiting the native villages. In 1778, the celebrated English navigator Capt. James Cook sojourned with the Nootka people of Vancouver Island. None of these visitors reported any traces of smallpox. By careful research, Fenn also dismisses the possibility that the mariners unwittingly introduced *Variola*, to spread after their departure. She detects no traces of epidemic in either their home ports or aboard their ships during voyages far longer than the incubation period. By canvassing the multiple European forays to tell her smallpox story, Fenn concisely, yet comprehensively, depicts the rich complexities of a part of North America generally left mysterious in our histories.

By eliminating Europeans, Fenn returns to the Shoshone as critical in transmitting the disease into the Pacific Northwest. European mariners detected that the Pacific natives traded up the Columbia River with the Nez Perce Indians of the Rocky Mountains. During their subsequent transcontinental expedition of 1804–6, Meriwether Lewis and William Clark noted that the Shoshone routinely traded with their neighbors, the Nez Perce. Fenn plausibly reads that relationship back into the previous generation to interpret the Shoshone and the Nez Perce as key links in the chain that brought *Variola* from New Mexico, up the Great Plains, into the Rocky Mountains, and down the Columbia to the Pacific. She explains: "Here the evidence regarding smallpox dwindles to nothing. But given *Variola*'s transit thus far, it takes no great leap to imagine the disease traveling so short a distance [from the Shoshone to the Nez Perce]." Once again, the smallpox story serves Fenn's larger ends: to reveal the continental shockwaves of colonialism far beyond the white faces; and to expose the enduring power of native networks of long-distance trade and diplomacy.

After canvassing the epidemic's spread across the continent, Fenn interprets its consequences. By her conservative estimate, during the war years, smallpox claimed the lives of 130,000 North Americans, most of them Indians. The epidemic killed far more people than did all of the battles in the long war. By disproportionately afflicting some native groups, the disease empowered neighboring groups that suffered less. Because the village Indians of the Missouri valley lived in greater concentrations, they died at a greater rate than did their enemies among the horse nomads. Exploiting their new advantage, the nomadic Lakota tribes destroyed many of the disease-weakened villages to become the most numerous and most powerful people in the northern Great Plains by 1800. Farther north, the Blackfeet similarly benefited from the greater deaths suffered by their rivals, the Shoshone to the west and the Cree to the east. The reduction of the Cree enabled the Blackfeet to obtain more guns directly from the British traders at Hudson Bay. Better armed than their enemies, the Blackfeet dominated the northern Great Plains, taking captives and hunting territory from the weakened Shoshone. At the start of the nineteenth century, the embattled Shoshone welcomed the Lewis and Clark expedition as an opportunity to obtain American allies and guns to even their scores with the Blackfeet. In the pattern of native rivalries, shifted by the epidemic, the expanding Americans found new opportunities to dominate the continent.

Ultimately, "*Variola* was a virus of empire," for, "in the long run, the pestilence seemed invariably to favor the great imperial powers of Europe and the United States." Especially the United States: with much help from smallpox in Virginia, the Americans won their revolution without conceding liberty to their many slaves. After the war, thanks to the further reduction of Indian numbers, the Americans more readily expanded their settlements westward, reaching the Pacific by the 1840s.

Fenn recovers and tells a story that is timely as well as sobering. Contrary to official and popular myths, smallpox is still with us. Advances in methods of inoculation and measures of public health did combine dramatically to curtail the disease during the twentieth century. Deemed eradicated in 1979 by the World Health Organization, smallpox last claimed victims in September 1978, when a medical technician died after contracting the virus from matter inadequately secured at a laboratory in Birmingham, England. In shame and despair, the laboratory's head committed suicide.

*Variola* will almost certainly kill again—if not by another accident, then by intentional proliferation as a biological weapon in war. After 1979, the World Health Organization reduced the officially authorized stocks of *Variola* to just two: one in the United States and one in Russia. Both were scheduled for destruction in 1999, but the American government balked. Suspecting a larger number of clandestine stocks in other nations, the American military preferred to preserve its own potential for biological warfare. If unleashed into our place and time, *Variola* will delight in human hosts far more crowded, rapidly mobile, capable of mass warfare, and free from the immunities of smallpox experience than in the eighteenth century.

# 4
# Martyrs to Venus

*October 28, 2002*

We usually think of colonial Americans as the passionless Puritans of Victorian stereotype. The humorist H. L. Mencken infamously described them as bedeviled by "the haunting, haunting fear that somewhere, someone may be happy." When asked to think of a colonial woman, we conjure up Hester Prynne, forced by Nathaniel Hawthorne to wear a scarlet letter for her adultery. Hawthorne and Mencken, in their own day, blamed the colonial past for repression while we recall their criticisms to congratulate ourselves for being oh so liberated and tolerant.

In this lively but uneven new book, historian Richard Godbeer challenges our traditional stereotypes of colonial America by recovering a remarkable volume of sexual discussion and debate, prosecution and evasion. The diverse colonists were more than just the Puritans of New England, and not even they were as puritanical as we have imagined. In both their sexual excesses and their anxieties, Godbeer's colonists seem surprisingly modern and accessible. Indeed, in their "complex and conflict-ridden sexual culture" Godbeer detects something very familiar: a "culture war, pitting different conceptions of sexual and marital etiquette against each other."

Godbeer discerns at least two sexual revolutions, and perhaps three, in early America. English colonization of New England began during the first revolution: a systematic drive by Puritan moral reformers to restrain the exuberance of Elizabethan England. They challenged an alternative, folk tradition of marriage that Godbeer characterizes as "pragmatic" and "popular." Avoiding the bother and the expense of official marriage and divorce, the pragmatic held their own private and informal marriages, impromptu separations, and convenient remarriages. Frustrated by official indifference to moral enforcement in England, many Puritans emigrated to found colonies in New England, where they could establish their vision of a "Bible Commonwealth." But they were accompanied

*Sexual Revolution in Early America,* by Richard Godbeer (Johns Hopkins University Press, 2002)

by enough moral reprobates to keep their new courts busy. The Puritan revolution also made little headway in the other, southern colonies, where ministers and magistrates were too few and far between to reform the popular tradition of loose and serial marriage.

Despite the limits of the Puritan revolution, Godbeer detects, during the eighteenth century, a second and radically different cultural revolution "toward a more individualistic marketplace of sexual desire and fulfillment, much to the horror of those who feared that greater personal freedom brought with it greater individual vulnerability." Premarital pregnancy surged, and a declining proportion of young men married the women they impregnated. And at century's end, horrified moralists mounted what could be described as a third revolution: a new celebration of female morality and premarital chastity in the name of the virtue needed to sustain the new republic founded by the American Revolution.

Although neat in concept, Godbeer's tripartite scheme often overrides the limits and complexities of the colonial evidence. His book also suffers from a division into episodic chapters that applies divergent methods to different colonial regions to reach inconsistent conclusions about the big picture.

Godbeer acknowledges that our own culture obsesses about sex in ways that would have been starkly alien to our colonial predecessors. They had no notion of "sexuality"—a concept that we have promoted to the core of human identity. In Godbeer's words, the colonists "viewed sex not as a product of sexuality but as a component of spirituality, cultural identity, and social status." Lacking the categories of homosexual and heterosexual, the colonists thought, instead, in terms of various acts, some moral (vaginal sex within marriage), but most immoral (a spectrum ranging from masturbation through fornication and adultery to sodomy and bestiality). They dreaded sodomy but characterized no one as fundamentally a sodomite, for they understood all sins as tempting everyone, even the most overtly godly. Such were the wages of universal, original sin in a culture immersed in the Bible rather than in Freud.

Despite that insight, Godbeer's entire project ultimately derives from our own culture's anachronistic curiosity to find sex and sexuality in the past. No matter his attention to historical context, Godbeer ultimately serves our voyeurism by highlighting the sexual as a distinct realm of human activity. Indeed, his book succeeds most fully as a sprightly description of sexual escapades, offering colorful anecdotes to tease our conventional expectations of stuffy colonists. In one seventeenth-century New England town, Samuel Terry provocatively disrupted Sabbath services by standing before a church window "chafing his yard to provoke lust, even in sermon time." Another New England court case reveals fornication between Hannah Green and William Clark: "a noise affrighted him and made him run away and he then carried away in haste her petticoat instead of his britches." Although Godbeer means to discredit the simple stereotype of the repressed Puritan, he exploits the persistence of that image in our minds, which affords us pleasure in discovering past sins.

Earlier scholars also balked at examining colonial sex—as a subject in its own right—from a fear that the sources were too scarce. Godbeer, however, forges ahead, "astonished by the richness of the material that survives on the subject." The problem is not that he lacks sources but, rather, that they are more misleading than he recognizes. Few diaries and letters survive from the colonial era, and fewer still frankly admit to sexual thoughts and acts. Generalizing from those scatological few to the larger colonial population is problematic, to say the least. More often, Godbeer must rely on hearsay accounts recorded by travelers, who keenly gathered news of scandals to deride the locales that they disliked. Or Godbeer depends on the recorded testimony from court cases brought by authorities or by aggrieved spouses seeking a divorce. The travelers' accounts and court cases provide plenty of seamy and steamy quotations, but taking them as representative skews our picture of colonial sexuality toward the sensational. Finding what he seeks, Godbeer proves reluctant to doubt any of his sources. That he discovers more conflict than consensus, more deviance than conformity, seems inevitable, given the nature of his sources—and his lack of interest in challenging them. Reading today's police log or tabloid newspaper certainly conveys a gritty reality obscured in other genres, but it is a reality that needs to be kept in proportion when characterizing an entire society.

Taking an episodic and anecdotal approach, Godbeer balks at designing quantitative tests that might give statistical precision and meaning to his broad implication of rampant illicit sex in the colonies. He observes that "it was not unusual for early Americans to pass from one cohabitational relationship to the next with scant regard for the formalities of divorce and remarriage." Does "not unusual" mean that most colonists did this? The statement is meaningless without some attempt to determine, for at least some sample of the population, the proportion of unofficial couples. Without statistical tests yoked to a research design, we have only a lot of colorful stories that may or may not be representative of the society.

When Godbeer does employ numbers, they appear out of context and convey a misleading sense of frequency. For example, he reports that "more than a hundred women were convicted" for bearing children out of wedlock in Essex County, Massachusetts, between 1640 and 1685. About 100 does not seem so many when divided by 45 years, to indicate only 2.2 such cases per year—in a county that had at least 5,000 inhabitants by 1685. If Godbeer provided comparable data for out-of-wedlock births from seventeenth-century England—or from contemporary America—we would certainly conclude that the New England Puritans were remarkably successful at reducing premarital pregnancy. Two cases per year in a populous county seems impressive only when run against our stereotypical expectation that those repressed Puritans had no illicit sex.

In interpreting varying levels of prosecution, Godbeer wants it both ways, regarding both a low and a high level as evidence for rampant illicit sex. In seventeenth-century New England, where he finds numerous prosecutions for fornication and lewd speech, Godbeer concludes that the authorities had their hands full coping with popular deviance and defiance. But in seventeenth-century Virginia, he regards the only known sodomy case as evidence that the overwhelmingly male population so regularly practiced sodomy, and so openly resented its sole prosecution, that the authorities never again dared to enforce the law. Similarly, in eighteenth-century Philadelphia, where all moral prosecutions were, for his purposes, inconveniently sparse, Godbeer insists that rampant promiscuity had worn down the authorities.

A specialist in the cultural history of seventeenth-century New England, Godbeer appears most comfortable and persuasive when analyzing particular episodes and texts drawn from that region and that century. In an especially insightful segment, he examines the case of Nicholas Sension of Windsor, Connecticut, in 1677. His prosecution for sodomy—a crime which carried the death penalty—seems to confirm Puritan rigidity and intolerance, but Godbeer reveals that for more than twenty years, Sension's neighbors had recognized and reproved his behavior without involving the court. Because Sension was otherwise a good neighbor and a prosperous farmer who acted only on young men of lower status, his townsmen balked at prosecuting him for a crime that carried the death penalty. Despite abundant evidence of multiple acts, the jury convicted Sension only of the lesser charge of attempted sodomy, which brought a public whipping and shaming instead of hanging. His Puritan neighbors persistently saw Sension as a wayward but redeemable sinner, no different from any other soul, rather than as a distinctive sodomite. During the seventeenth century, only two men ever suffered execution for sodomy in New England.

In addition to softening our image of the Puritans' moral enforcement, Godbeer ameliorates their cold image by recovering their sexual passion within both marriage and spirituality. In this emphasis, he follows the lead of Edmund S. Morgan, who made a similar case in 1942. Puritan sermons, poetry, and love letters celebrated marital and procreative sex in part to discourage all sexuality before or outside of marriage.

Never people to do things by halves, the Puritans extolled foreplay and orgasms by husband and wife. In a guide to marriage, Rev. William Gouge preached that sex "must be performed with good will and delight, willingly, readily, and cheerfully." Believing that conception depended on a female orgasm, ministers urged every husband to attend to his wife's desires. Another marital guide instructed: "When the husband cometh into the wife's chamber, he must entertain her with all kind of dalliance, wanton behavior, and allurements to venery."

More striking still, the Puritans expressed their spirituality in erotic terms that transcended gender. Ministers exhorted Puritans, male and female, to submit to "an eternal love affair with Jesus Christ." One young man asked in his diary: "Will the Lord now again return and embrace me in the arms of his dearest love? Will he fall upon my neck and kiss me?" Because souls were equal and either without gender or vaguely female, Puritan men comfortably spoke of submitting as brides to ravishment by Christ as their spiritual bridegroom. Godbeer concludes: "Puritan sensibility offered a way to spiritualize sex and sexualize the spirit in a glorious and torrid symbiosis."

New England's relatively dense pattern of settlement permitted close moral oversight by neighbors and by numerous ministers and magistrates. In the southern colonies, however, settlers were more dispersed and their churches and courts were fewer and usually more distant. In the colonial South, most of the ordained clergy were Anglicans rather than Puritans, but they sought a similar sexual decorum confined within the bounds of official marriage. In touring the raw and far-flung southern settlements, however, the Anglican missionaries could only fume in righteous frustration at their moral impotence. In 1766, the hyperbolic Rev. Charles Woodmason insisted that "concubinage [was] general" and that men engaged in "swopping their wives as cattle." Worst of all, "they will commit the grossest enormities before my face and laugh at all admonition." One especially impertinent settler stole and donned Woodmason's clerical gown before slipping into bed with a loose woman—who then brazenly circulated the story that Woodmason had ravished her.

Behaviors that Woodmason described as fornication, adultery, bigamy, and prostitution Godbeer characterizes as within the pragmatic and popular tradition of informal and serial marriage. Daunted by official fees and long, hard travel to the nearest minister, common settlers conducted their own marriage and separation ceremonies. Some even followed an old English custom of publicly selling a wife before witnesses to a new husband (apparently at her request) as a way to absolve the old husband of responsibility for her subsequent debts.

In the southern, middle third, of his book, Godbeer also turns, belatedly, to the relationship of sex and race. In contrast to other scholars of the history of sex and sexuality, Godbeer seems surprisingly uninterested in overtly applying a theory to organize his diverse evidence. Other colonial historians have focused on the construction of legal and customary barriers to sexual relations between white women and the racial "other"—Indians and enslaved Africans—as fundamental to a power structure that privileged white men. Rather than beginning there, or weaving that dimension into every chapter, as would befit the multiracial society of colonial America, Godbeer primarily examines sexuality within the white race. He confines discussion of interracial sex to two belated chapters: one about Indians, and the other about enslaved Africans. And in both cases, he offers relatively little about Indian or African concepts and patterns of sex, focusing instead on what white people wrote about, or did to, people of color.

Despite some rich sources, Godbeer's discussion of relations with Indians proves surprisingly superficial. He inconclusively concludes: "Rape was doubtless more common and relations in general more contested than the extant sources, with all their biases, suggest; but we should not ignore evidence for more positive interactions. Indians and Englishmen could and sometimes did enjoy each other, love each other, and live together in peace." No doubt, but a historian should discern some larger pattern and some trend over time, with some explanation for both, rather than simply describe, in conditional terms, two extremes that accommodate every behavior in between—which is to say nothing at all.

Godbeer's treatment of interracial sex between Africans and whites is clearer and more discerning, despite his heavy reliance for sources on the usual narrow set of suspects. The flamboyant diarists William Byrd of Virginia, John Gabriel Stedman of Surinam, and Thomas Thistlewood of Jamaica provide plenty of scatological color. Byrd famously "rogered" his wife on a billiard table and fondled "wenches" in the taverns, afterward praying for redemption in his study. Stedman reported that the jealous wife of a straying planter "put an end to the life of a young and beautiful Quodroon girl by the infernal means of plunging a red hot poker in her body, by those parts which decency forbids to mention." Between 1751 and 1764, Thistlewood recorded intercourse 1,774 times with at least 109 slave women, mostly by compulsion.

To his credit, Godbeer recognizes the exceptional nature of his few sources: "William Byrd may well have been unique in the extent to which he wrote about sex and the place that it occupied in his mental world." Godbeer also breaks important new ground by contrasting the attitudes of the elites in Virginia and Carolina toward the exploitation of slave women. Where the Virginia planters, including Thomas Jefferson, tried (ultimately, in vain) to keep secret their slave mistresses, the South

Carolina elites more frankly celebrated or debated their indulgence in enslaved bodies.

Godbeer finally examines, from three especially divergent angles, the sexual revolution he detects in eighteenth-century America. The southern and West Indian colonies vanish from the last third of the book; New England resumes its dominant role; and the previously neglected middle colonies (Pennsylvania, New York, and New Jersey) at last make a cameo appearance.

In eighteenth-century New England, premarital sex and pregnancy surged. Previous historical interpretations generally follow the trope first advanced by evangelical critics during the religious revivals of the 1740s: that New England had declined from Puritan piety to wallow in immorality. More sensibly, Godbeer depicts a triumph of moral pragmatism over the impossible purity of the initial Puritan agenda. Unable to prevent young people from engaging in premarital sex, rural parents sensibly sought some influence and information by encouraging the practice of "bundling." Instead of seeking sex in barns or byways, young people slept together, "bundled" in the paternal home. Although ostensibly partly clothed and supposed to limit themselves to fondling, the bundlers produced the surge in premarital pregnancy. Some ministers fulminated against the practice, but in vain and to the detriment of their influence and careers.

Parents defended bundling because it revealed whom their daughters slept with, so that in the event of pregnancy, they could bring effective pressure for marriage or a financial settlement. "In order to ensure that unwed fathers were held accountable," Godbeer explains, "it was essential that people other than the lovers themselves know that they had been involved with each other." A growing number of young women got only financial settlements for their out-of-wedlock babies, but those women suffered surprisingly little damage to their reputation; most quickly found another reputable man to marry. Godbeer describes the new rules of the game "as a pragmatic accommodation between the greater sexual freedom that young people now enjoyed and the desire of parents to maintain protective surveillance over their children."

In the next chapter, however, Godbeer gives his book a schizophrenic turn by narrating the same developments in a far more ominous tone. That tone registers his shift away from the social records of the preceding chapter entirely into cultural analysis of a literary genre. The morally didactic essays and novels of the postrevolutionary era depicted premarital pregnancy as an indelible stain, fatal to a woman's reputation and prospects for marriage. Seduced, impregnated, and abandoned, a young woman should wither in depression and illness into an early grave rather than suffer a prolonged life of disgrace, poverty, and prostitution.

Where literature had previously cast women as lusty temptresses, the new didacticism of the early republic depicted them as fundamentally more moral and vulnerable than men. That put the responsibility for chastity on women, who could and should resist the sexual temptations that overwhelmed men. "Let the fair remember," preached one essayist, "that their peace, dignity, and character chiefly depend on themselves." Such moralizing implied, in Godbeer's words, "that women could seduce men into virtue, a reversal of earlier writings that portrayed womankind as luring male victims into vice." He concludes that the didactic literature "sought nothing less than the moral reconstruction of the individual, especially of women, in order to meet the challenges of an increasingly permissive society."

Although an effective summary of the postrevolutionary literature, Godbeer's account of such woe and ruin radically contradict his previous picture of pragmatic families handling premarital pregnancy with little or no damage to their daughters' reputations. Should we conclude, then, that the stories were mere romances, indulged in imagination without connection—by either cause or effect—in behavior? No, Godbeer insists, "the changing tone . . . was not merely mimetic: the seduction genre appealed to Americans because it spoke to troubling issues with which they were all too familiar." Insignificant in one chapter, seduction and ruin become real, rampant, and troubling in the next.

To explain Americans' increasing anxiety over premarital sex, Godbeer also enlists political ideology. The American Revolution spawned a republican ideology that stressed the role of women in raising virtuous children capable of self-sacrifice for the common good. The apparently widespread seduction and abandonment of women therefore threatened the survival of the republic; preserving liberty required greater female morality and greater parental oversight.

In this explanatory reach to the American Revolution, Godbeer is in numerous company. Historians often credit every social and cultural change in the early republic to the effects of political revolution. The problem is that many of those changes also occurred in counterrevolutionary Great Britain. For example, eighteenth-century British writers invented, and then exported to America, the didactic literature of seduction and ruin. Indeed, the American popularity of British novels attests to the cultural limits of the American Revolution. Despite political independence, Americans remained culturally dependent on Britain as the literary metropolis that set the standards for manners and morals, particularly for the socially ambitious.

A more satisfactory explanation for the apparent coexistence of pragmatic courtship and literary hysteria finds that they derived from, and spoke to, two different generations in two distinct social orbits: one mid-eighteenth century, rural, and traditional; the other late eighteenth century, cosmopolitan, and upwardly mobile. The evidence for bundling comes primarily from New England's country towns, where most of the population lived, while the moral didacticism later emerged in the newspapers, magazines, and novels printed in the cities and commercial villages. The print media spoke first and foremost to the middle-class Americans who longed to perfect the manners and morality that composed "gentility"—a standard that derived from an idealized image of the British gentry as found in Jane Austen's novels.

This is not to say that the Revolution played no part. Prior to independence, only the colonial elite had mastered gentility, but the Revolution democratized aspiration, as middle-class people, in country towns as well as seaport cities, cultivated their own pretensions to gentility. Then, at century's end, a didactic literature that began in the cities found growing numbers of country readers eager to escape their reputation as bumpkins.

Regrettably, Godbeer does not seek data for premarital pregnancy at the close of the eighteenth and the start of the nineteenth century to compare with his earlier data. He needed to examine whether the didactic literature changed behavior in the countryside. Here his segregation of social and cultural methods in distinct chapters proves especially limiting. If he found that premarital pregnancies did not markedly decline in the era of didactic literature, perhaps those stories served as a vicarious outlet that vented anxieties in negative fantasies, thereby permitting young people to persist in premarital sex.

If Godbeer's final chapter, on Philadelphia, is accurate, the didactic essays and novels had no moderating effect on sexual behavior. He depicts postrevolutionary Philadelphia as sin city: "casual sex, unmarried relationships, and adulterous affairs were commonplace." Citing an "unbridled atmosphere" and a "polyamorous culture," Godbeer adds that "venereal infection ran rampant among the city's residents, and out-of-wedlock pregnancies also became increasingly common." But he presents little evidence to support his lurid caricature of the city. No statistical analysis supports his claims for out-of-wedlock pregnancies, and, in his only cited figure for venereal disease, he notes that clerks detected it in "around ten per cent" of those admitted to Philadelphia's hospital for the poor during a single year (June 1800–June 1801). One year and 10 percent of the city's most marginal people, including prostitutes, is no meaningful evidence for an epidemic in the city as a whole for a generation. To document brazen abandon among Philadelphia's women, Godbeer notes that "11 of 14 women cited for bastardy by the Philadelphia Quaker meeting between 1760 and 1780 were expelled because they refused to acknowledge that they had sinned." But a rate of less than one such case per year in a city with a population in excess of 30,000 seems better evidence for moral decorum than for a "polyamorous culture."

Godbeer primarily relies on a handful of divorce cases. Adultery and bigamy ran "rampant," but he cites only two divorce cases and must explain the virtual absence of prosecution by authorities of those crimes. Exaggerating Philadelphia's scale, he asserts that, "keeping track of marital histories in a large and chaotic metropolis was extremely challenging, so that bigamy and adulterous cohabitation seldom came to the courts' attention save in the context of divorce petitions." Similarly, two other divorce cases embolden him to declare that "some Philadelphia women evidently responded with enthusiasm to opportunities for non-marital sex that came their way or actively sought pleasure in casual encounters and transient affairs." But should we characterize an entire city as promiscuous primarily on the basis of charges hurled in a few divorce cases? Godbeer's response is circular: "not all allegations made by divorce petitioners and their supporters are necessarily reliable, but late eighteenth-century Philadelphians must have realized that claims of rampant promiscuity would appear only too credible." Only to those who took their reality from those divorce records.

Thus, Godbeer proposes radically contradictory readings of sexual culture in late eighteenth-century America. First, the inhabitants appear as pragmatists who shrewdly managed surging rates of premarital pregnancy. Next, they are consumed with anxiety over premarital sex and persuaded to indoctrinate their daughters to defend the republic with their chastity. Alas, although largely published in Philadelphia, none of this literature apparently affected behavior in that moral sinkhole.

The book's conflicting pictures of eighteenth-century culture reflect the author's own ambivalence about social criticism of contemporary forms of sexuality. Godbeer warns against our conservatives, "who argue that only certain kinds of sexual relationships should be accorded cultural legitimacy" and who "often point to colonial society as an ideal from which modern Americans have degenerated." By recognizing colonial America as a highly contested sexual culture, we cannot indulge in it as a golden age of moral consensus from which to fulminate against modern sins. But Godbeer contradicts that warning by occasionally expressing a surprising nostalgia for an organic and hierarchical colonial regime that he imagines preceded the libertarian sexual revolution that he (sometimes) finds in the late eighteenth century. Rather than celebrate the "permissive sexual climate" of his version of Philadelphia, Godbeer emphasizes the dark side: "as urban society became less organic and more individualistic, that left its members less protected as well as restricted by the corporate and hierarchic ties of the past."

For poor people, in particular, "individual freedom must have been a lonely and frightening experience." He cites the sad fate of Con McCue, a young Irish immigrant admitted in 1794 to the Philadelphia almshouse with a fatal venereal disease. The almshouse clerk recorded McCue's demise as "a martyrdom to Venus." Godbeer observes: "There were many such martyrdoms during this period in Philadelphia, undergone by men and women whose intimate encounters bore deadly fruit." The Puritans could expect no better vindication than Godbeer's depiction of a lurid Philadelphia.

5

# Sex and the City

*October 12, 1998*

So many elements of this compelling murder story seem so very contemporary. A stylish prostitute with a tony clientele is found dead in her burning bed. A trail of circumstantial evidence, including a discarded hatchet and a cloak, implicates a handsome young man with political connections. A fevered and unscrupulous press hypes the case throughout the nation, dwelling on the lurid combination of illicit sex and deadly violence. An immense throng attends a trial that features a celebrity defense lawyer at the peak of his powers. Appealing to class and gender prejudices, he assails the character of the victim and of her fellow prostitutes while casting his client as an innocent and misunderstood boy from an upstanding family. A surprise defense witness, an inept prosecution, and a biased judge strengthen the defense's case in the courtroom, but not in the court of public opinion. In a verdict that shocks the nation, the jury quickly acquits. Although he becomes a hero to other rakish young men, the acquitted reaps sustained scorn from moralizing editors, columnists, and readers convinced that the trial was a mockery of justice.

Yet this story of murder and injustice unfolded in New York City in 1836—a place in time with differences from, as well as resonances to, our own. Although the nation's largest city, New York had a population of only 270,000. Almost all dwelled in brick or wooden buildings of no more than four stories clustered in the lower third of Manhattan. Assault-and-battery cases were common; murder was not. In 1835, the city reported only seven homicides. Even the murder of a prostitute, so sadly routine today, could shock New Yorkers of the 1830s.

As a proportion of the population, prostitutes were more numerous, more conspicuous, and more tolerated than today. At least fifteen hundred prostitutes, and perhaps as many as ten thousand, worked in the city, most for low rates in the squalid slums of the Five Points District.

*The Murder of Helen Jewett: The Life and Death of a Prostitute in Nineteenth-Century New York*, by Patricia Cline Cohen (Alfred A. Knopf, 1998)

The more fortunate charged premium prices (three dollars to five dollars) and belonged to fashionable brothels woven into reputable neighborhoods. Helen Jewett lived and worked in the brothels of the expensive Fifth Ward, "the city's cultural and political center." City Hall and the Park Theatre were both a five-minute walk from her last residence, 41 Thomas Street. The property belonged to John R. Livingston, who belonged to the state's most prestigious family. His brother—who also lived in the neighborhood—had been secretary of state in Andrew Jackson's administration. The fashionable prostitutes frequented the city's theaters, which reserved special and conspicuous sections where they could meet their clients.

Women, not men, ran the brothels by leasing buildings from the likes of John R. Livingston. The more fashionable prostitutes made a good and independent living: $1,500 to $2,000 a year at a time when a young male clerk was lucky to earn $300. No other occupation then open to women paid nearly as well or permitted nearly as much autonomy and enterprise—provided, of course, that they met brothel standards and so could escape the grim and cheap life of streetwalking in the Five Points.

No law explicitly forbade selling sex, and so prostitution was not, strictly speaking, illegal. Vigilant police and magistrates could prosecute prostitutes for vagrancy or disorderly conduct. Few New York policemen and magistrates were so vigilant. Prostitutes had much more to fear from gangs of street toughs who occasionally ransacked the fashionable brothels, smashing furniture and windows, insulting and pummeling the women. These working-class men exercised both their misogyny and their resentment of class privilege.

A deft and thorough historian, Patricia Cline Cohen draws us into this alluring mix of the familiar and the strange. In her gripping opening chapter, "Snow in April," Cohen sets the vivid and tragic tone that sustains her entire book. With a steady accumulation of telling details, she carefully builds in the mind's eye the texture of New York and the diversity of its people. She shifts skillfully from the broader urban scene on a "cold, dark, and wet" Saturday night, April 9, 1836, to Rosina Townsend's brothel at 41 Thomas Street. Sensing something amiss, Townsend began to roam through her premises in the predawn hours of Sunday morning, April 10. Following a cryptic and troubling set of clues, Townsend ascended the stairs to the bedroom door of Helen Jewett. Pulled open, the door unleashed a billowing cloud of smoke from the burning bed that held Jewett's bloody and singed corpse. The alarm quickly spread through the house, into the neighborhood, and, by the end of the day, throughout the city. Even the mayor dropped by to investigate.

Suspicion immediately focused on Richard P. Robinson, a moody, dashing, and boyish (aged nineteen) clerk in a fashionable Manhattan fabric store. Townsend and two other prostitutes identified him as Helen's primary (but most volatile) customer. Two investigating policemen found a hatchet and a dark cloak behind the brothel along with clues that led them to Robinson's boardinghouse. After waking the suspect, the policemen hurried him back to the brothel to view the confusion and the corpse. "The officers scrutinizing his reaction were amazed to note his composure and impassivity," Cohen writes. Two doctors quickly performed an autopsy and assisted a hastily convened coroner's jury (twelve men plucked from the crowd gathered in the street) which ruled Jewett's death a homicide "by the hand of Richard P. Robinson." Despite his protestations of innocence, the officers arrested Robinson and hurried him off to the nearby city jail.

Robinson belonged to a new, large, and rapidly growing social group: aspiring young men living on their own in cheap, unsupervised boardinghouses in the city, far from their middle-class homes and parents in the small towns of New England and upstate New York. Robinson came from Connecticut, where his prosperous and reputable father was a farmer, real estate speculator, and state legislator. By day, the clerks worked for moralistic and tight-fisted entrepreneurs determined to teach them sobriety, thrift, hard work, and self-sacrifice. By night, the clerks were on their own, set free to taste the city's amusements and vices, especially the overlapping realms of the theater and the brothel. For an impecunious clerk, commonly paid four dollars a week, to afford the five dollar fee of a fashionable prostitute invited embezzlement. Robinson never seemed to lack for money.

By the end of the week, virtually every newspaper reader in the Northeast knew of Jewett's murder and Robinson's arrest. The case, Cohen notes, "afforded an opportunity to contemplate the forbidden, the taboo life behind the velvet curtain of her brothel. Sexuality infused this crime, inspiring both attraction and repulsion." The alluring combination of sex, violence, and mystery attracted a voracious and competitive press, especially the new, cheap, mass-market newspapers that sold for a penny.

The aggressive, resourceful, and often unscrupulous editor of the *New York Herald,* James Gordon Bennett, seized the lead by visiting the crime scene (setting a new precedent) and by focusing on his own visceral reactions as the very essence of the story. He invited readers to share his overwrought feelings as he viewed the perfect corpse: "It was the most remarkable sight I ever beheld—I never have, and never expect to see such another. . . . The perfect figure—the exquisite limbs—the fine face—the full arms—the beautiful bust—all—all surpassing in every respect the Venus de Medicis. . . . For a few moments I was lost in admiration at this extraordinary sight—a beautiful female corpse—that surpassed the finest statue of antiquity." Bennett put the dead woman, rather than the living suspect, at the center of the story, where she remained throughout the following uproar and trial.

A voyeur but more, Bennett also took inventory of Jewett's room and found surprising evidence of literary taste and aspiration. She collected the romantic novels of Lord Byron, Sir Walter Scott, and Edward Bulwer-Lytton; subscribed to highbrow literary periodicals; and decorated her walls with theatrical playbills and a print of Byron. Her worktable, "strewn with pens, ink, and expensive writing paper," and her trunk stuffed with over ninety letters to and from her lovers attested to Helen's elaborate and refined correspondence. "This had been a girl with not only beauty but talent and wit," wrote Bennett, "She was a remarkable character, and has come to a remarkable end."

Murdered but refined, such a prostitute sold newspapers, for she defied the dismissive stereotype of the vulgar and degraded whore, unworthy of a second thought. Rather than dismissing her death as inevitable, inconsequential, and irrelevant to their own lives, readers hungered to know more about her "remarkable character" as well as her "remarkable end."

New York's editors and readers fit Helen into an especially powerful trope in American culture during the 1830s. She became a murder victim after suffering a ruinous seduction, which drove her from respectable society. Despoiled of her virginity and denied a reputable husband, Helen fled into the dangerous demimonde of prostitution. Her seducer was thus the ultimate murderer, the man who drove her into harm's way at 41 Thomas Street.

Picking up where the newspapers left off, Cohen painstakingly tracks down and interprets the diverse, scattered, and often fragmentary local records from Jewett's youth in central Maine. Anyone who has worked with such documents will marvel at Cohen's resourceful ingenuity, dogged persistence, and judicious care in distilling from them the life and personality of a poor girl from an obscure family. From many local archives, she taps genealogies, military muster rolls and pension applications, probate inventories, local newspaper stories and advertisements, ephemeral pamphlets, tax rolls, land deeds, and vital and town meeting records. Such tedious and time-consuming research can, in lesser hands, make for dull reading. But Cohen draws readers into the excitement of the historian as detective, inviting them to assess the strengths and weaknesses of possible explanations.

Cohen reveals that "Helen Jewett" was an alias, the latest in a series that included "Helen Mar" in Boston and "Maria Stanley" in Portland, Maine. Until age eighteen, she was Dorcas Doyen, the daughter of an impoverished, drunken, and transient shoemaker. Born in the hardscrabble rural town of Temple, Maine, Dorcas moved with her family to the nearby commercial town of Augusta, on the Kennebec River. There, in 1826, at the age of twelve, she joined the wealthy and genteel household of Judge Nathan Weston, chief justice of the Maine Supreme Court. Although a servant, Dorcas was indulged with an education and the leisure time to read. In 1830, however, she abruptly departed, apparently after losing her virginity. Drifting to Portland, then Boston, and, ultimately, New York, she became a prostitute named Helen Jewett.

But what had propelled her out of Judge Weston's service and into prostitution? Cohen finds a clue in the travel writings published by Anne Royall. In September 1827, Royall called at the Weston mansion, introducing the future Helen Jewett to readers: "When I knocked at the door of judge Western [sic], it was opened by a little girl . . . who saluted with inimitable sweetness, and with a graceful wave of her hand, invited me to take a seat on the sofa. I knew her to be a servant, which surprised me the more. Stepping back as she opened the door, with an air of the most accomplished lady—I forgot to ask for the Judge, but began to question the little girl respecting herself." Evidently, the young Dorcas Doyen was a keen observer and mimic of the genteel ways on display in her master's household. A year later, she could read these words of praise in Royall's book, readily available in the Augusta bookstore of Harlow Spaulding. Cohen speculates: "Dorcas Doyen, the girl who read books to imagine a world beyond the pantry and laundry room, had now become a character in a book. The experience was bound to unleash ambitions—inappropriate ambitions for a poor shoemaker's daughter in Maine of the 1820s."

In nineteenth-century America, pious moralists castigated the reading habits of young people, who preferred romantic novels to devotional tracts. Novels bred dangerous illusions, they warned, rendering the young discontented with reality. It was especially disruptive to social order and public morals to awaken and empower the imagination of girls from the lower classes. A servant girl might take on airs and imagine escape from her allotted drudgery by romantic marriage to a dashing gentleman. Such a girl would all too readily succumb to the wiles of unscrupulous rakes, who would blast her reputation forever. Meanwhile, the gentleman's laundry would suffer.

Because historians are no longer pious moralizers of the traditional sort, they tend to take with a grain of salt nineteenth-century warnings against novels. But not Patricia Cohen, who suggests that reading really did launch Dorcas Doyen on the path to seduction, prostitution, and untimely death. By imagining herself to be more than a servant girl, to be the equal of her master's children, Dorcas Doyen set herself up for a fall—for she put herself on a collision course with the sexual and class codes of her society.

Occasionally, Cohen's dogged research treats dead ends with more respect and detail than they warrant. Determined to unmask the rogue who ruined Dorcas Doyen, Cohen devotes an entire chapter to assessing four suspects in seduction—but only one proves of any substance. As a single man, bank cashier, and the owner of an Augusta bookstore near the Weston mansion, Harlow Spaulding best fits Helen Jewett's hints at the identity of her seducer. Still at great length and diminishing plausibility, Cohen explores three extreme long shots, including Judge Weston. A boy named Sumner receives four pages, although he probably existed only in a fantastic biography of Helen Jewett crafted in 1849 by a disreputable journalist. The details of that biography ring just a tad suspect: after allegedly despoiling Dorcas, Sumner shipped out to sea, bound to the Philippines, where he killed a Jesuit priest, landed in jail, but escaped with the help of the American consul. Cohen remarks: "A search of the manuscript records of the American consulate in the Philippines shows that the appointed consul on duty in the 1820s left his post for the years from 1825 to 1829 for health reasons, and no one took his place. Clearly Wilkes invented that aspect of the story." Who knew there were records for the American consulate in the Philippines from the 1820s! How many other historians would have sought and found them? And all to test a patently implausible story. Here we find one of the leading pleasures of Cohen's book: the full and fair invitation to evaluate the twists and turns of sometimes intriguing, but sometimes misleading, evidence.

Popular literature and public opinion enforced a double standard by insisting that the seduced and abandoned woman was ruined for life—unfitted for any decent marriage. Because the culture considered men as innately lusty and women as naturally "passionless," the latter bore the principal responsibility for restricting sexuality and the primary burden for failure. Dorcas Doyen's fundamental problem was that, from close observation, she had developed a taste for the genteel life. After her fall, she might have lapsed back into obscurity by moving far from her Augusta reputation to become a mill girl in Massachusetts or a farm wife in Illinois. Instead, she chose prostitution. It alone promised the income that could purchase the props, if not the substance, of the high life: silk dresses, fine jewelry, theater tickets, gilt-edged writing paper, and bottles of champagne. Contrary to the then-prevailing myth of the seduced woman as innocent and passive victim, Helen Jewett chose her new life of prostitution.

Having learned genteel manners by careful observation in the Weston mansion, Helen Jewett could play the ruined lady, which was especially alluring to young gentlemen. By quoting long passages from letters discovered in Jewett's trunk in 1836, Cohen invites readers to share in their secrets and in her analysis. The letters reveal Jewett's talent for self-invention, for self-dramatization, and for manipulating genteel but callow young men. The most surprising revelation is that she expected and obliged her clients to treat her as their one and only true love. She rebuked one wayward customer: "my heart is full to bursting, that another should have been preferred to me when you have so often assured me that you loved no one else, and I think every one with me must acknowledge the singular and powerful force with which a girl innocent in herself clings to the belief of innocence in her lover."

The prostitute as innocent and jealous lover was no easy role to play. The submission of her clients was especially extraordinary, because they had to pay her very well and to accept, with seeming good grace, the fact that she had multiple paying partners. Helen Jewett reversed the sexual double standard that had driven Dorcas Doyen from Augusta while shielding Harlow Spaulding's name and reputation. She may have lost in Augusta but, until the very end, she prevailed in New York City. She chose whom she slept with, got top dollar for it, and commanded the romantic submission of her clients. With one conspicuous exception, "her clients presented themselves as respectful, even adoring men." They had to "court and flatter her, write love letters, and bring gifts." But, if they played by her rules, she rewarded them with her adoring attention and eloquent flattery. Helen assured one client: "In you I found high, generous, noble, independent feelings, such as I had never before met with. A woman should perhaps blush to make the avowal, but I saw and loved you, and my life became a new object, and when I say that I loved you truly, devotedly, disinterestedly, and still do, I only speak the truth, and you can yet be to me all that I in my fondness have wished you were." Cohen explains: "Her plan was to make each customer feel especially beloved."

Sex alone sold cheap; men would pay top dollar only for a fantasy that demanded more of them. By an entrepreneurial stroke of genius, Jewett turned her seduction into her greatest asset. She embroidered her past to exaggerate her gentility—inventing, for example, a boarding-school education in French, Italian, and music. And she narrated her seduction with all the pathos she could muster. Helen had discerned that her story of a fall from the highest social rank drove men mad with desire. They longed to protect her *and* to relive the role of seducer. One enraptured client wrote: "What a prize the villain had who seduced you at the Boarding School. How I should liked to have been in his place!" The pose of talented and innocent victim looking for that one true friend and lover was very good for business.

Only Richard P. Robinson saw through her, assuring a friend that New York's prostitutes "can tell piteous tales of their wrongs and sufferings,—

tricks of the trade, tho',—tricks of the trade, I do assure you." Robinson alone could violate Jewett's rules and get away with it. They met in June 1835, and for two months he conformed to her demands. But then their relationship became volatile: often angry, frequently reconciled, never entirely ruptured. Cohen explains: "They both lived on—indeed, thrived on living on—an emotional edge. Both experienced an intensity of feelings, not merely romantic or sexual longing, but dark, moody, depressive feelings as well, that they both enjoyed giving vent to." But the pleasure was increasingly attended with pain. Used to seducing and abandoning young women, Robinson resented his inability to make a clean break from Jewett.

At last, in late March 1836, he sought that rupture by returning her letters and by demanding his in return. When Jewett delayed, he dreaded that she meant to reveal his deepest secret—probably that he had embezzled funds from his employer. By flirting with blackmail, she overlooked the menace in his last letters: "I *have* feelings over which I have no control, and which, if trifled with in any way, would make me unhappy and almost crazy." Unwary, on the night of April 9, she welcomed Robinson into her bed, assuming another reconciliation—but under his long, dark cloak he hid a stolen hatchet. "Sometime between eleven at night and three in the morning, Robinson killed Jewett with a hatchet blow to the forehead," Cohen concludes.

Although arrested and tried, Robinson got away with murder. His employer hired the best criminal defense lawyer in New York, Ogden Hoffman, who argued that vicious prostitutes must have killed Helen in a fit of jealousy and then framed his client. A grocer provided Robinson with a shaky alibi: he had been buying cigars on the night of the murder. It also helped the defendant that the courtroom was packed with his peers, rowdy young clerks who openly rooted for their new hero. Best of all, Judge Ogden Edwards (grandson of the famous Calvinist minister Jonathan Edwards) was openly dismissive of the prostitutes' testimony, which he instructed the jury to ignore. The prosecutor did his part by declining to summon the men who had patronized the brothel on the night of the murder. As gentlemen, their testimony might have confirmed that of the lowly prostitutes. But, as gentlemen, their bodies had to be kept out of the courtroom and their names out of the newspapers. Their absence crippled the prosecution's case.

The trial lasted five days, long by nineteenth-century standards. On the fifth, the defense and prosecution dedicated over ten hours to their closing arguments, about a fifth of the total time devoted to the case. The jury consisted of a dozen white men drawn from the shopkeeper and professional class: the employers of clerks like Robinson. After deliberating for no more than fifteen minutes, the jury returned a verdict of not guilty. The courtroom erupted with applause. By acquitting Robinson, judge and jury defended both class and male privilege.

Acquitted in the courtroom, but convicted in the press, Robinson soon left New York for east Texas: the violent frontier land of escape from the law, the press, wives, and memories. Assuming the name of Richard Parmalee, he prospered as the operator of a saloon (Cohen tracked down his account book), the deputy clerk of the county court, and the owner of a stagecoach line. Marriage to a rich widow with a score of slaves and a plantation made Parmalee one of the ten richest men in the boomtown of Nacogdoches. As he became a pillar of the community, Parmalee gradually talked more freely, but always disingenuously, about his brush with the law and with notoriety. He died in 1855 on a visit to Louisville, Kentucky. In an obituary, the *New York Times* identified Parmalee as Robinson and insisted that he had died, in Cohen's words, "ranting and raving and speaking often of a Helen Jewett." Probably too good to be true, Cohen thinks.

And what of Helen Jewett? In a perverse way, Robinson's acquittal served her well. Because the jury's verdict defied abundant evidence and public opinion, the acquittal denied the case closure, keeping it alive in the public imagination as a powerful and intriguing mystery. In death, and especially in justice denied, Jewett garnered a large and mostly sympathetic celebrity—far beyond even her own dreams of grandeur. No other Maine shoemaker's daughter ever became so famous. Cohen observes: "She was her own self-made character, and all but the final stage of her literary career was under her own control. That final stage came after her death, when she truly passed over the line into fiction and became a tragic but exciting figure rendered in pamphlets, stories, and short novels." And on into the histories and historical novels of this century, including a prominent role in Gore Vidal's *Burr.*

Her physical remains fared less well. Later in the nineteenth century, her New York graveyard was obliterated to make a city park. In 1972, a backhoe, remaking the park into a playground, broke open the forgotten graves. "But Helen Jewett did not meet that backhoe," Cohen writes. "She was not in Walker Park . . . nor St. John's Burying Ground, not for long anyway. Four nights after her burial, medical students went at her grave with spades and pickaxes, removed her body in a bag, and carted it off for dissection at the College of Physicians and Surgeons on Barclay Street. A short time later, the *Herald* reported, her 'elegant and classic skeleton' hung in a cabinet at the medical school."

Cohen tells an extraordinary story endowed with power, pathos, and dignity. No post-modernist wallowing in doubt, she relentlessly seeks the truth and never shies from judging her subjects. She knows that Richard P. Robinson was guilty and she proves it. Her frank, no-nonsense voice is especially appealing. "Even in his relationship with Helen Jewett, George Marston evinced signs of being something of a dolt," she writes. "He was only seventeen and several months into a relationship with a woman light years ahead of him in her ability to manage both feelings and people." Cohen has an exquisite sense for detecting and unmasking the absurd and the disingenuous. After quoting James Gordon Bennett's over-the-top description of Helen Jewett's statuesque corpse, Cohen calmly observes: "To keep this rapturous vision of a dead Venus so pure, he shrewdly neglected the autopsy incisions made seven hours earlier, which surely disfigured the dead girl's chest and abdomen. Her 'beautiful bust' had been slit down the middle and probably peeled back to enable Dr. Rogers to reach her lungs, and no amount of skilled repair work could have concealed that laceration. Bennett's rhetorical strategy favored a sexualized corpse over a mutilated one." Unsentimental and candid, Cohen confidently guides readers into the dark recesses of a great American tragedy.

# Part II
# Souls

*6*

# In a Strange Way

*April 13, 1998*

In the spring of 1676, Narragansett Indians attacked and burned the colonial town of Providence in Rhode Island. In a subsequent parlay, one of the surviving colonists (Roger Williams) demanded to know the Indians' motives, and he recorded their three answers:

> [firstly] they Confessed they were in A Strang[e] Way.
> 2ly we had forced them to it.
> 3ly that God was [with] them and Had forsaken us for they had so prospered in Killing and Burning us far beyond What we did against them.

Most twentieth-century historians of that brutal conflict, known as "King Philip's War," dwell on the second answer: that the New England colonists' aggressive seizure of native lands had driven the Indians to attack. Without discounting that answer, Jill Lepore draws our attention primarily to the Narragansetts' cryptic and apparently psychological first answer, that they found themselves "in A Strang[e] Way."

Those chilling words seem to draw us into the heart of darkness. What enabled people—both Indians and colonists—to burn, plunder, torture, maim, kill, and mutilate their recent neighbors? How did they reconcile their minds to endure, and to inflict, such atrocities? And having endured and inflicted, how did they cope with and act on their memories? These are Jill Lepore's questions in this evocative, powerful, and provocative book about a little-known war that speaks to all wars. Because the colonists eventually won and had printing presses and archives, Lepore can more fully recover their answers to her questions, but she also makes every effort to re-create the silenced voices of the defeated. From 1675 to 1677, everyone in New England was "in A Strang[e] Way."

By current academic standards, Lepore's title seems defiantly retrograde. Few historians now believe in a singular American identity, past or present. And what could be more quaint than to seek that identity's

*The Name of War: King Philip's War and the Origins of American Identity,* by Jill Lepore (Alfred A. Knopf, 1998)

roots in colonial New England, the land of Puritans, Salem witches, the *Mayflower*, and Plymouth Rock? Such a search smacks of the WASP-ish ethnocentrism and filiopietism of late nineteenth-century Boston Brahmins, who celebrated their deeper regional roots and their Anglo-Saxonism to hold newer immigrants at bay. Today's historians usually look for multicultural roots and multiple identities in more exotic locales: in Santa Fe, in St. Augustine, in New Orleans, in the Chesapeake or Iroquoia—anywhere but stuffy old New England.

Moreover, as scholars piously debate the proper names for things, Lepore dares to employ the traditional—and recently suspect—phrase "King Philip's War." Bestowed by the Puritan victors, that name seems to blame the war of 1675–77 on its most famous Indian victim and mis-names him with an Anglicism (his original name was Metacom or Meta-comet). That name also exaggerates his power by calling him a "king"—an alien concept to natives who called their multiple and limited leaders "sachems." Searching for something more sympathetic to the defeated, recent scholars have invented an apparently more neutral alternative: "Metacom's Rebellion."

But Lepore clings to the now-provocative "King Philip's War" precisely because it highlights the power of the literate colonists to impose their meanings on their victory. She wants readers to confront the tangled processes of naming and remembering that render words so tricky and so powerful. Lepore understands that unraveling the past's mysteries is much more than a matter of renaming them. She prefers to highlight the historical ironies and the cultural baggage of older names. "'King Philip's War' is not unbiased," she observes, "but its biases are telling." Indeed, there is an exorcising quality to Lepore's invocation of King Philip's War, as if it were healthier to showcase than to flee its masquer-ading qualities.

By mustering her unconventional book under a conventional title, Lepore runs the risk that casual readers will expect to find a standard political and military history of events that adheres to a strict chronol-ogy. She avoids the sort of omniscient narrative that begins with causes, proceeds into a linked sequence of battles, climaxes in one crucial en-counter, and culminates in an analysis of consequences. Instead, Lepore tells episodic and thematic stories out of time and bracketed by a schol-arly analysis that ranges far and wide to find parallels and echoes in later centuries. Thus she begins with a gruesome episode of torture and exe-cution from the last months of the war and then backtracks to the war's origins more than a year earlier. And these stories are open-ended, defy-ing closure because their sources remain cryptic or incomplete.

Rather than bemoaning this lack of certainty, Lepore takes (and gives) exuberant pleasure in the past's multiple possibilities. She possesses that special insight of our most enduring historians: a flair for finding strange and ironic episodes whose details reveal the past's most fundamental and painful contradictions.

*The Name of War* primarily offers a history of history making that reveals how, over three centuries, diverse people (but mostly colonists and their descendants) have variously, selectively, and subjectively narrated the war to manage their horror and to give meaning to their lives. "How wars are remembered can be just as important as how they were fought and first described," Lepore observes. When the Puritan ministers Increase Mather and William Hubbard framed the first narratives of the war as a demonic uprising against God's chosen but wavering people, they completed the conquest. Indeed, Lepore argues that violent action and its interpretation are reciprocal in war: "it is the central claim of this book that wounds and words—the injuries and their interpretation—cannot be separated, that acts of war generate acts of narration, and that both types of acts are often joined in a common purpose: defining the geographical, political, cultural, and sometimes racial and national boundaries between peoples."

The war began in June 1675, after the Plymouth colonists hanged three prominent Wampanoag Indians convicted of murdering a Christian Indian who was an informer. Infuriated by the executions, the principal Wampanoag sachem, Metacom/Philip, invoked two generations of colonial abuses and Indian resentments to draw most of the Algonquian tribes of New England into a war intended to destroy the newcomers. A succession of bloody and fiery raids assailed fifty-two of the region's ninety colonial towns, destroying twelve of them and killing or wounding perhaps a quarter of the colonists. Facing obliteration, the colonial rulers rallied their forces, including a coerced minority of Christian Indians.

To prove their loyalty and zeal, Christian Indians had to bring in two scalps or heads. Those who would not or could not fight were confined on a cold, barren island in Boston harbor, where hundreds died from exposure, malnutrition, and disease (or were stolen by slavers).

In 1676, the colonists turned the tide by destroying the villages of their Indian foes, massacring men, women, and children. After Metacom/Philip's death and mutilation in August, Indian resistance waned, as hundreds surrendered to the victors' justice. Triumphant but embittered, the colonial authorities executed the Indian leaders and enslaved their women and children for sale in the West Indies. Only those Indians who had assisted in subduing their kin were permitted to remain in southern New England, as a tiny and maligned minority within small reservations surrounded by the victors. Defiant survivors had to flee northward to take refuge among northern New England's tribes, which preserved their independence and hostility into the mid-eighteenth century.

The brutality of the war and the near-totality of the colonial victory combined virtually to erase a physical and cultural landscape of partial accommodation between the natives and the newcomers. Before the war, most colonists and Indians had warily accepted that they should try to find some way to coexist. Before 1675, there was no clear frontier separating Indians and colonists, in geography or in culture. Indian villages and settler towns were intermixed in much of southern New England. Indeed, to the dismay of their leaders, many colonists had borrowed some Indian ways, particularly a shifting and dispersed pattern of settlement that put many closer to Indian villages than to Puritan churches. At the same time, under the pressure of the growing colonial numbers and power, many Indians were trying to adopt English ways, including a measure of the Puritans' especially demanding form of Christianity.

Some Indians tried to preserve some of their land and autonomy by moving into "praying towns" supervised by Puritan missionaries, principally Rev. John Eliot. By drawing Indians into praying towns, the missionaries hoped to preserve native lives from more vindictive colonists, as well as to save their souls from hell. Prewar New England's mix of native and settler communities was no multicultural utopia; the imbalance of power demanded far greater sacrifices and far more traumatic changes from the natives. But this uneasy set of accommodations was preferable to the slaughter, slavery, and isolation that followed.

In the early 1670s, this strange new world of shifting and overlapping cultures—English and Indian—was disturbing to purists among both the colonists and the natives. Puritan leaders worried that their dispersed settlers were degenerating into quasi-savages from immersion in the forest and their association with the Indians. And many native sachems blamed their people's dwindling numbers, shrinking domains, declining wildlife, and deteriorating prowess on their neglect of traditional beliefs and ceremonies. All this decay seemed to show that their spiritual power was ebbing. To restore that power, they needed to reject the invaders' God, reunite all Indians in the performance of ancestral ritual, and drive out the corrupting colonists.

And so, to purify themselves and their land, the militant sachems rose up in rebellion in 1675. Precisely because the colonists had labored so hard to remake the landscape, to "clothe" it in the churches, houses, fences, barns, and cattle of English Christianity and civility, the Indian rebels systematically and theatrically burned, killed, mutilated, and desecrated all those marks of possession. Taught by missionaries, some Indians knew enough English and Christianity to mock dying Puritans with blasphemy: "Come Lord Jesus, save this poor Englishman if thou canst, whom I am now about to kill." The rebels regarded every dying colonist, every burning house, every desecrated church as accumulating evidence that the English God was no match for their own returning spiritual power. Recall, the explanation of the Narragansett Indians that they destroyed Providence because, in Roger Williams's words, "God was [with] them and Had forsaken us for they had so prospered in Killing and Burning us far beyond What we did against them."

The colonists were horrified at the rapid destruction of their hard-earned property, at the ready effacement of their culture from the land, at the imminent prospect of a resurgent Indian landscape, and at the unavenged blasphemy of Indian voices. Only by counterattacking with unchecked brutality could they vindicate their God and prove their own worthiness to worship him. The ravages of their landscape and the mockery of their God freed the colonists to demonize and dehumanize the Indians as satanic wolves or snakes. Only by destroying them without mercy could the colonists reaffirm their own devotion to Christianity and English ways. Every dead Indian and burned wigwam manifested the resurgent power of the Puritan God and his renewed approval of his chosen people, the New England saints.

In this grim equation, unchecked brutality toward savages was the ultimate proof of Christian civilization. Infuriated by the Narragansetts' boasting, Roger Williams retorted that "God had prospered *us* so that wee had driven the Wampanoogs with Phillip out of his Countrie and the Nahigonsiks out of their Countrie, and had destroyed Multitudes of them in Fighting and Flying, in Hung[e]r and Cold, etc.: and that God would help us to Consume them." And in both the course of events and the history writing about them, Roger Williams had the last word (until Lepore).

War and victory freed colonial leaders to indulge their darker ambition utterly to destroy or to subdue Indians on the battlefield and in collective memory. Indeed, the two types of victories, bloody and wordy, were reciprocal. "If war is a contest of both injuries and interpretation," Lepore writes, "the English made sure that they won the latter, even when the former was not yet assured."

During and immediately after the war, prominent Puritan ministers rushed their histories into print in both England and New England. They vindicated the colonists' atrocities as godly reprisals, and they justified a New England ethnically cleansed of Indians. Rev. William Hubbard warned readers to waste no sympathy on the dead or enslaved Indian children: "Being all young Serpents of the same Brood, the subduing or taking [of] so many ought to be acknowledged as another signal Victory, and Pledg[e] of Divine Favour to the English." Hubbard wanted no criticism from distant England to inhibit the bloody work of preserving New England and vindicating the Puritan God. Increase Mather attributed the war to a just and angry God provoked by the Puritans' prewar degeneracy:

"Christians in this Land have become too like unto the Indians, and then we need not wonder if the Lord hath afflicted us by them." Only by establishing a new distance from Indian ways, Indian thoughts, and Indian bodies could colonists bolster the Englishness and the Christianity that their God demanded. Lepore concludes that, "in the end, their writings proved to be pivotal to their victory, a victory that drew new, firmer boundaries between English and Indian people and between what it meant to be 'English' and what it meant to be 'Indian.'"

Only a few Puritan missionaries regretted their countrymen's ruthless new determination to treat all Indians as unredeemable savages. These dissidents were a tiny, nearly silenced minority, threatened with death when they spoke up. A grieving John Eliot saw no point in trying to challenge his history-writing colleagues who gloried in the slaughter and the slavery of Indians. He confined himself to private and futile pleas for the lives of Christian Indians deemed insufficiently loyal by the authorities. His more reckless colleague, Rev. Daniel Gookin, did write a history of the war that sympathized with the sufferings of the Christian Indians trapped between the belligerents. But no one would publish his manuscript until the next century.

Drawing sharp new boundaries on the land and in their minds, the Puritans consigned the Indian survivors to shrinking reservations, and they redefined the natives as immutably inferior—barely deserving of life and hardly worth the effort to convert. The victors virtually obliterated the prewar world of cultural ambiguities and social accommodations. The colonists and their heirs proved unrelenting in their new determination to separate and dominate, and so Lepore regards King Philip's War "as a critical step in the evolution toward an increasingly racialized ideology of the differences between Europeans and Indians." Indeed, she even credits the Puritan victory for "the worldview that would create, a century and a half later, the Indian removal policy adopted by Andrew Jackson."

Here she claims too much for this one war, however bloody, in New England. Southern historians can counter that seventeenth-century Virginians had already fought a succession of equally brutal Indian wars that contributed at least as much to the emergence of American racism. Andrew Jackson of Tennessee derived his unforgiving views of Indians more proximately and more probably from a Virginia tradition that needed no lessons in hatred from the Puritans. Lepore's claim highlights the new twist on the old regional chauvinism long characteristic of colonial historians. In past generations, Virginia's and New England's historians competed to claim the birthplace of democracy; but now they contend over when and where racism emerged. The common denominator is a persistent pride in their chosen region as more important in defining nineteenth-century America—which used to be known as a land of liberty, but is now increasingly seen as a domain of inequality and injustice.

If we narrow Lepore's claims to New England, however, she is surely right about the powerful legacy of King Philip's War. As they waged further wars to conquer northern New England's defiant Indians, the colonists revived their vindictive memories. Every new conflict evoked grim and determined retellings of the Puritan version of King Philip's War as a holy war. Every New England generation needed to prove that it was as worthy as its heroic forbears, who had survived savage attacks and had rallied to destroy the demonic minions of King Philip. In the late seventeenth century, tourists went to Plymouth not for the now-celebrated rock, but to gape at and mock King Philip's skull, bleaching on a post beside the road. At the close of that century, the visitors included Cotton Mather, who followed in his father's footsteps to become a minister and historian. He also inherited his father's rage, for Cotton Mather wrenched off and took away King Philip's jawbone, thus completing the silencing of the rebel sachem.

A century later, the rage of New Englanders receded in favor of a patronizing retrospection. Once the region's Indians seemed entirely subdued and virtually invisible, New Englanders reinvented their myth of King Philip. No longer needing an Indian villain, they recast King Philip as the noble savage, admirable but tragic. The nineteenth-century version reflected an insistence that all Indians were clearly doomed to a rapid extinction that was mandated by a divine providence. In that utter confidence, northeastern Americans indulged in a new sentimentalism about dead Indians that was the ultimate declaration of total victory.

In 1829, the New England playwright John Augustus Stone collaborated with the bombastic actor Edwin Forrest to craft a play entitled, *Metamora; or, the Last of the Wampanoags.* Once again renaming Metacom, the playwright allowed him a proud defiance, because the point of the play was to kill him off as the last of his tribe and as an omen for the fate of all other Indians. Moreover, by applauding the depiction of "Metamora" as an American patriot resisting English colonists, nineteenth-century audiences could see themselves as his truly deserving heirs while impugning the Indians of their own day as a degraded, drunken, and dwindling few unworthy of their noble ancestor. Thus the play was the consummate indignity heaped on King Philip: remaking him into a witness against the survival of America's living Indians.

In fact, Indians survived the horrors of colonial and nineteenth-century America, even in New England. Until recently, however, local Indians had a very hard time getting other New Englanders to see them. In 1876, the governor of Rhode Island celebrated the bicentennial of

King Philip's War with a speech that pronounced "the red man" as "wiped out"—despite the conspicuous presence near the podium of two Wampanoag women in full Indian regalia. This willful blindness is the subject of Lepore's consummate story: her epilogue, which reexamines "Northmen's Rock" (or "Viking's Rock") on the shore of Mount Hope Bay in Bristol, Rhode Island.

In 1835, the locals first detected a strange inscription on the rock. Antiquarians leaped to the satisfying conclusion that the carvings were runes, and therefore proof that Vikings had visited New England precisely in 1007. This discovery reassured the white folk by lengthening their pedigree in the New World. Consequently, nobody paid much attention in 1920, when an iconoclastic psychology professor from Brown University debunked the Norse myth by demonstrating that the carvings were Cherokee and translated into English as "Metacomet, Great Sachem." If so, the inscription postdated 1821, when Sequoyah invented the Cherokee syllabary, and predated 1835, when the rock first attracted notice. It was probably carved by a Cherokee named Thomas Mitchell and his Wampanoag wife, Zerviah Gould, who claimed descent from King Philip. They married in 1824 and lived in nearby Massachusetts. The story of Northmen's Rock perfectly serves Lepore's larger story about the persistence of Indians, the distinctiveness of their memories, and the distortions of their dominators. Today's residents of Bristol continue to call the stone "Viking's Rock."

Although surviving documents dictate that Lepore concentrate on the stories told by colonists and their descendants, she makes the most of every scrap of evidence to recover traces of Indian voices. We have some twenty published accounts from the war's contemporaries, in addition to more than four hundred letters. Almost all were produced by wealthy and prominent colonists; none is by an Indian. In reexamining the self-serving stories told by the colonists, Lepore struggles to bring toward the center the native voices that they marginalized. For example, she retells the famous tale of Mary Rowlandson, a Puritan minister's wife who suffered and survived Indian captivity in 1676. Redeemed both physically and spiritually from her ordeal, Rowlandson published, in 1682, a recounting of her ordeal under the pious title, *The Soveraignty and Goodness of God.* The first American best seller, Rowlandson's captivity narrative contributed to the dehumanization of the Indians as utterly alien and demonic. Recalling their attack on her town, Rowlandson described, "Christians lying in their blood, some here, and some there, like a company of sheep torn by wolves. All of them stripped naked by a company of hell-hounds, roaring, singing, ranging and insulting, as if they would have torn our very hearts out."

Lepore muddies this racial polarization by restoring to Rowlandson's captivity story the prominent and mediating role played by a Christian Indian known as James Printer. Converted by John Eliot, Printer obtained his name by serving that missionary as a translator and typesetter for his Cambridge press. In 1675, Printer and the other residents of the praying town of Hassanemesit were forcibly drawn into the war by their rebelling kinsmen. After helping to take Rowlandson prisoner, Printer brokered the negotiations for her ransom by Puritan authorities. Recognizing the tide turning against the militants, Printer deserted, bringing the heads of two dead Indians to purchase his amnesty from the Puritans. Returning to Eliot's press, he probably helped to set the type to publish Rowlandson's captivity narrative. In the delicious ironies of Printer's and Rowlandson's intertwining experiences, Lepore detects the continued entanglement of Indians and colonists even as the latter sought a complete obliteration of the other.

Still, Lepore cannot complete her retelling because she cannot recover what intrigues her the most: what ran through Printer's mind as he worked with Rowlandson's powerful words, so deadly to the world of accommodation. "It is impossible not to wonder what he thought. Did he measure Rowlandson's sufferings against his own?" If so, it must have been painful to realize that neither his master nor the public would suffer Printer to publish his own, more extraordinary, story. The Puritans wanted to read of their own people surviving captivity, not of the far more numerous, horrific, and permanent enslavements endured by Indians.

Time and again, Lepore's bold efforts to recover the lost centrality of Indians dissipate into intriguing possibilities for want of evidence. What became of those captured natives exported by the hundreds in slave ships for sale to the sugar planters of the West Indies? The most likely destination, the English colonies of Barbados and Jamaica, quickly barred the importation of enslaved New England Indians. Although desperate for additional slaves for their profitable but deadly plantations, the West Indian masters deemed the New England Algonquians "a people of too subtle, bloody, and dangerous inclination to be and remain here." So where did the slavers take them? Our colonial informants are mute, because they did not care what became of the Indians once they were sold, so long as they never came back, which they apparently never did. Lepore can only speculate: "Turned away at port after port, it is possible that slave ships from New England simply dumped their now valueless cargo somewhere in the Caribbean Sea, or abandoned groups of New England Indians on uninhabited islands."

This is where our history writing seems headed: into provocative meditations about possibilities suggested, but left uncertain, by stray slivers of evidence. Until recently, historians allowed the well-documented elite to speak for all colonists and left the Indians' thoughts in the obscurity of the record or to the obloquy of their enemies. Today, historians ask larger questions based on slimmer evidence than did their predecessors. For this reason, we lack the certainty that formerly characterized the writing of history. This new, more speculative, and open-ended mode of history writing can thrive when the historian is as honest, thoughtful, and imaginative as Jill Lepore.

7

# Crucibles

*November 10, 2003*

The Puritans of colonial New England puzzle or appall us for having believed in witchcraft unto the death of its suspects. Their witch-hunting infests our popular memory as an original, national sin: as something we can congratulate ourselves for outgrowing *or* as a cautionary reminder of our lingering potential for collective folly and cruelty. We would like to consider ourselves as more rational and scientific than they, but can we be so sure? We cannot shake the anxiety, as Arthur Miller insists in *The Crucible,* that we conduct latter-day witch-hunts against imagined traitors within. So we never think about Puritan witch-hunting without making it about ourselves.

With mixed results, historians try to transcend such "presentism" by scrupulously reconstructing the cultural context of the past, treating the Puritans on their own terms rather than as inferior or interior versions of ourselves. In their time, a belief in witches followed logically from seventeenth-century conditions and assumptions pervasive in Europe as well as the colonies. Early modern people did not dwell in the disenchanted universe of pure reason (nor, of course, do most contemporary Americans—witness the popular credulity for the existence of angels, ghosts, and space aliens). The Puritans saw and heard wondrous signs of God's purpose and the devil's menace: ominous lights in the sky, prophetic dreams, multiple suns, eclipses, comets, deformed newborns, speaking infants, poltergeists, unseen and portentous voices, eerie coincidences, apparitions of warring armies or ships in the sky, and cases of blasphemers and Sabbath breakers suddenly struck dead. Given God's omnipotence and Satan's malignity, all such "remarkable providences" seemed pregnant with a divine meaning that the Puritans struggled to decipher as a guide to communal security.

The colonists shared the European conviction that Satan recruited humans to become his servants—his witches—by having them sign their

*In the Devil's Snare: The Salem Witchcraft Crisis of 1692,* by Mary Beth Norton (Alfred A. Knopf, 2002)

names in blood in his book. By selling their souls, witches obtained magical power to harm and to kill their enemies on earth. When cattle or children sickened and died, the New England colonists suspected witchcraft by some in their midst. To protect the community, the Puritan magistrates had to identify, prosecute, and execute witches—by hanging rather than the burning of popular myth.

Witchcraft made perfect sense to a premodern people vulnerable to an unpredictable and often deadly nature beyond their control: a world of fires, floods, windstorms, droughts, crop blights, livestock diseases, and human epidemics. Unpredictable and deadly afflictions demanded explanation, some attribution of cause that might protect people from further suffering, or at least console them with resignation to God's will. No Puritans wished to believe that misfortune lacked supernatural meaning, for random accident would confirm their helplessness and their isolation in a world without God. Witchcraft was also plausible because some colonists did dabble in the occult to tell fortunes and to cure, or to inflict, ills—but there is little reason to believe that such "cunning folk" worshiped Satan or that they possessed more than the ominous power of threatening suggestion.

The victims of affliction usually blamed aggressive and contentious individuals—particularly poorer folk and older women who acted with an assertion deemed beyond their assigned social station. Females constituted the majority of both the accusers (mostly young) and the accused (mostly older). The disproportionate prosecution of women attests that their words had power in Puritan communities, but also demonstrates the considerable unease generated by that power—and points to a generational tension between young and old.

Although the belief in witchcraft was pervasive and continuous, the prosecution of witches was only sporadic and localized, occasionally erupting in a few especially fractious towns, where long memories nurtured grudges and suspicions. Rather than rush to judgment, the authorities usually contained suspicion short of a trial by scrupulously following legal procedures in gathering evidence and examining witnesses. Even when a case proceeded to trial, it was no easy matter to prove witchcraft. The New England colonists prosecuted ninety-three witches, but executed only sixteen—until 1692, when a peculiar mania at Salem dramatically inflated the numbers.

Salem was an especially troubled township, internally divided into two parishes with distinct communities and churches: the commercial seaport of Salem Town, and the farming hinterland of Salem Village (now Danvers). The latter was particularly rancorous, as inhabitants squabbled over farmland and a succession of ministers with short tempers came and went. January 1692 in Salem Village, two teenaged girls in the household of Rev. Samuel Parris began to suffer fits and hallucinations. Encouraged by local adults, principally the confrontational Parris, the girls accused a growing number, and an expanding orbit, of witches. Taken with deadly seriousness by the county magistrates, the accusations ultimately led to formal charges against 144 people (38 men and 106 women) from twenty-two towns. The prosecutors secured 54 confessions, which provided the critical evidence to convict and execute 20 people (14 women and 6 men). No previous episode could compare in scale or intensity. Ending in early 1693, the spree left such bitter feeling and guilty consciences that New Englanders abandoned judicial witch-hunting.

Despite historians' avowed rejection of presentism, every new history of Salem witch-hunting offers a particular theory that resonates with contemporary American concerns. In 1974, Paul Boyer and Stephen Nissenbaum published the provocative and influential *Salem Possessed: The Social Origins of Witchcraft.* Troubled by American materialism, they found a tension between the peasant values of Salem Village and the nascent capitalism of Salem Town. Two years later, popular interest in psychotropic drugs influenced Linda R. Caporael's argument, published in *Science* magazine, that ergot poisoning caused the hallucinations and the paranoia of Salem in 1692 (a shaky interpretation much recycled in pop histories in print and on television). In 1987, feminism informed Carol F. Karlsen's *The Devil in the Shape of a Woman: Witchcraft in Colonial New England,* which more clearly discerned Puritan misogyny in the selective and disproportionate prosecution of assertive women. And now Mary Beth Norton reflects historians' current drive to recover the importance of Indians, and especially of the violence by and against them, in the making of American culture and society.

Norton is an especially productive and influential scholar, specializing in the history of women in colonial and revolutionary America. As a feminist, she initially felt drawn to the Salem story because it pivoted around female protagonists: the accusing girls and the accused witches. In Puritan society, the reinforcing hierarchies of gender, age, and wealth ordinarily cast young women working as household servants at the social bottom. They were supposed to labor in humble and silent obscurity, deferring to their male elders and betters. In Essex County, Massachusetts, in 1692, however, a set of teenaged girls, most of them servants, inverted the social hierarchy by claiming the supernatural power to discern witches. They boldly spoke out in church and court—in the centers of community power ordinarily shut to them except in the role of passive audience. The accusing girls implicitly challenged patriarchy by calling the tune for the prosecuting magistrates and by imperiling the reputations and the lives of some high-status men and women. Norton remarks: "women took center stage at Salem: they were the major instigators and victims of a remarkable public spectacle."

But deeper research persuaded Norton that she needed to proceed beyond the women to focus on "the hitherto neglected men accused in 1692," especially Rev. George Burroughs. The writing of colonial social history has reached a new stage when a leading feminist scholar can conclude that her peers have so successfully rescued colonial women from obscurity that—at least for the Salem story—we have lost sight of pivotal characters because they were men.

Norton also transcends the usual focus of historians on Salem Village, where the crisis began, by moving outward to the rest of Essex County, where that crisis culminated. It was the town of Andover, rather than Salem, that generated the largest number of accusations. "Thus the term *Salem witchcraft crisis* is a misnomer," Norton explains, "*Essex County witchcraft crisis* would be more accurate." But old terms die hard; witness the subtitle of Norton's book: *The Salem Witchcraft Crisis of 1692.*

In a third break with previous scholars, who depict a unified and steadily expanding crisis, Norton divides the crisis into two starkly different stages, with mid-April 1692 as the line of demarcation. In the early stage, the Salem Village episode resembled previous outbreaks: accusations were few, local, and conventional—targeting the usual suspects: quarrelsome older women and some of their husbands. And the authorities initially proceeded cautiously, skeptically probing the evidence before prosecuting. All of that changed in late April, when the number of accusations suddenly soared, ascended the social hierarchy, and spread throughout Essex County and beyond. Something happened in April to render the Salem outbreak unprecedented in scale and consequences. For Norton, explaining that escalation in April trumps in importance the outbreak in January in Salem Village.

To account for the escalation, Norton emphasizes the confession, on April 19, by Abigail Hobbs, a teenaged refugee from Falmouth (now Portland) in Maine, then a frontier region governed by the colony of Massachusetts. In early 1692, most of Maine's settlements, including Falmouth, suffered destruction by the Wabanaki Indians and their French allies, sending demoralized refugees to Essex County. Under pressure from other accusing girls and the county judges, Hobbs confessed that she had met the devil in Falmouth and signed his book. "Those who heard her confession readily grasped the connection between Satan and the Wabanakis," Norton announces; Hobbs's "confessions pointed everyone's attention toward events in Falmouth, and on the Maine frontier, with striking results." A night later, on April 20, Ann Putnam—one of the leading accusers—had a horrific vision that identified the devil's viceroy in Maine as Rev. George Burroughs, a former resident of both Salem Village and Falmouth. Nothing could have been more sensational and shocking to Puritans than to discover that a minister had betrayed God and his Christian people to serve Satan. So it is striking that, instead of dismissing as incredible the spectral testimony of two young women, the magistrates made the most of it, arresting Burroughs for trial in Salem for his life.

Alas for George Burroughs, he had made too many enemies, had sparked too much damning gossip, and had been in the wrong places at the wrong times. Although a Harvard educated minister, Burroughs held unorthodox religious beliefs and behaved in unconventional ways. He never sought ordination, did not baptize his children, and neither offered nor received the other ritual sacraments. Local gossip implicated him in abusing, and perhaps murdering, his first two wives. His checkered ministerial career included a contentious stint in Salem Village during the early 1680s, when he had lodged with the family of Ann Putnam, who reflected parental gossip in her vivid accusations. He moved northeast to the frontier settlement of Falmouth, where Burroughs knew Mercy Lewis and Abigail Hobbs, who later fled to Salem as refugees and there became leading witch accusers. His enemies suspected demonic premonition when Burroughs twice left frontier communities, including Falmouth, shortly before their destruction by Indians. The suspicious also detected a satanic bargain when Burroughs displayed a prodigious strength that transcended his short and wiry build.

Burroughs, his enemies charged, plied satanic magic to lead the dual attacks on New England: Wabanaki on the margins and witches at the core. To save themselves, the Puritans had to destroy Burroughs and his network of witches. Convicted of witchcraft, Burroughs died on the Salem gallows on August 19. Cotton Mather exulted: "Our good God is working of miracles."

When the Salem magistrates readily prosecuted a minister, the floodgates opened, allowing accusation to flow far and wide and up the social ladder to imperil other colonial leaders. "What linked them all—and what nearly all historians have failed to recognize—was the relationship of their targets to the Indian wars on the Maine frontier," Norton maintains. The new suspects included Capt. John Floyd, a militia officer defeated by the Wabanaki, and Capt. John Alden, a mariner suspected of trading ammunition with Indians in return for sexual favors.

Norton attributes the expanding Salem witch-hunt to the shock felt by the Puritan colonists at their stunning defeats on the northeastern frontier. Seeking revenge for stolen land, traders' cheating, and colonial insults, the Wabanaki rapidly destroyed most of Maine's farms and towns with fire and massacre. Shocked out of their complacent sense of superiority over pagan savages, the Maine settlers blamed neglect by their colonial rulers based in Salem and Boston. Anguished colonists wondered why military assistance was too little, too late and conducted by incompetents. And surely, the refugees reasoned, the simultaneous outbreak of witchcraft in Essex County could be no random coincidence.

To save themselves, the colonists had to determine what they had done to offend their vengeful God, who had lifted his protection to permit rampaging Indians and witches to smite his chosen but sinning people. The Puritans felt compelled to purify their ranks by forsaking their blind indifference to Satan's evident minions working within. And those minions, Norton reasons, could best be found among the men blamed for the military follies on the Maine frontier.

The residents of Essex County had particularly strong reasons to link witchcraft within to the Indian menace without. The county's magistrates who investigated and tried the witches also speculated in Maine land and commanded the militia expeditions that failed so miserably to defend the frontier. And the towns of Essex County became crowded with distraught and disoriented refugees fleeing ravaged homes, mourning dead relatives, and looking for someone to blame. "Unable to defeat Satan in the forests and garrisons of the northeastern frontier," Norton asserts, "they could nevertheless attempt to do so in the Salem courtroom."

During the spring of 1692, the Essex County magistrates, principally Jonathan Corwin and John Hathorne, made fatal decisions that empowered the accusers to escalate a local crisis into a countywide, communal obsession. Breaking with the tradition of separate, skeptical examination of accusers and accused, the magistrates brought them all together in public court to watch the fits fly. Rational deliberation and legal procedure vanished at the public hearings, as the girls erupted in painful outbursts and vivid hallucinations when provided with an audience and faced by the suspects. Those physical outbursts and the "spectral evidence" of the girls' visions became critical confirmation of the charges. But to clinch their cases, the magistrates needed confessions, which the communal settings promoted.

Under intense public pressure, including from spouses and relatives, many suspects broke down at the hearings, offering lurid confessions that confirmed the authority of the girls and that named new witches for prosecution. The magistrates compounded the incentive to confess by sparing the confessors from trial, provided that they testified against the more defiant suspects such as George Burroughs. Some confessed witches subsequently explained that at the communal hearings they were told: "We were witches, and they knew it, and we knew it, which made us think that it was so." One elaborated that she "became so terrified in her mind that she owned, at length, almost anything they propounded to her." A Dutch merchant resident in Boston marveled: "Throughout the countryside, the excessive gullibility of the magistrates has caused that which the tormented or possessed people bring in against someone together with other trivial circumstances to be taken as substantially true and convincing testimony against the accused."

By allowing the accusers to dominate the proceedings, the magistrates abdicated some of their power, and most of their discretion, to tormented teenaged girls who professed access to a higher, supernatural power. Norton elaborates: "Thus in the invisible world the afflicted, in effect, assumed the role of magistrates. They listened to the testimony of spectral witnesses (the murder victims) and extracted the confessions that Hathorne and Corwin could not." Ironically, Norton makes an unintended case for elite patriarchy as a lesser evil—given the irrational destruction of life that marked the triumph of the young female accusers. Had the magistrates defended the power of patriarchs, the girls would have been kept in quiet obscurity, and twenty Puritans would have lived longer lives to natural ends.

Why did the magistrates defer to the girls? Norton answers that the Puritan elite subconsciously recognized their responsibility for failing to defend Maine against the Indians. Vulnerable to charges of supernatural betrayal, the judges slavishly followed the girls, determined thereby to prove their true zeal against New England's spectral enemies. The judges, Norton writes, "attempted to shift the responsibility for their own inadequate defense of the frontier to the demons of the invisible world, and as a result they presided over the deaths of many innocent people." She boldly concludes that, "had the Second Indian War on the northeastern frontier somehow been avoided, the Essex County witchcraft crisis of 1692 would not have occurred. This is not to say that the war 'caused' the witchcraft crisis, but rather that the conflict created the conditions that allowed the crisis to develop as rapidly and extensively as it did."

Norton proposes an ingenious argument, but it is not quite as original as she insists, early and often. Although she can justly claim to have explored the Maine connection, and the Essex-wide dimensions, in unprecedented detail, she scants credit due to previous scholars who, in briefer versions, anticipated her accomplishment. For one example, Norton does not acknowledge Christine Leigh Heyrman's *Commerce and Culture: The Maritime Communities of Colonial Attention, 1690–1750,* which appeared in 1984 and called attention to both the Andover accusations and to the psychological impact of the frontier war on the witch-hunt.

Norton's Maine connection works better as partial coloration than as a single explanation for the whole complex and messy crisis. If ties to Maine, especially refugees, were pivotal, why were afflictions more intense, and accusations more numerous, in hinterland communities (Andover, Topsfield, and Salem Village), where refugees were relatively few, than in the seaports (Boston, Newbury, Ipswich, and Salem Town), where they were most numerous? And if the shock of frontier war shaped the visions of witches within, why was there no witchcraft outbreak during King Philip's War of 1675–76? That earlier frontier conflict killed more colonists, destroyed more towns, and affected more of New England than did the Second Indian War of 1689–97. Although offering plenty of misery, the Second Indian War had an even more miserable precedent in recent memory, which must have taken some of the shock out of its less destructive sequel. Norton's solution is to lump the two wars together in the minds of 1692, which raises the question of why it took the Puritans so long to react to the greater, earlier shock.

In driving her thesis, Norton makes the most of her evidence—and then some. She shifts to the foreground every circumstantial link between Maine and Essex County, between Wabanaki and witches, while shunting to the background the evidence and events, especially those internal to Salem Village, which loom larger in previous accounts. Where other historians highlight the original accusers from Salem Village, especially Abigail Williams and Ann Putnam, Norton favors the subsequent accusers from Maine, especially Mercy Lewis and Abigail Hobbs. In assessing the twenty executed witches, Norton emphasizes the two who had lived in Maine rather than the eighteen who had not. To explain the prosecution of George Burroughs, Norton makes more of his Maine residence than of his heterodox religious beliefs, which so horrified his enemies and seem primarily to have motivated his prosecution.

In sorting the accused, she makes much more of those directly associated with the Maine military campaigns than of the larger number who had no such association. This selective emphasis is especially striking because, with the conspicuous exception of George Burroughs, the Maine connected were often accused but rarely tried. Captain Alden broke jail with surprising ease, while the magistrates eventually dropped their case against Captain Floyd. For Norton, the broad pool of tenuous accusations—which featured the Maine connection—seems more significant than the smaller subset of especially serious cases carried through to trial, conviction, and execution, where Salem Village predominated. Fundamentally, she focuses on escalation over origins and on accusations over convictions.

Norton's argument often hinges on a speculative reading of snippets from Puritan testimony or commentary. Some afflicted girls saw spectral witches roasting victims on a spit, which Norton takes as resonating their dread of flaming tortures by rampaging Wabanaki. Plausible, but hellfire was long associated with witches' satanic power. To clinch her point,

Norton needs to demonstrate that torture by burning was a more common motif in 1692 than in previous witch testimony in New England.

Similarly, when accusers described the devil and demons as black, Norton says that they were thinking of Indians: "Thus the frequent references to the 'black man' by confessors and the afflicted establish a crucial connection between the witchcraft crisis and the Indian wars." Maybe, but it was a very old convention, predating contact with the Indians, for medieval and early modern Europeans to paint their devils as black. And "tawny," rather than black, was the usual coloration given by colonists to Indians. Apparently only one accuser explicitly described the devil as "not a negro, but of a tawney, or an Indian colour."

At some key junctures, the speculative evidence thins to nothing. On June 10, 1692, the Essex authorities hanged their first Salem witch: Goodwife Bridget Bishop. The next day, Indians attacked the frontier town of Wells. Norton speculates: "Did anyone view the attack as revenge for Goody Bishop's execution? It would have been easy for New Englanders to reach such a conclusion, but no such reasoning is recorded in surviving documents." Similarly, Norton concludes that the judges "quickly became invested in believing in the reputed witches' guilt, in large part because they needed to believe that they themselves were *not* guilty of causing New England's current woes." But in no surviving document does a judge confess to this reasoning, nor did any of their contemporaries suggest such a judicial psychology of projection, which seems more modern than Puritan.

Norton responds that the silences in the documentary record indicate a purge of embarrassing documents by authors or their descendants: "the holes in the documentary record are too consistent and specific to be explained in any other way." By imagining that the Puritans did write explicit evidence for her argument, but then suppressed it, she sustains her pose of scrupulously reflecting their world rather than her own modernity. Faulting other historians for applying "modern-day terminology to the incidents," she counters: "I have deliberately omitted attaching contemporary labels to the participants and their actions. Instead, *In the Devil's Snare* focuses on describing and analyzing the crisis in seventeenth-century terms." If this were literally so, Norton would endorse the Puritan explanation that the devil really did employ witches to torment their bodies and minds.

In fact, as a twenty-first-century author, Norton cannot simply borrow the past's terms and categories. By plunging into archives to analyze documents within the rational conventions of modern scholarship, she inevitably interprets an alien past for contemporary readers seeking a secular explanation. By accounting for the witch-hunt in terms of mass hysteria following military defeat, Norton speaks to us rather than for the Puritans. In sum, she is too skilled a historian literally to practice her oft-repeated but misleading declaration of seventeenth-century authenticity. And given her own creativity at connecting the dots of circumstantial and rhetorical evidence in ways that no Puritan could, why would Norton wish to deny the impressive modernity of her effort?

Norton explicitly denies the pertinence of modern psychology to seventeenth-century minds, but modern psychology implicitly shapes her interpretation of the tormented (and tormenting) girls, as well as of the projecting judges. Only at the book's end, in a retrospective, does Norton render explicit her assumptions that the original afflictions "were genuine" and that the later confessors, especially the war refugees, manifested "post-traumatic stress disorder." But she also finds "prearranged collusion" in the synchronized visions that doomed George Burroughs, and so Norton concludes that, eventually, "some of the afflicted accusers, reveling in the exercise of unprecedented power, began to augment and enhance their stories." Although credible to modern readers, none of these judgment calls echo seventeenth-century terms.

In her quixotic pursuit of a premodern sensibility for her explanation, Norton organizes her book in a manner meant to segregate her roles as narrator and historian. In the body of the text, printed against a white background, she gives a detailed, day-by-day recapitulation of the events in Essex County during 1692, with minimal analysis but many flashbacks to conflicts on the Maine frontier. She apparently intends to plunge readers into the spontaneous confusion of the unfolding events as an antidote to the heavy-handed "modern" interpretations that she disdains. But Norton intermittently interrupts her narrative for briefer passages, boxed and printed on shaded pages, in which she becomes the analytical historian, overtly explaining her methods and interpretations.

Norton apparently assumes that most readers want their story "pure" with an invitation to skip past easily identifiable, and presumably boring, bits of scholarly explanation. In practice, however, her shaded interludes are tighter, more lucid, and more compelling than the body of her narration, which suffers from long, repetitive stretches recapitulating testimony and random events. The innumerable snippet quotes, excessive detail, and blizzard of minor characters often lack any clear connection to her larger interpretation—other than in the claim to immerse the reader in the (confusing) past. In fact, the historian as detective explicitly weighing the evidence is the role that best serves Norton, better than she recognizes, and far better than her predominant, but distracting, attempt at narrative verisimilitude. Freed from confinement in a few boxes, the analytical mode would have brought clarity and discipline to the whole text, framing and winnowing the details, giving forest to the trees.

In the end, Norton falls short of her greatest ambition: to provide the master key to the Salem witch craze, to present a supreme interpretation that sweeps all other contenders into the dustbin of history. In fact, we will never find closure for the mysteries of the Salem witch-hunt. Neither readers nor historians can resist taking the Puritans' measure at their most mysterious—as believers in Satan's infernal world and in his destructive traffic in human lives and souls—for we long to know human nature at its worst and the past at its strangest. As our own culture evolves, we will revise our relationship with the Salem witch-hunters with renewed attempts to fathom a world that may be lost, or that may be all too close at hand.

# 8
# A Seeking People

*March 20, 2000*

Historians used to treat the colonial period as a precocious preparation for an independent and distinctive United States eager and able to ignore Europe. They argued that the Atlantic divide and the American environment obliged the colonists to shed their European ways and to create an "exceptional" new culture and society. Captured by their new continent and isolated by the broad Atlantic, the colonists increasingly ignored Britain as irrelevant, until they readily severed the vestigial and irritating tie during the American Revolution. In effect, the Revolution simply brought the political structure into line with the cultural and social independence that had already been achieved.

But, of late, historians have argued for an alternative, for an "Atlantic perspective." They emphasize the continuing interdependence of the colonies and Britain until they were painfully divided by the Revolution. Clustered along the coast, most colonists faced eastward toward the ocean and across to Europe, rather than westward into the continent. Indeed, the continental interior of dense forests, Indian peoples, and uncertain dimensions was far more mysterious and daunting than an ocean passage. British colonists knew, often by direct and multiple experiences, that the Atlantic was regularly traversed, but no colonist knew how to cross the North American continent.

Far from operating as a barrier, the Atlantic was an eighteenth-century bridge that routinely tied colonists to correspondents and institutions in Great Britain. Because overland transportation was painfully slow, difficult, and expensive, eighteenth-century people and goods moved most easily in ships over water. A Virginian dwelling beside Chesapeake Bay had faster and surer access via the Atlantic to news and goods from London than did a rustic dwelling in an obscure village in northern Britain. In the eighteenth century, the British Empire was essentially a regulated network of ships and sailors carrying cargos of consumer goods

*Inventing the "Great Awakening,"* by Frank Lambert (Princeton University Press, 1999); *Daughters of Light: Quaker Women Preaching and Prophesying in the Colonies and Abroad, 1700–1775*, by Rebecca Larson (Alfred A. Knopf, 1999)

and bundles of letters, newspapers, and books. By virtue of their maritime and commercial orientation, most colonists were far better integrated into the empire than were the Highland Scots.

During the first half of the eighteenth century, the colonists grew closer to the economy and culture of the home country. Between 1690 and 1740, the quantity of transatlantic commercial shipping tripled and newspaper and book publication exploded in both Britain and the colonies. The expanding network of merchant ships carried a growing volume of correspondence and print, enhancing the transatlantic exchange of information. Instead of growing more Americanized over time, the leading colonists became more Anglicized. They looked to London as the great metropolis and the arbiter of all fashion, intellectual as well as material. Until the botched British attempts to "reform" the empire during the 1760s and the 1770s, the colonists generally felt comfortable within a transatlantic empire that served them so well.

Subscribing to the "Atlantic perspective," Frank Lambert and Rebecca Larson treat the empire as unified by the ocean, rather than divided by it. "The American colonies did not form a separate nation before the American Revolution," Larson reminds, "but were part of the British empire, not only politically, under British government, but culturally, as 'part of the expanding periphery of Britain's core culture.'" Instead of limiting their topics and research to the colonies, both authors follow people and ideas to and fro across the Atlantic. In effect, Lambert and Larson do not allow the future United States retroactively to define the boundaries of eighteenth-century colonial culture—which was, in fact, transatlantic and increasingly so. In particular, they can see that the colonies and Britain shared in a mid-eighteenth-century surge in evangelical religion previously considered uniquely American.

The exceptionalist version of colonial history made much of a dramatic set of religious revivals that peaked during the early 1740s. Labeled the "Great Awakening" (or the "First Great Awakening"), this spate of revivals allegedly produced a distinctively American religious culture that made the American Revolution possible and necessary a generation later. Scholars used to treat the Great Awakening as an integrated and synchronized set of revivals that brought evangelical Protestantism into almost every corner of colonial America. In 1982, however, an iconoclastic religious historian, Jon Butler, dismissed the Great Awakening as an "interpretative fiction," belatedly created during the 1840s to lump together many different, limited, and local revivals spread over a thirty-year period.

In partial agreement with Butler, Lambert concedes that the concept of a Great Awakening was invented to exaggerate the connections between and the scope of local revivals—but he also insists that the invention predated the 1840s by a century, originating with the revivalists of the 1740s, who did report (in the lower case) "a great awakening." The name belonged to their larger invention: a new mode of evangelical revivalism unprecedented in ambition and effect. By delivering especially emotional sermons and conducting prolonged evening prayer meetings, the revivalists brought congregations to the emotional brink of "conversion": the moment when an exhilarating sense of divine grace filled a soul emptied by despair. Without that "New Birth," a soul remained destined to eternal hellfire, and the revivalists believed that only terror could bring people to the liberating shock of conversion. But, Lambert notes, the revivalists insisted that they were mere "instruments that God used for his ends, and not the engines of the work."

Determined to credit God alone, the revivalists also obscured the critical importance of their publications in constructing models of revival preaching and evangelical conversion. By sharing increasingly standardized accounts of local revivals, evangelical ministers developed a common style and set of expectations. Then, in the similarity of their local revivals, they found the consummate proof that all belonged to God's Work rather than to their own. Ironically, that conviction increased their exertions to make the most of God's power while it flowed in the land. The illusion of human passivity and complete divine power compelled the evangelists to demand more of themselves and of their congregants. In sum, Lambert examines "how revivalists themselves wove their own web of meaning which convinced them and thousands of others that they were participating in a glorious 'Work of God.'"

Revivals came only to churches and communities that expected and worked for them—all the while insisting that God alone could revive their faith. Owing to varying ethnic mixtures and seventeenth-century origins, the distribution of denominations varied from colony to colony and region to region. Some denominations—principally, the Congregationalists of New England and the Presbyterians of the Middle Atlantic colonies—nurtured revivalism, while others—chiefly the Church of England in the southern colonies—did not. Many Presbyterian and Congregationalist communities sustained a cycle during which, over a generation, surges in emotional fervor and new conversions alternated with longer intervals of lower energy and fewer New Births.

Until the 1730s, these cycles were localized, varying in intensity and duration from community to community. And revivalism was controversial and divisive. Some Presbyterians and Congregationalists and most Anglicans distrusted evangelical revivalism as too emotional, disruptive, and volatile. They preferred more gradual and rational conversions carefully guided by a patient and learned minister. It was during the 1730s that the local revivals became more coordinated and better publicized, capturing wider attention as a common work of God. The process began in the Raritan Valley of eastern New Jersey, with revivals among the Presbyterians and the Dutch Reformed. A leading New Jersey revivalist, Rev. Gilbert Tennent, reported the inspiring news to his New England correspondents, including Rev. Jonathan Edwards of Massachusetts. Ambitious and evangelical, Edwards emulated Tennent by preaching revival with a greater intensity. By dramatically renewing his Northampton congregation, Edwards inspired other Congregational revivals throughout the Connecticut Valley of western Massachusetts and central Connecticut. In Northampton, the revival ebbed in 1735, after the death by suicide of Edwards's own uncle, who had despaired of ever achieving conversion.

Yet that revival persisted and grew by breaking into print. Edwards wrote a vivid account, entitled *A Faithful Narrative of the Surprizing Work of God*, which leading Congregationalists published in London in 1737 and in Boston in 1738. *A Faithful Narrative* linked the Connecticut Valley and Raritan Valley revivals, overriding their distance in time and place to depict God as acting throughout the colonies, and perhaps the entire Protestant world. Widely and avidly read in Britain and the colonies, *A Faithful Narrative* provided models of evangelical preaching and conversion to guide subsequent revivals, which then seemed all the more impressive because of their similarity to one another and to their precedents in *A Faithful Narrative*. Evangelicals read the similarities as manifesting God's uniform power rather than as evidence of Edwards's influential account. Lambert insists: "the *Faithful Narrative* was the vessel that carried the spore of a great awakening from America to Britain in 1737."

The English readers of *A Faithful Narrative* included George Whitefield, a young Anglican minister who had developed an evangelical style at odds with the dominant tone of the Church of England. Inspired by Edwards's account, Whitefield developed an innovative career as an itinerant evangelical, touring England and Wales to reach laboring people ignored by mainstream Anglicans. Drawing crowds too large for churches and made up of people uncomfortable in them, Whitefield preached conversion to thousands in the streets, fields, and parks. Never before had so many people assembled to hear preaching, and never before had so many felt so emotionally engaged in the performance.

Echoing across the Atlantic, the swelling volume of evangelical print escalated revivalism on both shores of the Atlantic. Edwards's words had crossed the ocean into print in London to inspire Whitefield. In turn, London newsprint passed in ships to the colonies to convey sensational and inspirational accounts of Whitefield's impact in England. His immense crowds in London assured Whitefield of an eager audience in the colonies, for the colonists paid cultural deference to the great metropolis as the source of fashion. The more they read about him, the more the colonists longed to hear and see Whitefield preach.

In 1739, Whitefield crossed the Atlantic to tour the colonies, ostensibly to raise funds for an orphanage in Georgia, but mainly to export his form of evangelical theater to new audiences. His American tour reflected the transatlantic integration of the British Empire into an increasingly common market of goods and ideas. Whitefield benefited from the proliferation of shipping and newspapers, the improved network of roads, and the greater density of settlement, which promised larger crowds. His preaching tour also furthered the process of integration by enlisting colonists into the first transatlantic and intercolonial cultural movement. Traveling from Maine to Georgia for two years, Whitefield probably was seen by most of the colonists. Lambert observes: "The evangelist arrived as a long-expected, fashionable import, and colonists eagerly anticipated his coming much the way late-twentieth-century Americans await the latest rock star."

Although nominally an Anglican, Whitefield was primarily sponsored by Presbyterian ministers in the middle colonies and by Congregationalists in New England. They shared his evangelical Calvinism, and hoped that Whitefield's sensational preaching would provoke a renewed wave of conversions. Although people of many denominations attended his immense open-air services, Whitefield evoked a relatively tepid response beyond the Presbyterian and Congregational orbits. The Anglicans were especially cool, distrusting his emotional preaching and ecumenical support, and so Whitefield drew his smallest crowds and made the slightest impact in the southern colonies.

Despite those limits, his preaching disseminated and coordinated revivalism in more places and with greater fervor than ever before. In Philadelphia, Whitefield exhorted: "Would any Thing I could do or suffer influence your Hearts, I think I could bear to pluck out my Eyes, or even to lay down my Life for your Sakes. . . . But such Power only belongeth unto the Lord—I can only invite; . . . It is his Property to take away the Heart of Stone, and give you a Heart of Flesh." Especially in New England, the revivals of 1740–42 greatly exceeded those of the 1730s in emotional intensity and geographic range. Whitefield's spectacular impact alarmed religious conservatives, who preferred a more cautious and reasoned faith. They denounced his itineracy as a dangerous innovation and disdained the emotional audiences as "enthusiastic," an eighteenth-century pejorative that denoted madness and fanaticism.

To counter the conservative contention that the revivals were erratic and random, Rev. Thomas Prince, an evangelical Congregationalist from

Boston, collected dozens of reports describing the local revivals in remarkably similar terms. From 1743 to 1745, Prince published these accounts in his magazine, *Christian History*. The similarities reflected the influence of a questionnaire circulated by Prince and based on Edwards's models of revivalism and conversion as codified in *A Faithful Narrative*. "The result was that, *as reported*, local revivals assumed a greater degree of uniformity than they did *as experienced*," Lambert remarks.

No American chauvinist, Prince compiled similar revival accounts from Germany, Scotland, England, and Wales to demonstrate the common pattern to God's power. As was characteristic with colonists, he claimed importance for American developments by placing them in a transatlantic context. Feeling provincial, colonists needed the reassurance that God was active in the home country. In 1749, a New England minister explained to a Scottish correspondent: "It would tend to cause this concert [of revivals] to prevail much more here, if we could hear that it was greatly spreading and prevailing on your side of the Atlantick, where it was first begun, and from whence it was first proposed to us. On the contrary, it will undoubtedly be a discouragement to people here, if they hear that the matter decays and languishes, or is come to a stand." It is especially revealing that the New England minister deferred to Britain as the source of the expanding revivalism, which actually had begun in New Jersey.

By emphasizing literary inventions, Lambert often questions the authenticity of "a great awakening" beyond the accounts framed by the evangelicals. He is most persuasive in showing how the accounts framed popular expectations to stimulate remarkably common revivals. By believing in their own story, the evangelicals did make a Great Awakening. Often, however, Lambert undermines that insight by doubting that anything knowable operated beyond the published tissue of cultural constructions: "Historians, then, who seek to explain the state of religion in mid-eighteenth-century colonial America confront an array of fictions, inventions, and counterinventions, from which they construct their own 'interpretive fictions.'"

By his own design, Lambert cannot find a Great Awakening beyond the web of print produced by one segment of American evangelicals. His book relies almost exclusively on printed works by or about Congregationalists and Presbyterians—to the neglect of unpublished documents and of sources from the other denominations. Relying on the standard printed sources long familiar to historians, Lambert gives them an interesting interpretive twist, but he rarely ventures into the archives to find new manuscript evidence that could more dramatically improve our understanding of the Great Awakening.

Merely tweaking the conventional Congregational and Presbyterian version of the awakening, Lambert relies on the usual suspects—Tennent, Edwards, Whitefield, and Prince—and the standard events—the Raritan and Northampton revivals, Whitefield's tours, the conservative reaction, and Prince's compilation. As a result, he misses the opportunity, suggested by recent scholarship, to find an authentic and restless spiritual hunger that transcended denominational bounds and relied primarily on oral performances that only rarely passed into print. Taking his Congregational and Presbyterian sources too literally, Lambert awards them a monopoly over revivalism and joins them in pronouncing the revivals dead by 1745. Had he taken a more daring plunge by investigating local churches and by seeking documents made by more obscure people, Lambert might have discovered a far more vibrant, extensive, and enduring Great Awakening—something far more real and powerful than an endless mirrored hall of interpretative fictions.

As Rebecca Larson demonstrates for the Quakers, the evangelical fervor of the mid-eighteenth century affected almost every Protestant denomination. Lambert especially neglects the more radical, and less print-oriented, wing of colonial evangelicals: the poorly educated but charismatic Separates and Baptists, who became the most dynamic American revivalists after 1745. During the 1750s and the 1760s, they carried the legacy of the Great Awakening southward far beyond its origins in New England and New Jersey. One symptom of Lambert's limited perspective is his complete omission of Isaac Backus, the preeminent Baptist leader to emerge from the Great Awakening.

Although ostensibly addressing a more modest topic, Rebecca Larson offers a deeper and more daring probe into colonial religious life. To recover the long-obscured lives of Quaker women preachers, she ventures far beyond print sources into a diverse array of previously untapped manuscript letters, diaries, journals, and church records from many archives in both Great Britain and the United States. From new sources, she documents ordinary people with extraordinary experiences to reveal eighteenth-century spirituality from a provocative new angle. Instead of the oft-studied Congregational and Presbyterian ministers, Larson introduces a diverse and intriguing new cast, including Susanna Freeborn of Rhode Island, Esther Palmer of New York, Catharine Payton of England, and Abigail Craven of Ireland.

More than an exceptional few, at least thirteen hundred Quaker women served as preachers between 1700 and 1775 in the transatlantic British Empire. They reached large audiences, for Quakers composed the third- (or fourth-) largest denomination in the colonies, after the Congregationalists, Anglicans, and perhaps Presbyterians. During the early eighteenth century, Quakers concentrated in Rhode Island, eastern Pennsylvania, western New Jersey, and the North Carolina backcountry.

Many more Quakers lived in Great Britain, especially in Wales, Ireland, and northern England.

Quakers zealously worked to maintain the connections between their distant meetings throughout the empire. Regular correspondence and a steady cycling of traveling preachers linked the Quakers into "one transatlantic community." Larson notes: "The itinerant ministers became shared points of reference for far flung Friends on opposite sides of the Atlantic, helping to forge a common Quaker culture with their preaching." Like the Congregationalists and the Presbyterians, colonial Quakers deferred to the cultural authority of preachers from Britain. In Boston, the English preacher Mary Weston noted: "Many Friends were at [the meeting], expecting some great Things from a Londoner." But colonial Quaker preachers also enjoyed a cachet in Britain among Quakers curious about their more exotic fellow seekers from America.

Larson's female preachers are especially compelling because they contradict so many common assumptions in American religious history and American women's history. We lament, with good cause, that so few records produced by early American women survive; but Larson finds numerous women who left surprisingly extensive and revealing documents. Most colonial women rarely ventured beyond their home farms and villages, but Larson presents women who traveled thousands of miles, enduring the dangers and rigors of the Atlantic and of the frontier. Historians usually postpone to the mid-nineteenth century the struggle by women to speak in public before audiences that included men; Larson reveals women who routinely and authoritatively preached to audiences of both genders, all ages, and curious non-Quakers as well as devout Friends.

Larson demonstrates the importance of Quaker women in exposing and testing the limits of convention long before the nineteenth-century female reformers. All other Christian denominations barred women from the ministry. To justify a male monopoly on preaching, they cited the Apostle Paul, who insisted: "But I suffer not a woman to teach, nor to usurp authority over the man, but to be in silence" (1 Tim. 2:12); "And if they will learn any thing, let them ask their husbands at home; for it is a shame for women to speak in the church" (1 Cor. 11:3). But Quakers found alternative scriptural injunctions, including one by the Apostle Paul: "There is neither male nor female; for you are all one in Jesus Christ" (Gal. 3:28).

The Quakers began as a radical religious movement in Britain during the 1650s, a decade of political upheaval that fomented apocalyptic expectations. Sensing the approaching millennium, devout seekers felt God's power within their own souls and distrusted external authorities, including pompous bishops and learned ministers. The seekers called themselves the Friends of Truth and rallied to the charismatic preaching of George Fox, a common tradesman who felt divinely inspired. They became commonly known as "Quakers" because one of their preachers claimed that they alone quaked before the power of God.

The Quakers insisted that every true Christian found and nurtured an "Inner Light" that provided access to the Holy Spirit. The Inner Light offered immediate, divine revelation and guidance that trumped even the Bible and certainly all learning obtained in this world. Rejecting a paid and learned clergy, the Quakers practiced an egalitarian worship by gathering to hear the Inner Light through the voices of the truly converted and specially inspired. The gender of the body did not matter, for the words came from God.

After 1670, as the apocalypse began to seem less imminent, the Quakers moderated their public fervor and institutionalized a hierarchy of meetings to achieve a greater conformity. Larson notes: "The uninhibited, ecstatic, confrontational Quaker preacher of the mid-seventeenth century was evolving into the more introspective quietist of the eighteenth century." But, because the Quakers clung to their belief in the Inner Light and the equality of all souls, they preserved female preaching and established parallel meetings for women to share in the church governance. At the same time, thousands of Quakers emigrated to the colonies, stretching their network of meetings across the Atlantic.

Any Quaker could speak in meeting, but a few especially articulate and inspired people took the lead. Formally recognized as "Public Friends," the adepts sat as a group on an elevated gallery in front of the congregation. When a Public Friend felt summoned by God to travel to preach to other meetings, he or she applied to her local meeting for a certificate affording permission. Receiving no salaries, the Public Friends worked at some temporal employment and, during journeys, depended on the charity of meetings and of prosperous patrons. Welcomed by their hosts, the traveling Public Friends brought new voices to distant meetings, which helped renew fervor and maintain the ties of a common faith. And their published memoirs circulated among Quakers, holding up female as well as male preachers as paragons of spirituality.

Meetings had to watch carefully for signs of special inspiration in any member, male or female. The members discouraged idle prattlers and ambitious blowhards devoid of a divine calling—but members also needed to encourage anyone who apparently offered "immediate revelation of the Spirit of God," lest they defy the Holy Spirit in his choice of preachers. And God chose obscure people, including women, almost as often as he favored prosperous men. In 1718 in rural Pennsylvania, for example, Jane Fenn, a young and impoverished maidservant, felt a divine call to preach, an inner voice that commanded: "I have chosen thee a vessel from thy youth to serve me, and to preach the Gospel of salvation to many people; and if thou wilt be faithful, I will be with thee unto the end of time, and make thee an heir of my kingdom." Feeling unworthy, she struggled to suppress that divine call for fear of embarrassing herself and offending her meeting. But the members of the meeting noted her struggle and encouraged her calling. Fenn's patrons included a male preacher and her wealthy employer, who released Fenn from service and financially supported her travels throughout the colonies and to the British Isles. No other denomination would have done the same for a woman, especially one of such low status in the world.

Ironically, by claiming submission and service to God, select women obtained greater confidence and authority in a society that ordinarily limited their options. In 1724, Elizabeth Webb wrote to the son of another female preacher: "Thy mother is become very courageous in riding thru deep waters and over rocky mountains beyond what I could expect. She says fear is taken away from her and that she is borne up by a secret hand." Although not self-consciously feminist, they expanded the usual female sphere of activity as an effect of their divine calling. Quaker fathers and husbands relinquished their patriarchal claims on daughters and wives and accepted their long absences while preaching in distant places. Often, Quaker husbands had to care for infant children when God summoned their wives away to preach. The priority of divine service appeared when the Philadelphia Yearly Meeting authorized Ann Dillworth to visit England as a preacher but denied the similar application of her preacher husband—apparently because he seemed insufficiently inspired.

Larson challenges the usual assumption that eighteenth-century Quakerism had grown so spiritually inert that the Friends felt alienated from the evangelical Great Awakening. She shows that the Quakers engaged in the same struggle between maintaining group cohesion and encouraging a potentially divisive fervor. The female preachers certainly wrote and preached in an evangelical vein meant to provoke spiritual conversions; they, too, expected sinners to pass from despair into resignation before receiving liberating grace. With all the fervor of other evangelicals, mid-century Quaker preachers denounced spiritual indifference and exhorted moral reform, stricter church discipline, and renewed conversions. Mary Weston sounded remarkably like Jonathan Edwards in her "dreadful Apprehension of being cast into the Lake that burns with Fire and Brimstone" for "gratifying my vain Mind in the Delights, Pleasures & Pastimes of a deluding World." Mary Peisley seemed to echo Gilbert Tennent when she denounced most Quaker elders as "dry, withered, fruitless trees, twice dead, plucked up by the roots, being rich in words and expressions of former experience, but out of the power of Truth."

In their own ways, the Quakers anticipated and contributed to the Great Awakening. Their itinerant preachers of transatlantic celebrity long preceded Whitefield and probably prepared his way. Quakers also annually gathered by the thousands from great distances to hear conversion preached by multiple preachers in open settings decades before Whitefield and his many emulators. In their long-standing emphasis on conversion, extemporaneous preaching, and a divine calling to preach (instead of relying on reason, written sermons, and a learned clergy), the Quakers established the style that evangelical Congregationalists and Presbyterians later emulated in a louder vein. After hearing Rachel Wilson preach in England, George Whitefield introduced himself to praise her as a kindred spirit. Although Frank Lambert ignores the Quaker sources from a conviction that the Society of Friends resisted revivalism, Rebecca Larson reveals that from 1732 to 1734 their Philadelphia Yearly Meeting recognized one hundred new preachers—an unprecedented surge indicating a burst in fervor simultaneous with the Raritan and Northampton revivals.

Far from avoiding the Great Awakening, the Quakers more fully lived up to the radical social implications of the revival challenge to secular authority. Far more than their Congregational, Presbyterian, and Baptist counterparts, Quaker preachers obliged their churches by demanding sweeping social reforms. Under pressure from their meetings, most colonial Quaker leaders reaffirmed their pacifism by withdrawing from politics in wartime. In 1758, the Philadelphia Yearly Meeting barred Quaker slaveholders from church leadership, and in 1776, it prohibited them from membership. In a society premised on slavery, the Quakers became the lone denomination systematically to seek abolition during the eighteenth century.

By the 1760s, female Public Friends were attracting remarkable public attention and respect from non-Quaker audiences and officials. Indeed, the female preachers drew larger and more diverse crowds than did their male brethren. In 1769, the English Quaker Rachel Wilson toured the colonies, everywhere drawing packed houses and newspaper praise from non-Quakers. In Newport, Rhode Island, a Congregational minister extolled Wilson as "a pious sensible woman." Despite her gender, Wilson enjoyed broader public and official support than did Whitefield on his later tours of the American colonies.

The increased attention paid female Quaker preachers reflected the more evangelical and ecumenical orientation of the popular culture in the wake of the Great Awakening. Larson notes: "the new religious intensity had unified as much as it had divided, by fracturing barriers between religious groups." Less bonded to their own denominations and more eager for spontaneous spirituality, colonists (and Britons) more readily sampled the increasing variety of traveling preachers. By the 1760s, thousands of non-Quakers were as prepared to hear God through a sojourning female Quaker as from their resident, male, and learned minister. Wilson aptly characterized her many non-Quaker listeners in Boston as "a Seeking pepol."

Neither Frank Lambert nor Rebecca Larson finds a colonial culture alienated from Great Britain and headed for revolution. By revealing the common transatlantic religious culture of the eighteenth century, they suggest that the American Revolution ruptured a shared world, reversing instead of fulfilling the social and cultural trends of the previous half century. The pacifist Quakers certainly experienced the revolution as a catastrophe that disrupted their cherished contacts across the Atlantic. That revolution then created a nationalism that has long needed to reconfigure its colonial past into a steady trajectory away from Great Britain and into the American continent, obscuring the lost transatlantic world of George Whitefield and Rachel Wilson.

9

# Midnight Ramblers

*February 5, 2001*

During the late eighteenth and early nineteenth centuries—an age of revolutions—Americans were, literally, dreamers. They earnestly experienced, described, and discussed their dreams and visions. Instead of reflexively dismissing a dream as "only a dream," most Americans suspected supernatural meaning, either divine providence or satanic manipulation. Such dreams demanded explanation and action, for to ignore them was to risk an early death, court eternal damnation, or lose some golden opportunity. Guided by angels, Joseph Smith Jr. sought—and claimed to find—the golden plates of a newer testament that became the Book of Mormon. After envisioning a spectral battle in the sky, Nat Turner organized a bloody slave rebellion in Virginia in 1831 that made the Civil War almost inevitable. Inspired by dreams and assisted by magic spells, hundreds of common farmers dug for buried treasure throughout the hinterland. Young people looked to dreams to learn whom they would marry. Most common of all, souls traveled in dreams to see heaven and hell and to seek the secrets of salvation from angels.

The most self-conscious dreamers wrote autobiographies and had the means, or obtained the sponsors, to secure publication. Uncommon before 1740, such "self-narratives" proliferated after the American Revolution, as printing presses multiplied and as common people felt more important and more curious about one another. Some two hundred published narratives, most featuring recounted dreams, provide the basis for Mechal Sobel's daring new book, *Teach Me Dreams: The Search for Self in the Revolutionary Era.* An Israeli scholar educated in the United States, Sobel combines the insights of both an insider and an outsider to American history. In one nation or the other (or perhaps in both), she has developed a special sensitivity to the interdependence of peoples who profess their separation and enmity. In a previous book, *The World They Made Together: Black and White Values in Eighteenth-Century Virginia,*

*Teach Me Dreams: The Search for Self in the Revolutionary Era,* by Mechal Sobel (Princeton University Press, 2000)

which appeared in 1987, Sobel reveals the surprisingly deep influence exercised by enslaved blacks on a culture ruled by their white masters. Built on that predecessor, *Teach Me Dreams* finds African spiritual practices oozing into southern evangelical Christianity.These included shouting and dancing to express a more joyful spirituality. Above all, Sobel finds that blacks and whites dreamed obsessively about one another.

The book itself has a dreamlike quality in its repetitive organization and its broad swings in tone and approach. The prose oscillates between passages of feverish opacity, bursts of creative insight, and biographies of compelling characters. Sobel rescues from obscurity an array of fascinating personalities, including Deborah Sampson, who dressed as a man to serve in the revolutionary army; Sarah Osborn, who developed a popular ministry disguised as a school; Jonathan Brunt, "a fear-ridden madman" consumed with rage against women; and William Grimes, a former slave who contemplated bestowing his whip-scarred skin to the United States government to "bind the Constitution of glorious, happy, and *free* America. Let the skin of an American slave bind the charter of American liberty!" In sum, Sobel's book cannot be read quickly and easily, but patience will provide rewarding surprises.

To interpret these early American dreams, Sobel moves beyond Freud, applying, instead, the more recent and more empirical theories of Charlotte Beradt, Heinz Kohut, Ernst Lawrence Rossi, and Christopher Bollas. Studying dreams recorded in Germany during the 1930s, Beradt concludes that people conformed to Nazi demands in their dreams before embracing them in action. Drawing from Kohut, Sobel concludes that dreams develop and maintain a sense of identity. Rossi provides a useful measure for a dreamer's level of self-reflection, from the lowest (dreams without people) up to those with "multiple levels of awareness"—dreams that promote the greatest "psychological growth." From Bollas, Sobel draws the notion that the "self" does not simply emerge in complete antithesis with an "other"—but also covertly steals ideas and emotions in a process of "introjection." In dreams, people repel an opposite identity, to mask their own introjections of envied attitudes and behaviors. In sum, Sobel and the theorists treat dreams and their narration "as technologies of the self": as subconscious tools to exercise inner tensions and then to work through them to a greater self-awareness (albeit while saddling themselves with hidden costs).

Once upon a time, American cultural historians wrote about the emergence of "individualism." Now they analyze the development of the self in relation to an other. More than a matter of words, the shift registers a darker view of our national past. In former histories, American individualism seemed a bracing response to the material abundance and the dangerous challenge of an open frontier, which demanded initiative as it offered liberation from older creeds and constraints. Associated with wide-open spaces and opportunities, individualism seemed upbeat, expansive, and available to all (except, of course, Indians and enslaved blacks). In stark contrast, the self is a more sobering concept that demands an inner, psychological explanation. No product of shared abundance and opportunity, the varieties of self reveal, instead, the powerful divisions of race, class, and gender in our history. The white, middle-class man necessarily constructs a different sense of self by polarizing against all whom he considers his opposites: blacks, the poor, and women. By defining them as shiftless, immoral, and weak, he seeks to become industrious, virtuous, and strong. Of course, he also must serve as the consummate other for an impoverished black woman. By regarding him as domineering and dull, she can cherish community and spontaneity. In the process of creating a self, everyone learns "to reject aspects of their potential" by projecting them onto an imagined "anti-Me."

Today most people take for granted the inner consciousness called the "self" as the supposed controller of emotions and actions. We earnestly believe that we can improve by self-action, given the proper books, tapes, reflection, therapy, and support. In our overwhelming self-consciousness, we assume that past peoples felt and thought as we do.

Cultural historians, however, depict our contemporary sense of self as a modern construction. Before the eighteenth century, they maintain, Europeans and their colonists had a weak and porous sense of self, one subject to the demands of their communities and their social superiors—but especially to the tricks of the devil and the ultimate providence of God. The few surviving narratives written by common people present a life experienced passively as one surprising crisis after another, all revealing helplessness before the ultimate and inscrutable power of fate and the divine. "They did not see themselves," Sobel notes, "as having fashioned their lives or as being responsible for their selves." Indeed, self was their enemy, their other, best suppressed as a snare fatal to Christian salvation.

This began to change after 1740, as people gradually reimagined themselves as assertive actors at center stage in lives with individual patterns and profound significance. To explain this shift in consciousness, Sobel cites the voluntary choice in allegiance promoted by evangelical churches, the active citizenship celebrated by the republican revolution, the individuating demands of a more commercialized economy, and the increasing interaction between the races as the black population grew. But she ultimately locates the process of change in particular lives. Dreams were central to the "refashioning" of American selves—but, according to Sobel, they only mobilized "self-fashioning" only when the dreamer identified an "alien other" located the dream in her or his life story and found validation by an "outside authority."

Troubled by social and political changes in their world, often in ways obscured to their conscious minds, Americans of the revolutionary era struggled with dark feelings, which found a focus in dreams about an enemy, the alien other. In dreams, whites felt attacked by imaginary blacks for what had been done to them. Similarly, blacks vented their nocturnal rage in dreams of thieving, cheating, abusive whites. Gender also polarized dreams, as men and women imagined one another as alien others, which helped propel an increasing distinction, during the day, in gender roles.

Americans evidently did not sleep lightly, for Sobel reports an array of grim and violent dreams full of fear and loathing. The revolutionary cross-dresser Deborah Sampson dreamed that she was attacked and "drenched in blood" by an immense serpent. She whacked the snake to bits, only to see the pieces reaggregate as a raging ox. Sampson killed it a second time by bludgeoning the ox into "gelly." Sobel plausibly reads this dream as evidence that Sampson dreaded sexual assault and, thereafter, meant to defend herself by dressing as a man.

In 1770, the Quaker preacher John Woolman dreamed that "a man had been hunting and brought a living creature to Mount Holly of a mixed breed, part fox and part cat." To provide "flesh to feed this creature," the dream whites seized an elderly black man: "raising a long ladder against the house, they hanged the old man" and butchered the remains. Although appalled, the dreaming Woolman felt paralyzed and unable to articulate his horror: "And being in great distress I continued wailing till I began to wake, and opening my eyes I perceived it was morning." Later that day, Woolman described his horrific dream to a close friend, who confessed that he had dreamed that same night of a butchered black man hung up in a smokehouse. Sobel interprets their dreams as expressions of guilt at how little they had done to challenge slavery.

Regarding such dreams as especially profound, and perhaps divine, people recalled and scrutinized them for guidance, for some change that they needed to make in their lives. They felt compelled to narrate their especially vivid and troubling dreams, usually orally, sometimes in print. Over time, these narratives assumed a more dramatic form, with a climax and resolution effected by self-action. Sobel explains that "threats to the self were coped with in dreams and then in the narrated lives. Change in the self was often worked out on the dream-screen, and this change was then played out in the narrative report of the waking life. In crucial dreams . . . an alien other was targeted and a dream-screen commitment was made. Many people awoke determined to act on this recognition and commitment." Pressured to re-create themselves as autonomous individuals, men felt a stress that induced dreams of women as weakening temptresses. By overcoming such women in their dreams, and by narrating the victories to their peers, men moved closer to the demanding ideal—but at a painful cost to their relational and empathetic potential.

To honor their dreamed commitments to a new self, people needed a legitimating forum—a social group to evaluate and vindicate both the dream and the changes. Religious groups, especially upstart Protestant denominations, provided the most effective "outside authority." By demanding and examining conversion stories, which often included the spiritual interpretation of dreams, the churches "helped the individual reframe the past and begin a new path in life." In effect, they confirmed that the dream was valid and worthy of spurring life changes.

But such groups also narrowed the ambivalent meanings of dreams, further demonizing the alien other. Far from celebrating the triumph of the modern self, Sobel sees a tragic legacy: "as a result of the growing need to develop an individuated self, irrational hatreds came to further dominate our lives." In her closing note, she urges a break from "our binary systems of white/black and male/female, in order to reframe reality. Perhaps the way lies through a new appreciation of individual dreams and collective myths."

Almost all of Sobel's evidence derives from published narratives, only rarely from manuscript diaries, journals, and reminiscences kept in archives. This raises the probability that her sources were heavily filtered by the demands of readers, publishers, editors, and financial sponsors, who expected a certain conformity to the specifications of a genre: the pious biography of a repenting sinner. Rather than address the constraints of literary form and the publishing market, Sobel insists: "In this study I have taken the narrators at their word."

She also does not offer systematic criteria for selecting the two hundred published accounts—a subset of the many hundreds written in America between 1740 and 1840. Featuring people preoccupied with racial and sexual difference, the texts seem chosen to confirm her argument rather than more randomly to test it. In the process, Sobel gives very short shrift—a mere paragraph—to the powerful dream-culture of Indians and its interplay on the frontier with the dreams and visions of evangelical settlers. Rather than explore the major role of Indians and whites as self and other in their different dreams, she "focuses on black-white interaction inasmuch as this relationship was *the* defining self-other relationship for most of the narrators in this study and has remained central in American culture since that time," which is to say that black-white relations were central to those narratives that she chose to investigate.

Sobel insists that the range of authors—in race, class, and gender—offers a representative cross section of American society. If so, readers will conclude that, during the revolutionary generation, most people became preachers—for the narratives largely derive from religious seekers justifying their sense of calling to a ministry. As Quakers, Baptists, Methodists, and Disciples of Christ, most of the authors belonged to upstart religious groups that especially cherished dreams as a source of divine authority superior to the official authority of learned and powerful men in this world. And Sobel's authors tend to be people with especially unconventional claims to the ministry—blacks, women, and the poor—who could find authorization only in a divine dream or vision. Although important and rapidly growing groups, these religious seekers did not necessarily speak for the majority of Americans, who professed a faith more skeptical of dreams: Presbyterians, Congregationalists, Anglicans, and rationalists.

By necessity, Sobel's interpretations of the dreams are highly subjective and speculative. Where Freud detected sex within every dream, Sobel finds pervasive the race consciousness that she seeks. Sarah Beckhouse Hamilton, a young woman in South Carolina, dreamed of heaven, seeing "a great company of shining people in white robes, with white palms in their hands. They all sung with melodious harmony, such singing as I had never heard before." Sobel interprets: "All these references suggest that Hamilton saw the heavenly host as African American: 'Singing such as . . . never heard before' was a response often made to Africans' singing, and the 'white palms in their hands' can be understood as a pun which conflated the palms of Palm Sunday with the white palms of Africans' hands. The 'shining people' may well have been another reference to Africans, who used oil to anoint their skin." Maybe Sobel is right, given the subsequent twist in Hamilton's life. Suddenly rejecting a proposed marriage to a wealthy planter, she instead became "a lay leader in a black and white congregation." On the other hand, shining (white) people, glorious singing, and white palm fronds were commonplaces of the spiritual dreams narrated by dozens of northerners who never made Hamilton's choice and never had much to do with blacks.

Fundamentally, Sobel investigates dreams to get at racial thinking. Consequently, she explores some texts that illuminate racism—even if devoid of dreams for analysis. For example, she understandably (and insightfully) recapitulates the luridly compelling narrative of William Otter, who gloried in his powerful physique, thorough racism, and talent for mockery. A white artisan in urban America during the early nineteenth century, Otter felt a violent rage toward women, toward the Irish, and—especially—toward blacks. A professional slave-catcher, he became covertly but thoroughly familiar with the haunts of fugitives: black taverns, dance halls, boardinghouses, and churches. When not tracking blacks for business, he tormented them for pleasure. Once he thrust a goat, blindfolded and daubed in excrement, into a crowded black church. As the alarmed worshipers bolted through the windows, Otter and his gang of white thugs pummeled them with sticks and whips. Narrated with unrepentant glee, his tales sought the applause of whites who needed rage to mask their apparent envy of black cultural spontaneity. Sobel concludes: "He wrote his narrative as though it were the script for a blackface minstrel show in which he played the role of master trickster." Analyzing Otter is critical, for he appears as the lone example of a major category in her schema: "Conflicted Self-fashioning." Unfortunately for this purpose, Otter recorded no dreams to provide the master key to his (arrested) psychological development.

With more ingenuity than consistency, Sobel finds a dream for him in an anonymous account printed in 1835 by *The Southern Literary Messenger*. Seized by two "large, gaunt blackamoors," the dreamer painfully lost his nose to their spinning grindstone. Adding insult to injury, the blacks mocked the dreamer by singing a minstrel ballad. Awaking in a sweat, the narrator focused his outrage on the ballad, which he insisted had been "*stolen . . . from the white black-face minstrelsy stage.*" Associating this dream with Otter, Sobel insists: "The writer of this dream report, while far more self-conscious and far more intellectual than Otter, revealed himself as his compatriot. It was 'the cruel mockery' that the author felt he had suffered at the hands of blacks that most hurt him. Their hearty African laughter dishonored him and spurred him to break his bonds."

In an aside and a note, however, Sobel reveals that some scholars attribute the published dream to Edgar Allan Poe. Given Sobel's causal emphasis on Otter's class position as a laboring man in competition with blacks, it seems arbitrary to analyze the literary construct of an educated gentleman as if it were Otter's dream.

Because her interpretations of dreams can only be speculative, Sobel cannot *prove* her largest claim: that these particular dreams served as the crucial pivot for a society-wide transformation of revolutionary and enduring dimensions. Instead of a social science proof, Sobel presents a powerful evocation of a troubled America for common people, a divided land ordinarily obscured by mythic celebrations of the Revolution as a boon for everyone. She has boldly probed a strange, demanding, and promising subject, paving the way for others. By exploring the conspicuous nexus of race, gender, rage, dreaming, and self-fashioning in one particular set of narratives, Sobel has certainly identified a critical set of raw nerves in our history and a daring new approach to the understanding of our past.

## 10

# Worlds within Words

*July 29, 2002*

Nations, Jill Lepore reminds us, are linguistic projects troubled by lingering divisions. In Europe during the eighteenth and nineteenth centuries, the creators of France, Spain, Germany, Greece, and Italy invented traditions of homogeneity in blood and culture. Nationalists worked to suppress profound regional variations in language by instituting centrally directed instruction in a single, systematized "national" language. Swabians and Bavarians became Germans as their schools taught Hochdeutsch—a northern dialect. In France, Bretons and Gascons had to learn Paris's language.

But the construction of nation through language rarely achieves closure. Although compelled to learn English, the Catholic Irish resented subordination within the British Empire. Although indoctrinated in Castilian Spanish, the Catalans and Basques clung to their own languages and dreams of autonomy. Closer to home, many Francophones pursue Québec's secession from Canada's Anglophone majority. And our own Cassandras dread the growing numbers of American Hispanics as a linguistic threat to national unity. These alarmists insist that America risks a Canadian division along cultural lines unless we renew, codify, and enforce the domination of English.

Although the particular fear of Spanish is relatively new, the anxiety over our linguistic bonds reaches back to our national origins in revolution. The English names and faces of the leading revolutionaries—the Founding Fathers—mislead our national memory to imagine a united people homogeneous in culture. Indeed, we usually credit our current ethnic and linguistic diversity entirely to nineteenth- and twentieth-century waves of immigrants. In fact, English folk were but the largest minority in the ethnic mosaic of eighteenth-century America.

Although English in government, the colonies had attracted (or dragooned) thousands of Scots, Scotch-Irish, Irish, Germans, Dutch, Swedes,

*A Is for American: Letters and Other Characters in the Newly United States,* by Jill Lepore (Alfred A. Knopf, 2002)

Finns, Swiss, Welsh, French Huguenots, and enslaved Africans—to say nothing of the Indians, who spoke several hundred distinct languages. In 1744, Dr. Alexander Hamilton, a Scottish immigrant, marveled at the diversity of Philadelphia: "I dined at a tavern with a very mixed company of different nations and religions. There were Scots, English, Dutch, Germans, and Irish; there were Roman Catholicks, Church men, Presbyterians, Quakers, Newlightmen, Methodists, Seventh day men, Moravians, Anabaptists, and one Jew." No recent innovation, American multiculturalism has very deep roots. Working with census data, Lepore calculates that "the percentage of non-native English speakers in the United States was actually *greater* in 1790 than in 1990."

Consequently, those English-named and English-speaking Founding Fathers worried about how to construct a unifying sense of nationalism among a diverse and contentious people recently drawn together and violently wrenched from the British Empire. "If there is a country in the world where concord . . . would be least expected," Thomas Paine explained, "it is America. Made up, as it is, of people from different nations, accustomed to different forms and habits of government, speaking different languages, and more different in their modes of worship, it would appear that the union of such a people was impracticable." In a peevish moment, Benjamin Franklin anticipated modern worriers by demanding: "Why should Pennsylvania, founded by the English, become a colony of aliens, who will shortly be so numerous as to Germanize us instead of our Anglifying them?"

By recalling these fears, Lepore corrects the patriotic, school-book version of the American Revolution, which depicts a homogeneous and united people led by supremely self-confident statesmen of English descent. She highlights, instead, the cultural divisions of Americans and the pervasive anxieties expressed by America's leaders between the Revolution and the Civil War. They worried that the new nation was too big and its people too different to hang together for long. They realized that American nationalism was new and fragile—and more artifice than instinct. By recovering the Founders' dread of division and their contentious struggles to create bonds of nation, Lepore renders them more human, more pertinent, and more familiar. In the past, as in the present, America has been paradoxically, indeed, perversely, united by a cultural debate over our differences.

For Noah Webster, a Yankee pedagogue and gadfly, the new nation could not endure without greater linguistic uniformity. In 1786, he asked: "A national language is a national tie, and what country wants it more than America?" English was the nation's principal language, already adopted, at least in part, by most of the recent immigrants and slaves, but as the language of the British Empire, English linked Americans to their colonial past. Americans were, Lepore writes, "too much like the English and not enough like one another; Americans shared very little by way of heritage, custom, and manners, and what little they did share, they shared with England." To sever that linguistic tie to colonialism, some visionaries proposed making French, or even Greek or Hebrew, the new national language. But Webster regarded such proposals as both impractical and incomplete. In 1789, he asserted that "*language,* as well as government should be national. America should have her *own* distinct from all the world."

Webster's goal was dual: a linguistic uniformity among the American people, north and south; *and* a linguistic distinction from the King's English. He proposed a new system of phonetic spelling that would, he insisted, dissolve sectional and ethnic distinctions in pronunciation—while fomenting an ever-widening distinction from English. "There iz no alternativ," he argued. His more radical spelling proposals reaped scorn—one critic mocked the author as "No-ur Webster." By subsequently diluting his system, Webster became the nation's most widely read and taught author. First issued in 1783, his patriotic *American Spelling Book* became standard in schools throughout the nation, selling ten million copies by 1829.

During the late 1850s, Jefferson Davis, then a United States senator from Mississippi, insisted that Webster had achieved his fondest dream of unifying the country. "Above all people we are one," Davis insisted, "and above all books which have united us in the bond of a common language, I place the good old spelling book of Noah Webster." During the next decade, however, Davis presided over the southern Confederacy in the Civil War, which killed more than half a million Americans. The dead included two of Webster's grandsons, who fought on opposite sides. As it turned out, no spelling book could compensate for the divisive power of slavery, which unraveled the union in more bloodshed than even the Founding Fathers had feared.

Lepore musters Noah Webster in the first and foremost of the seven character sketches that compose her new book, *A Is for American,* a Plutarchian cultural history of our national origins. The other characters include William Thornton, a West Indian planter who settled in America and promoted a "Universal alphabet" to facilitate communication between European and African languages. Sequoyah was an uneducated but brilliant Cherokee silversmith who never learned English but instead developed an effective syllabary and writing system for his native language. Thomas Hopkins Gallaudet pioneered in the education of the deaf by founding residential schools that developed American Sign Language; Abd al-Rahman Ibrahima was a southern slave who displayed literacy in Arabic to achieve celebrity, freedom, and a return to Africa.

Samuel F. B. Morse developed the world's first system of instantaneous communication over vast distances, the telegraph and Morse Code. Alexander Graham Bell, improved upon the telegraph by inventing the telephone - and thought that he could improve on Gallaudet by suppressing sign language among the deaf in favor of an alternative called "Visible Speech." Most of the seven promoted symbolic systems meant to promote a sense of American nationalism.

Recurrently playing on the double meaning of "character"—as both personal quality and written symbol—Lepore describes her book as "a story about how a few early Americans tried to use letters and other characters—alphabets, syllabaries, signs, and codes—to strengthen the new American nation, to string it together with chains of letters and cables of wire." The seven also appeal to Lepore's talents as a teller of stories rich in cultural implication; she has been drawn to biographies "rich with irony and passion and a certain kind of flawed earnestness." Well-meaning but myopic, they are protagonists plausible in our own time.

The seven lives reveal American history as an enduring tension between two versions of patriotism: one optimistic and universalist (which we often now call "Wilsonian" after Woodrow Wilson); and the other more pessimistic and inward (think Pat Buchanan). Derived from the Enlightenment, the optimistic version sought improved communication systems and technologies to unify and uplift people throughout the world, which generally meant rendering them more like Americans in their religion and politics. The pessimistic version dreaded that foreigners bore a cultural contagion best defeated by enforcing a linguistic uniformity within the nation.

Lepore's biographical subjects varied considerably in their linguistic forms of nationalism. William Thornton most consistently expressed an enlightened universalism, offering his new alphabet as a means to world peace and global Christianity. Webster, Morse, and Bell gravitated toward the more pinched version of linguistic patriotism. Although they initially expressed or inspired universalist dreams, the three eventually became strident nativists and cranks, ever more alarmed by the passing years that brought old age to them and new waves of immigrants to the nation.

Abd al-Rahman and Sequoyah, by contrast, never subscribed to American-led universalism. On the contrary, their linguistic strategies defended the cultural separatism of their own people. By developing a Cherokee writing system, Sequoyah resisted the corrosive acculturation into American ways promoted by learning English. Favoring Cherokee traditionalism and isolation, he willingly moved west—in contrast to his nation's mixed-blood, English-speaking leaders, who assimilated American ways in the vain hope that acculturation would enable them to persist in their Georgia homeland in defiance of covetous white frontiersmen.

To escape from American slavery, Abd al-Rahman displayed his Arabic literacy and pretended to a Christian zeal to convert his people—a pose that sent him back to Africa, where he could, instead, practice his Muslim faith. Neither an innovator nor a system builder, Abd al-Rahman is the wild card in Lepore's deck, primarily included for some literal and figurative color.

By creating American Sign Language, Thomas Hopkins Gallaudet also defied the pervasive nationalist pressure for linguistic uniformity. Prior to Gallaudet, deaf Americans seemed incapable of education. In Britain during the eighteenth century, a few reformers tried to teach the deaf to lip read, with limited success. More successful were the clusters of deaf people, in various countries, who developed local systems of hand signs. Following their cues, the French educator Charles-Michel de l'Epée developed a signing system that his students taught to Gallaudet. Adapting French Sign Language, Gallaudet created American Sign Language and founded a residential school for the deaf in Hartford. Gallaudet's school and system vastly improved the ability of the deaf to communicate with one another and to learn from their teachers; but critics, including the educational reformer Horace Mann, blasted Gallaudet for colluding in the linguistic distinction of the deaf from their fellow Americans.

Although the deaf were relatively few, the notion of any linguistic nation within the larger republic appalled nationalists. Their fears found some confirmation in 1855, four years after Gallaudet's death, when a deaf admirer, John J. Flournoy, proposed creating in the West a new state called Gallaudet. Although Flournoy was the scion of a wealthy planter, he had failed miserably in three races for Georgia's state legislature. Ambitious but frustrated, he sought his own state, limited to deaf people (who also had to be white). "We will have a small republic of our own, under our sovereignty, and independent of all hearing interference," Flournoy proclaimed. He even insisted that the hearing children of deaf parents would have to leave his state of Gallaudet, a proposition that appalled almost everyone. Nothing came of Flournoy's implausible scheme other than to heighten criticism of American Sign Language as the seeds of separatism.

Rather than pose as blandly objective, Lepore holds—and shares—blunt opinions about her human characters. She particularly despises Noah Webster: "a failed schoolmaster, a passionate flutist, a lousy lawyer, an intriguing essayist, an inexhaustible lobbyist, a shrill editor, a pompous lecturer." He was, she concludes, "an arrogant, self-promoting pedagogue" and "a tight-lipped, supercilious, embittered patriarch." Aggrieved by prolonged exposure to Webster's pompous writings, Lepore cannot bear to concede his integrity and insights. She depicts the more genial, cosmopolitan, and optimistic William Thornton as an admirable anti-Webster: "Thornton was worldly; Webster was not. . . . Thornton was expansive; Webster was not." Both men were early abolitionists, but Lepore splits hairs to celebrate Thornton while denigrating Webster: "Yet, if Webster concerned himself with the matter of slavery, he expressed no interest in African languages. And he never linked his antislavery sentiment to his work on spelling reform."

Lepore is much easier on Thornton, despite his Panglossian scheme to transport and colonize freed American slaves in Africa. A logistical nightmare, a financial impossibility, and a moral travesty, African colonization was bitterly opposed by most African Americans *and* by Noah Webster. He aptly blasted African colonization as "a flagrant act of injustice, inferior only to the first act of enslaving their ancestors." Given that he was far more correct than Thornton on the big question, why fault Webster for failing to forge a tenuous link between opposition to slavery and spelling reform? But in fairness to Lepore, anyone who has suffered through a committee meeting—in business, the law, politics, or academia—will recognize how difficult it is to concede that the biggest jerks can occasionally make the best point.

Although far more likeable, Thornton, it has to be said, could be a fool. Smitten by the French Revolution, he excused its atrocities in a fawning letter to the dictator Robespierre: "In extraordinary cases you are warranted in the use of extraordinary means." With scant concern for practicality, Thornton later promoted a federal union of all nations in North and South America, with a capital on the Isthmus of Panama. Aside from designing the United States Capitol, Thornton accomplished little that has endured. After an initial sensation in 1793, his master work, *Cadmus: or, a Treatise on the Elements of Written Language,* quickly faded from print and memory, while Webster's school book and dictionary have persisted through multiple revisions to our own day. The lightweight Thornton may have been the nicer guy, but Webster mattered—and still matters—far more.

Lepore delights in irony and finds a treasure trove in the life of Samuel F. B. Morse. A frustrated artist, Morse turned, in 1832, to experiments applying electromagnetism to communication and to developing a coded system of dots and dashes keyed to the alphabet: the Morse Code. A xenophobic nationalist, Morse meant for his telegraph and code to remain military secrets held by the federal government to combat America's purported enemies—the Catholic powers of Europe. But the penny-pinching Congress balked at purchasing them, obliging Morse to sell his patent rights, instead, to private investors, to his immense financial benefit. A shrewd business partner and a voracious commercial demand spread the telegraph across the continent to the Pacific and across the Atlantic to Europe, making Morse immensely wealthy.

Many commentators, then as now, naïvely detected world peace and harmony in technological determinism. In 1858, an especially optimistic proponent of the telegraph boasted that the transatlantic cable "binds together by a vital cord all the nations of the earth. It is impossible that old prejudices and hostilities should longer exist, while such an instrument has been created for an exchange of thought between all nations of the earth." Poppycock, thought Morse, who dreaded foreigners, especially Catholics, as a menace to the American republic, which he conceived of as properly and perpetually Protestant. Of course, the real danger to the Union came from within, from the highly Protestant southern states wedded to slavery and to the English language. Nor was Morse satisfied when his telegraph became a military asset to the Union during the Civil War as a tool for suppressing southern secession. Indeed, the inventor despised Lincoln, defended slavery, and sympathized with the South. "Our country is dead," he gloomily observed in 1862. No linguistic technology, neither Morse's code nor Webster's school book, could hold together a house divided, one half free and the other committed to slavery.

During the 1860s, as the United States blew apart, a Scottish professor of elocution named Alexander Melville Bell developed a new thirty-four character alphabet that he called "Visible Speech." Reviving Thornton's ambition, the system promised to express all of the sounds in every language to facilitate Christian missionaries and British imperialists around the globe. Bell's famous son, Alexander Graham Bell, adapted Visible Speech to teach the deaf to speak. After immigrating to Boston in 1871, the younger Bell also experimented with the telegraph to reproduce sounds, culminating, in 1876, with the first telephone. The funding came primarily from Gardiner Greene Hubbard, the wealthy father of Mabel Hubbard, a young deaf woman who had become Bell's student and would become his wife. The Bell Telephone Company enriched the couple, enabling Bell to retire from business during the 1880s to devote his time to founding the National Geographic Society and to promoting his own system for deaf education.

In old age, Bell succumbed to the dread that had haunted his predecessors Webster and Morse: that cultural divisions within the United States would widen to undermine the nation. Although patron to a geographical society that collected, packaged, and disseminated global information, Bell liked foreigners best at an exotic distance—where they could not breed with Americans. Although an immigrant, he felt superior to those who came to America from non-English-speaking lands. "The only hope for the American race," he wrote in 1920, "lies in the restriction of immigration."

Like most learned men of his generation, Bell fell hard for Social Darwinism and its affinity for scientific racism and eugenics. Despite his deaf wife and his commitment to deaf education, Bell worried that sign language isolated the deaf from other Americans and encouraged them to procreate with one another, which would culminate in "a deaf variety of the human race." Perhaps to prove his point, Bell took up as a hobby the selective breeding of cats to produce a set of blue-eyed and white-furred animals that were deaf. And Bell preached against Gallaudet's system of teaching American Sign Language in distinct, residential schools for the deaf. In 1913, Bell wrote: "I believe that, in an English speaking country like the United States, the English language, *and the English language alone,* should be used as the means of communication and instruction." With the best of intentions, but the worst judgment, Bell damaged for a generation the most effective mode of teaching the deaf.

This short book is smart and suggestive—but inconclusive. Readers will enjoy an intriguing journey through several colorful lives narrated with insight, but they will gain little sense of the big picture: of the process and destination in the changing modes of national communication and debate. Lepore's style is atmospheric, offering flavor rather than argument, evocation instead of demonstration, and anecdote rather than data. She presents personal essays built around historical personalities without advancing a unifying argument about change through time.

In a brief epilogue, Lepore races from Bell to the digital age, where computers mediate communication. Rather than detail the processes by which our society moved from telephone to computer, she hastily concludes with two contemporary characters, the ubiquitous megamogul Bill Gates and Jeff Hawkins, who invented the Palm Pilot, a hand-held computer with its own alphabet, trademarked as "Graffiti." Taking for granted an age of global American power, both commercial and military, Gates and Hawkins are far less fearful for the national project than were their seven predecessors in Lepore's book. Driven mainly to accumulate more capital and to justify their profits, Gates and Hawkins vaguely ennoble their enterprises in the tropes of Enlightenment universalism, benignly depicting computer-driven globalization as a great harmonizer of opportunity, democracy, and prosperity.

Rather than contradict these dubious claims, Lepore abruptly ends her book with an elegiac sentiment: in the "transformation from a 'republic of letters' to a 'digital economy,' we've replaced characters with numbers." Given Lepore's own flair with characters, let's hope not. Indeed, the eloquent quirkiness of *A Is for American* attests that her concluding sentiment is misleadingly ominous. And Lepore's success in founding and editing a creative Web magazine called *Common-place* reveals the enduring possibilities for words in a medium defined by numbers.

# Part III
# Empire

*11*
# The Virginians
*June 25, 2001*

During the 1580s, Queen Elizabeth I ruled a relatively small and poor kingdom. England lagged far behind Spain, which had surged to wealth and power by developing the first transoceanic empire, conquering and exploiting the Indian peoples of the Caribbean, Mexico, Central America, and Peru. American gold and silver enabled the Spanish emperor to build the largest army and navy in Europe. Alarmed by Spanish power, the other Europeans felt compelled to seek their own share in the American riches. From the Spanish example, the English courtier Sir Walter Ralegh concluded: "That hee that commaunds the sea commaunds the trade and hee that is lord of the trade of the world is lord of the wealthe of the world."

The quickest way to obtain American wealth was to steal it on the high seas, after the Spanish had conveniently mined the gold and silver and loaded it onto ships. Lacking a substantial navy, the impecunious English queen covertly encouraged private investors—a mix of ambitious aristocrats and London merchants—to send armed ships to attack and plunder the Spanish ships homeward bound from the Caribbean. But piracy was a hit-or-miss proposition. Ralegh understood that, to secure a steadier flow of enriching overseas commerce, England needed its own American colony. In the short term, such a colony could serve as a base for the English pirates. In the longer run, the ideal colony would provide mines of precious metals and plantations of hot-climate crops—sugar, cacao, and tobacco—that commanded high prices because they could not thrive in cool and damp England.

In search of such a colony, Ralegh financed voyages that probed the Atlantic seaboard of North America. In honor of their queen's celebrated virginity, the English named as "Virginia" the entire coast between Florida and Canada. They found Virginia unoccupied by the Spanish, who had their hands full managing the vast lands, the many people, and

*Big Chief Elizabeth: The Adventures and Fate of the First English Colonists in America,* by Giles Milton (Farrar, Straus and Giroux, 2000)

the rich mines to the south, in Mexico and Peru. But the Spanich did not want piratical and heretical neighbors like the Protestant English. To preserve Virginia as an Indian country, the Spanish vowed to destroy any English colony.

Ralegh's colonial venture was, like second marriages, a triumph of hope over experience. Previous English bids at American colonization had failed miserably. In 1583, Ralegh's hot-tempered half-brother, Sir Humphrey Gilbert, organized an expedition of five ships bearing 260 men to colonize some spot along the vast shoreline of Virginia. Sailing first to Newfoundland, Gilbert and his vessel foundered, with all hands, in the North Atlantic.

On Gilbert's death, the queen's charter to colonize Virginia passed to Ralegh. Overcoming birth into a Devonshire family of genteel poverty, Ralegh had risen spectacularly in wealth and influence by using his dazzling charm and quick wit. Gifted at both flattery and self-promotion, he caught the queen's attention and won her affections. Handsome and dapper, Ralegh eclipsed the other ambitious courtiers who clustered around the monarch. Middle-aged and trapped in a public virginity, the queen delighted in flattering flirtation with handsome and intelligent younger men. No one played the game better than Ralegh, who wrote sonnets likening the queen to the goddesses of antiquity.

For his charms and pains, Ralegh reaped royal favor in the form of lucrative monopolies, important offices, and rambling mansions. No one in England could sell wine or woolen broadcloth without paying for a license from Raleigh. Appointed to command the queen's bodyguard, Ralegh enjoyed unmatched access to Elizabeth and her patronage. Less successful but higher-born courtiers seethed at his extraordinary success and influence, while common people resented the higher cost of their clothing. A rival denounced Ralegh as "the best hated man of the world."

Ralegh devoted some of his new wealth to his Virginia schemes. In London, he attracted and patronized a talented coterie of experts, principally the young polymath Thomas Harriot, an adept mathematician, linguist, and ethnographer. In 1584, Ralegh and Harriot sent two ships, commanded by Philip Amadas and Arthur Barlowe, across the Atlantic to probe the American coast for a suitable site to colonize. They chose Roanoke, an island nestled within the Pamlico Sound formed by North Carolina's Outer Banks, a long and treacherous set of sandbanks. Impressed by the security that the Outer Banks promised against Spanish attack, Amadas and Barlowe overlooked how difficult it would be for English ships to supply Roanoke. They also overestimated the fertility of the soil as "the most plentiful, sweet, fruitful, and wholesome of all the world." Better yet, wishful thinking reported docile, welcoming Indians: "We found the people most gentle, loving and faithfull, void of all guile and treason, and such as lived after the manner of the golden age." But the English possessed plenty of guile, luring aboard ship two young Indian men, named Manteo and Wanchese. Taken to London, they taught Harriot their complex Algonquian language and afforded insights into the lands and the peoples of Virginia.

In 1585, Ralegh prepared a second, larger expedition to colonize Roanoke Island. Command belonged to Sir Richard Grenville, a fiery and showy martinet. An acquaintance noted: "He was of so hard a complection [that] he would carouse three or four glasses of wine, and in a braverie take the glasses betweene his teeth and crash them in peeces and swallow them downe, so that oftentimes the blood ran out of his mouth." His assistants included Simon Fernandez, an able but quarrelsome Portuguese navigator; Ralph Lane, a hardened veteran of England's brutal conquest of Ireland; John White, a skilled map maker and artist; the scientist Harriot; as well as Manteo and Wanchese, who returned to serve as interpreters. Ralegh remained in England to tend to the doting queen.

The voyagers quickly discovered the folly of Roanoke as a site for colonization. Frequent storms trapped wooden ships against the treacherous Outer Banks, which became a graveyard for growing numbers of sailors, anchors, and vessels. One gale breached the primary ship, spoiling most of the provisions on board—provisions needed to sustain the colonists through the first year until their harvest the following summer. The disaster rendered the colonists dependent on supplies of corn, beans, squash, and venison wheedled from the Indians dwelling around Pamlico Sound. The demanding colonists put to the test the assurances of Amadas and Barlowe that the Indians were meek and generous innocents.

When frustrated in this fantasy, English commanders became enraged and certain of their superiority in both virtue and weapons. After visiting one Indian village in force, Grenville missed his cherished silver drinking cup. Blaming Indian theft, he returned to teach them the favorite lesson of imperialists: their power to punish whatever frustrated their will. He burned the entire village and trampled its growing crops, threatening the inhabitants with starvation. This was hardly the smartest move for a small band of intruders who needed the goodwill and the food of the much larger native population. Grenville could not have cared less, for he sailed away in August, leaving Ralph Lane behind to govern the colonists and to bully the Indians.

The Indians were also shocked by new diseases unwittingly introduced by the newcomers, who bore the more virulent pathogens of Europe. Harriot reported: "Within a few dayes after our departure from everie such [Indian] towne, the people began to die very fast, and many in [a] short space." The "disease was so strange that they neither knew what it was, nor how to cure it." Both the English and the Indians attributed the deadly epidemic to supernatural power. The English credited their God, who, they said, favored the new colony. The Indians suspected magic exercised by the colonists to (in Harriot's words) "kill and slaie whom wee would without weapons." Many Indians sought to deflect or to capture that magical power by attending the colonists' religious services to repeat their prayers and sing their psalms.

By spring, Roanoke's nearest chieftain, Wingina, ran out of patience. Disease continued to kill his people and the English continued to demand food, long after the Indians had exhausted their harvest from the previous fall. Seeking security in distance, Wingina withdrew his people from Roanoke Island, resettling on the mainland, where he negotiated alliances with other native peoples who shared his anxiety about the aggressive newcomers. Governor Lane interpreted Wingina's moves as treachery. Drawing on past experience brutalizing Irish rebels, Lane prepared a preemptive strike.

Pretending to offer a peaceful parley, Lane surprised Wingina's village, killing all of Wingina's subordinate chiefs. Dodging the first volley, Wingina bolted into the woods, with two of Lane's men in hot pursuit. To the governor's relief, his men soon returned carrying Wingina's bloody head. An apparent victory, Lane's attack doomed his settlement by confirming the hostility of the many other Indian villages scattered around the sound.

A few weeks later, the fortuitous arrival of Sir Francis Drake's English flotilla enabled Lane and the colonists to abandon Roanoke and return home. In their hasty departure, sailors threw overboard most of the precious samples, maps, drawings, and notebooks so painstakingly collected by White and Harriot during the previous year. The hasty also forgot, and left behind, three laggard colonists—the first of the "lost colonists." To find space for the embarking colonists and (some of) their baggage, Drake jettisoned about three hundred African and Indian slaves whom he had gathered in raids on the Spanish Caribbean. Marooned on a strange shore, they either starved to death or survived by incorporating into local Indian populations: no one knows, for the English did not care. Later that summer, Grenville stopped by with reinforcements only to discover Roanoke abandoned. To keep the fort in repair, he left behind fifteen soldiers when he sailed away.

In 1587, Ralegh dispatched a new expedition that applied the lessons learned from Lane's failure. In contrast to Lane's bellicose men, the new colonists included a core group of families with seventeen women and nine children. Less threatening to the natives, familial colonists would also better develop self-supporting farms. Instead of the military Lane, the new governor was the civilian John White. Best of all, Ralegh forsook Roanoke in favor of Chesapeake Bay, which offered more fertile land beside an array of navigable rivers and good harbors.

But the best-laid plans fell prey to the expedition's navigator, Simon Fernandez, who unceremoniously dumped the colonists ashore at Roanoke so that he could get on with the more profitable business of attacking Spanish ships. The colonists found themselves among natives alienated by past bad treatment. The fifteen soldiers had all vanished except for the skeleton of one evidently slain by the Indians. The fate of the rest was as uncertain as that of the three colonists forgotten in 1586 (or the three hundred slaves marooned that year). Soon, the Indians killed one of White's men. Belatedly adopting Lane's approach, but lacking his brutal skills, White mistakenly attacked the only Indians who were still friendly. Thereafter, he felt a desperate need for reinforcements and for more supplies from England. Departing for England to plead that case, he left behind the other colonists, including his married daughter Eleanore Dare and a newborn granddaughter named Virginia.

White found England preoccupied with fending off attack by a massive Spanish fleet: the infamous Armada. Although eventually victorious, the English could spare neither ships nor supplies for Roanoke until 1590, when White returned to find the settlement abandoned. A lone clue was carved into a tree: the word "Croatoan," the name of a nearby island. But the mariners refused to test the treacherous waters to investigate Croatoan, sailing away instead, with a dismayed and grieving John White. Their departure rendered lost the latest set of colonists (the third, if you're keeping score).

Under the terms of his charter, Ralegh risked losing Virginia if it remained unoccupied by colonists for seven years. He needed to find his lost colonists, or at least to pretend that they remained alive. Pretending was easier and cheaper than finding, especially after Ralegh suddenly fell out of royal grace and deep into debt in 1592. Grown complacent with royal favor and weary of unconsummated love talk with an aging queen, Ralegh covertly impregnated and married one of her maids of honor—a double betrayal in the eyes of a possessive monarch. Discovering their secret, she imprisoned both Raleghs, man and wife, in the Tower of London.

Ralegh vainly sought an early release by reviving his mawkish flattery; he longed to "behold [the queen] riding like Alexander, hunting like Diana, walking like Venus, the gentle wind blowing her fair hair about her pure cheeks, like a nymph; sometime sitting in the shade like a goddess, sometime singing like an angel, sometime playing like Orpheus." After four months, the queen partially relented, freeing the couple but barring them from her court and offices.

Far worse followed in 1603, when the queen died and was succeeded by a distant relative, who ruled as James I. A coarse and frugal man, the new king despised the charming and profligate Ralegh. Accused of treason and convicted in a fixed trial, Ralegh suddenly waxed popular as the victim of the unpopular new king. Although James stayed execution to avoid creating a popular martyr, Ralegh remained imprisoned in the Tower for another decade.

King James transferred the Virginia charter into new hands, the London merchants known as the Virginia Company. In early 1607, they sent across the Atlantic about one hundred colonists in three ships. This time, the navigator, Christopher Newport, dutifully sailed to the Chesapeake to establish a new settlement, named Jamestown, on a river called James, both in honor of the new king. Although more fertile and accessible than Roanoke, Jamestown compensated with its own flaws, principally the surrounding swamps, which supplied the colonists with fetid drinking water and millions of malaria-bearing mosquitoes. Sapped of energy, the colonists failed to exert themselves as farmers. As supplies ran low, they counted on extorting provisions from the Indians.

Unfortunately for the English, the Chesapeake natives were even more numerous and better organized than their Roanoke kin. The Chesapeake's paramount chief, Powhatan, had secured command over about thirty small tribes, a total of twenty-four thousand Indians. Shrewd and ruthless, Powhatan responded to force with force, usually keeping the English cooped up in their swampy settlement, where mosquitoes, foul water, starvation, and infighting took a grim toll. During the first year, a colonial officer heard the "men, night and day, groaning in every corner of the fort, most pittifull to hear." A coup sacked the colony's first governor when it was discovered that he had hoarded a roasted squirrel.

Conditions temporarily improved during the second year, thanks to the blustering but effective leadership of Capt. John Smith, who compelled his men to perform more work and the Indians to give them more food. On Smith's return to England in 1609, colonial indolence and Indian hostility increased, with deadly consequences. During the winter of 1609–10, the starving colonists boiled and ate their shoes. A few exhumed and consumed their newly dead comrades. One man even killed and devoured his wife. By spring, only sixty of the fall's five hundred colonists remained alive. The haggard survivors abandoned Jamestown but, en route downriver, they were intercepted by a new governor, Lord De La Warr, arriving by sea with reinforcements.

De La Warr compelled the reoccupation of Jamestown and adopted a genocidal policy of raiding Powhatan's villages to massacre men, women, and children. The grim war persisted until 1613, when the English captured Powhatan's favorite daughter, the teenaged Pocahontas. Held in Jamestown, she accepted English ways, including a colonial husband.

Marrying John Rolfe in 1614, she assumed the Christian name of Rebecca. Weary of war and eager to see his daughter again, Powhatan wishfully interpreted the marriage as the sealing of an alliance of equals.

In 1616, the Virginia Company brought John and Rebecca Rolfe to England for a promotional tour. On display, their marriage and newborn son suggested a new era of interracial peace and harmony, which affords Giles Milton a conveniently happy ending to his hitherto sordid tale: "With no more need for warfare or bloodshed, the search could once again begin for the lost colonists of Roanoke." Happy but misleading. Exposed to new diseases, Rebecca/Pocahontas died in 1617, at the age of twenty-one. Powhatan expired a year later, and his authority passed to his half-brother Opechancanough, whom Milton strangely miscasts as a peacemaker.

A boom in tobacco cultivation, initiated by John Rolfe, rendered Virginia profitable and newly attractive, drawing hundreds of immigrants, who invaded Indian lands. Outraged, Opechancanough led a surprise uprising in 1622 that killed 347 men, women, and children—nearly one third of the Virginia colonists. In grim retribution, the English destroyed Indian crops and towns and slaughtered the inhabitants. In 1623, the starving survivors entered peace negotiations, but the English poisoned their alcohol; incapacitated, the 250 Indians at the parley were easily finished off by English swords.

From a population of twenty-four thousand in the Virginia lowlands in 1607, the natives dwindled to just two thousand by 1669. The survivors occupied small reservations within a Virginia landscape dominated and transformed by a colonial population that had surged to forty-one thousand by 1670. Far from peace and racial harmony, seventeenth-century Virginia brought a systematic depopulation and dispossession to the native peoples, as well as massive losses of colonial life to disease—and the introduction of growing thousands of African slaves at century's end. Milton should have recognized that his story was a tragedy of deadly exploitation.

After prematurely concluding his narrative on an upbeat note, Milton appends an epilogue that returns to the mystery of those lost Roanoke colonists, especially the approximately one hundred left behind by John White in 1587. Milton reveals that by late 1608 the Jamestown colonists had learned from Indian informants that dozens of English people had taken refuge in an Indian village that defied Powhatan's rule. Apparently, the refugees had been wiped out in 1607, when Powhatan's warriors destroyed that village. By belatedly revealing this discovery in the epilogue, Milton arbitrarily keeps alive the suspense of his previous two chapters, in which he roundly criticizes Jamestown's governors between 1609 and 1616 for doing so little to find the lost colonists. If they knew the lost colonists to be dead, why should they have been looking for them? Milton also employs sleight of hand in accounting for how the tale became known. He insists that Powhatan first confessed the truth to Capt. John Smith, who dared not reveal it to his countrymen: "Smith knew that news of the slaughter had to be kept secret, since it was certain to prove deeply embarrassing to King James. He, after all, was still celebrating the fact that he now had a vassal king in America. If news leaked out that Powhatan was actually a mass murderer, James would be a laughingstock of England." This is utter nonsense. Like any seventeenth-century ruler, King James was very familiar with terror and massacre as instruments of state; he dealt regularly with warlords who had done in Ireland what Powhatan did in Virginia. Nor did his public expect better.

And the story of the destroyed lost colonists *was* published in England during the king's reign—but not by Smith. Although Milton masks the fact, the story actually appeared in print in England in 1612, in a conspicuous book by William Strachey, an official of the Virginia Company. Neither Strachey nor his company felt that they were embarrassing James in the slightest. Nor did the king take affront. So why would Smith have censored himself on a story that had already been prominently and safely published?

In fact, Smith never claimed in his own writings that Powhatan revealed the secret to him. Not until 1625 did another writer, Samuel Purchas, insist that Powhatan had so confessed to the captain. Purchas published after the bloody 1622 uprising, which encouraged reviving the atrocity story of the lost colony and tracing it by anecdote directly to Powhatan's lips. Of course, Milton could not reveal Purchas's role and motive without mentioning the bloodshed of 1622, which he left out of his own book by choosing a happy ending in 1616.

An English author of popular history, Giles Milton musters an array of amusing anecdotes (some of them true) and many striking quotations (mostly accurate). His vivid style renders into neon an already colorful cast of characters and dramatic action. His Queen Elizabeth "swore like a trooper, picked her teeth with a gold toothpick, and delighted in coarse jokes." Capt. John Smith's "head was crowned with a shock of red hair, and his face was so covered in beard and whiskers that he looked more like an animal than a man." Aboard one of Drake's ships, an unfortunate steward "was caught with his hose around his ankles and two young lads in his bunk."

That Elizabethan men wore codpieces is a matter of special and recurring fascination for Milton. A courtier named Robert Dudley "had come within a codpiece of depriving the Virgin Queen of her much-vaunted epithet." As for King James, "When he was nervous, he had an alarming habit of fiddling with his codpiece." Liking his joke so much, Milton later repeats it. When popular opinion rallied to the convicted Ralegh, King James "after fiddling with his codpiece, heeded the popular sentiment." Milton's breezy style quickly suffers from repetition.

Turning a clever phrase and framing a graphic image often trump the evidence. Determined to caricature King James I (admittedly, a tempting target), Milton reports as fact the malicious inventions of the monarch's enemies: "He was so malcoordinated at table that it was said to be possible to identify every meal he had eaten for seven years by studying the scraps of dried food stuck to his clothes." When Rebecca/Pocahontas called on the king, she found, Milton asserts, "a dirty and rather disheveled fifty-year-old with food in his beard and stains on his waistcoat." Slanderous exaggeration was the stock-in-trade of disappointed courtiers, and amplified (rather than analyzed) by Milton, it becomes the gist of his tale.

Milton seems as lost as the colonists in weighing the strengths and weaknesses of his highly partisan and often incomplete sources. Judging from his appended bibliography, Milton relies on a mix of other popular histories and the English scholarship of past generations. He avoids more current and compelling works, particularly by American specialists on Indians during the initial encounters with the colonizers. Informed by anthropology, recent scholars have partially recovered the complexities of native culture, which belie their stereotyping as primitives dwelling in an untouched wilderness.

Milton's slim understanding of Indian culture proves especially distorting in recounting the fabled story of Pocahontas rescuing Capt. John Smith from an execution ordered by her father in late 1607. Following Smith's self-promoting account, Milton, insists that Powhatan was so stunned by the spontaneous and chivalrous act of his daughter that he abruptly reversed course, saving and adopting the captain as a kinsman. Scholars of Algonquian culture more plausibly interpret the mock execution as a carefully scripted adoption ceremony, from beginning to end. Paralleling Powhatan's similar treatment of conquered Indian chiefs, the ritual was meant to subordinate Smith and his colonists to the rule of the paramount chief. Misunderstanding the terms of his consent, Smith returned to Jamestown and his bullying ways. Milton can see the policy behind the colonists' subsequent coronation ceremony giving Powhatan an English-made crown of copper, the better to claim that he was a tributary of King James. But Milton cannot recognize that Indians had their own policies of power and rituals of subordination—or that an eleven-year-old girl almost certainly did as her father ordered.

Despite his shallow understanding of native culture, Milton claims an uncanny ability to read the minds of particular Indians. Powhatan "was so shaken by the doom-laden prophecies of his elders that he decided that [Capt. John] Smith would be safer dead than alive." But Pocahontas wanted Smith to live because "she found herself captivated by the English settlers and their magical array of tools and instruments and wished to learn more about their strange ways." In both cases, Milton's imagination ranges far beyond his sources into a fantasy that implausibly contrasts the motives of father and daughter. In fact, she did her father's bidding because they both wished, by hook or by crook, to obtain a share in the dangerous technology of their invaders.

Oblivious to current scholarship, Milton instead echoes the world view of Rudyard Kipling's day, casting his tale as a struggle between English "civilization" and Indian "savagery." On the one hand, Milton dismisses as promotional bunkum any reports that emphasized the humanity and civility of the natives: "Their hardest task was to present the Indian population in a positive light." On the other hand, he endorses every account that depicts Indians as alien, primitive, and repellent. Adopting the imperial gaze, Milton writes: "The old men looked so bizarre that even Harriot could scarcely conceal his sniggers . . . The women looked even more extraordinary. They were strongly boned and had partially exposed breasts, and might have been considered attractive had it not been for their razored heads and tattooed cheeks." Harriot, "for one, was never going to share his eider-down with a shaven-headed maiden." Manteo serves as Milton's exception to prove the savage rule: "For the first time, England had forged an Indian in its own image, a tattooed and shaven-headed tribesman who was now so civilised that he would salute the flag of St. George. He spoke English, wore breeches and a doublet, and had even rejected his panoply of gods and devils." Rather than investigate native spirituality, Milton mocks it, referring to "a native population whose interest in the Bible had so far been limited to stroking their bellies with its vellum jacket."

Milton consistently deprecates the native culture as primitive and even absurd. The Algonquian name for a chief, *weroance,* was, in Milton's view, "both barbarous and slightly comical." And Powhatan's council house "was nothing to write home about; constructed from branches and twigs, it was little more than a large wooden shack." No reader will discover from Milton that Indian housing was more efficient—quicker to build and warmer to live in—than the clunky and costly structures of the English. Nor does he note that the Indians' more productive methods of horticulture and fishing enabled them to subsist—unlike their unwanted and obtuse guests, who so abjectly failed to support themselves in a new land.

The imperial gaze often leads Milton to endorse the imperial myth that the invaders were the innocent victims of savage cruelty. He describes the Roanoke woods as "home to a growing band of vengeful and warlike tribesmen." He fundamentally blames their chief for the worsening relations: "a capricious individual," Wingina kept "busy making mischief" for the English, eventually provoking Ralph Lane's righteous revenge. But the only evidence for Wingina's treachery comes from Lane's self-serving account; the fairer Thomas Harriot felt that his commander overreacted. Given that Lane pretended to parley in order to surprise and butcher Wingina and his subordinate chiefs, treachery at Roanoke seems more clearly English than Indian.

Although almost all of the violent deaths in 1586 at Roanoke were of Indians slain by the English, Milton mischaracterizes the natives as "neighbours who showed an alarming propensity for murder and bloodshed." No pacifists, the Indians were certainly human in their capacity for violence and cruelty—but Milton distorts by suggesting that they were innately less trustworthy and more brutal than their invaders. We need not romanticize the Indians to recognize that they suffered far more than they inflicted in the exchange of bloodshed and destruction.

In the pages of *Big Chief Elizabeth,* the Indians remain inscrutable in their violence because Milton fails to investigate their cultural context and recent experiences. In 1607, Capt. Newport's expedition reached the Chesapeake only to experience an "unprovoked ambush" by Indian archers. Milton does not explain that for decades European mariners had visited the Chesapeake, occasionally killing or kidnaping natives. By 1607, the Algonquians had plenty of provocation to drive away new intruders.

Given his understanding of Indians as fickle, remorseless, and brutal, Milton evaluates colonial leadership in terms of machismo. According to Milton, the militarist Lane knew how to handle Indians: "Bold, decisive, and supremely confident, he marched a phalanx of forty soldiers into the village and seized the chieftain." By contrast, Milton derides White as a weakling for first attempting a diplomatic solution when the Indians killed one of his colonists. Where the sword-happy Lane gets the benefit of the doubt, the more cautious White receives a double dose of authorial contempt for departing from Roanoke. After depicting the governor as compelled to leave by colonists wearied by his weakness, Milton contradicts himself to insist: "At a critical juncture in the fortunes of the colony—and with hostile forces gathering apace—White had voluntarily abnegated his responsibilities." A fairer assessment of the two governors would find White tragically overmatched at Roanoke by a mess largely of Lane's creation: the brutal and unprovoked murder of Wingina and his subchiefs the year before.

In assessing the subsequent leaders of Jamestown, Milton similarly prefers the bellicose to the pacific. In 1608, Christopher Newport secured a desperately needed interlude of peace and supplies of food by offering in trade what Powhatan wanted most: metal tools and weapons. Despite the trade's substantial benefits for the beleaguered colonists, Milton derides Newport's "foolish policy" for diminishing a military advantage. He prefers Newport's confrontational successors, especially Sir Thomas Dale, whose "brutally effective leadership had shaken Jamestown out of its torpor. . . . The tribes nearest to the settlement had been all but neutralised and the threat of violence had subdued even the belligerent Powhatan—at least for the time being."

Downplaying moments of intercultural exchange and diplomacy, Milton instead highlights Indian violence, dwelling on long and gruesome descriptions of their torturing and massacring the innocent English. When the historical record proves insufficiently lurid, Milton imagines an even bloodier scene of helpless colonists victimized by relentless savages. Imagining the last day for the largest set of lost colonists, Milton insists:

> The onslaught, when it came, probably followed a depressingly familiar pattern. . . . The ambush must have come without any warning: a hail of arrows, a scream from the forest, and a ferocious and terrifying assault. The Indians would have formed themselves into small bands whose task was to single out the toughest of the English. These poor victims would have been seized and bound before the tribesmen "beat out their braynes" with wooden cudgels. Only when the strongest men had been slaughtered would they have turned their attentions to the weak, the sick, the women and children. Some, perhaps, were "broyled to death"—slowly burned on a bed of charcoal. Others would have been stripped and flayed alive. Only the fortunate would have been killed in the initial onslaught on the village.

Designed to complete the reader's identification with the English and alienation from the Indians, this graphic fantasy reveals far more about Giles Milton than about the tragic mystery of the lost colonists. A fuller and fairer understanding of native culture renders much of Milton's scenario implausible; although they tortured and executed captured men, the Indians preferred to adopt and assimilate women and children. As killers, they were more discriminating than the English, who mastered in Ireland and exported to America the intimidating massacre of entire towns.

Milton's ethnocentric lapses are all the more jarring because he sometimes adopts a more reflective and judicious tone. Contradicting his former praise of Lane's militarism at Roanoke, he later observes: "the settlers' brutal treatment of the Indians had been an act of incalculable folly. Only when it was too late did the English realise that their colony was doomed to fail without the active support of the native tribesmen." Such passages suggest that Milton's delight in clever and graphic prose betrays his wiser and more humane judgment as a historian.

I intend no blanket rejection of popular history, which can do a world of good. Readers need history rendered accessible. Heaven knows, academic historians could pay more attention to their literary craft. And independent scholars such as Giles Milton can produce gripping works of history that are honest and profound. The problem comes when a pop historian casts adrift from the creative tension with evidence that gives history its mystery and depth. Why not imagine that colorful effect and scrupulous investigation can be kept in tandem, serving each other?

*12*
# Devil in a Blue Dress
*August 3, 1998*

We begin with a mysterious painting, an eighteenth-century portrait apparently of a wealthy but dour middle-aged woman wearing a lovely blue dress. But the label affixed identifies the subject as Edward Hyde, Viscount Cornbury (1661–1723), the royal governor of colonial New York and New Jersey from 1702 to 1708. Conspicuously hung in the New York Historical Society, the painting seems to confirm scandalous rumors that Cornbury routinely displayed himself in public in women's clothing.

Historians used to uphold prim morals and were quick to accept the charge of the viscount's transvestism. It seemed of a piece with better-documented evidence of Cornbury's arrogance, greed, corruption, and mismanagement. Historians generally considered him "the worst governor Britain ever imposed on an American colony." Given our common assumption that royal governors were corrupt bullies and twits who drove the colonists to revolt, the worst of such a bad lot must have been a consummate rogue, indeed.

No accusation was be too bad to believe of Lord Cornbury. In 1935, a historian dismissed him as a "degenerate and pervert who is said to have spent half of his time dressed in women's clothes." In 1976, *American Heritage* published a scathing account of Cornbury entitled, "His Most Detestable High Mightiness." According to that account, he routinely dressed as a woman and delighted in "lurking behind trees to pounce, shrieking with laughter, on his victims."

Biographies of royal governors rarely provoke much popular interest, but the Cornbury scandal promises a broader audience for Patricia Bonomi's intriguing and carefully crafted book. Instead of writing a conventional biography, Bonomi frames her narrative with the charges against Cornbury. She then shapes a sustained historical brief for his defense. While benefiting from our salacious interest in the most lurid charge against Cornbury, she ultimately spoils the party by debunking

*The Lord Cornbury Scandal: The Politics of Reputation in British America,* by Patricia U. Bonomi (University of North Carolina Press, 1998)

the painting and the other evidence of his cross-dressing as fictions manufactured by his political enemies. Her Cornbury was a good man and an upstanding governor who never donned a blue dress.

While depriving us of a wonderful scandal, Bonomi compensates with an intriguing detective story that exposes the weaknesses in the case against Lord Cornbury. A judicious and resourceful historian, she relentlessly pursues, and scrupulously assesses, the scraps of evidence. In the process, she illuminates the operation of political power in the colonial past and the nature of history writing in the present.

Bonomi examines Cornbury's aristocratic youth and family connections in England to establish innocence by association. She suggests that he was too well connected to the conservative, the powerful, and the wellborn to have gambled his precious reputation on public peculation and a silk dress. His grandfather was the first Earl of Clarendon and the Lord High Chancellor, second only to the king in English power during the early 1660s. His aunt Anne married the king's brother, the Duke of York, who inherited the throne in 1685 and reigned as James II until overthrown in 1688 by a coup known by the victors as the "Glorious Revolution." The Hyde family weathered the political storm because Cornbury had become an army colonel with an exquisite sense of timing. By shifting his loyalty at the opportune moment, he assured the military triumph of the new monarchs, King William and Queen Mary. It helped his transition that aunt Anne was long dead and that her daughter was the new Queen Mary and, therefore, Cornbury's first cousin. Betrayal of an uncle by a former marriage was easier when it benefited a cousin by blood. When Queen Mary and King William died childless, her sister Anne inherited the throne, reigning from 1702 to 1714.

The patronage of his regal and female cousin rescued Lord Cornbury from his increasingly insistent English creditors. To recoup his fortune, he sailed across the seas to the distant, but potentially profitable, post as governor of New York and New Jersey, on the American margins of the empire. Although recalled by the imperial bureaucracy after a contentious administration, Cornbury's conduct impressed his queen, who rewarded him with a two thousand–pound pension on his return home in 1710. She also promoted him to her Privy Council and to the Board of Admiralty—the two preeminent institutions of British imperial rule. Bonomi insists that Queen Anne would never have so honored Cornbury if there had been any substance to the sensational charges against him as a royal governor.

His dual governorship presented special difficulties. At the start of the eighteenth century, the empire's managers tried to rationalize colonial administration in hopes of mobilizing more resources to build a larger army and navy—the better to prosecute Britain's escalating warfare with the powerful French Empire. As a result, Cornbury demanded more in taxes and in militia service from the colonists than had his relatively lax predecessors. Moreover, New York was vulnerable to attack because of its especially strategic location astride the Hudson valley, the corridor of invasion between the British settlements along the Atlantic seaboard and their French and Indian enemies to the north in Canada. Cornbury struggled to meet the daunting costs of frontier defense because New York was virtually bankrupt. His predecessors had mismanaged the colonial treasury, and the elected assembly representatives curried popularity by minimizing taxes. Their constituents were farmers and artisans who cared less about the empire than about their own pockets.

New York's politicians were also bitterly polarized by the local legacy of the Glorious Revolution. The Dutch-speaking majority resented the English-speaking minority, which dominated the colony after its conquest from the Netherlands in 1664. In 1689, a majority champion, an ambitious merchant and militia captain named Jacob Leisler, exploited the political turmoil in England to seize power in New York. Making himself governor, Leisler infuriated the Anglophile faction. Aided by troops sent from England, the Anglophiles took their revenge in 1691 by securing Leisler's arrest, trial, conviction, and execution for treason.

Thereafter, New York's leaders rancorously divided into Leislerian and anti-Leislerian factions. Every new royal governor felt obliged to pick a faction to reward and another to punish usually rejecting the faction favored by his predecessor. The Earl of Bellomont had favored the Leislerians, so Lord Cornbury embraced the anti-Leislerians. Cornbury also reaped political trouble by attempting to govern the restive colonists of New Jersey, who wanted their own governor rather than accept rule by New York's.

Given such daunting difficulties, any royal governor would have made enemies, but Cornbury made more than his share. A military man, he tried to govern by command, treating subordinates brusquely and heaping contempt on critics. A Tory by family politics, he irritated the Whigs, who prevailed in New York politics. As a Tory, Cornbury favored a high church and an authoritarian sovereign—unpopular positions in the colonies. Whigs, by comparison, were more libertarian in politics and more latitudinarian in religion and morality. Cornbury also made enemies by aggressively pursuing every paying perquisite of his office, irritating other royal officers with their own needs and greed. During his controversial administration, Cornbury tangled with an array of equally contentious opponents, ranging from Presbyterian and Anglican ministers to royal naval captains, and from land speculators to auditors for the imperial treasury. "Clearly Cornbury relished wielding power, was impatient of insolence, and was not loath to quickly intervene in the chain of command," Bonomi observes.

In addition to being numerous, Cornbury's enemies were ruthless and creative. Writing to their political friends in England, they charged the governor with browbeating his opponents, with taking a bribe, and with embezzling defense funds to build a pleasure house by the sea. More insidiously, they suggested that Lord Cornbury frequently appeared in public in women's attire, thereby discrediting his office and dishonoring his monarch. Robert Livingston claimed that hundreds of spectators daily witnessed their governor promenading "in Women's Cloths." Lewis Morris insisted: "the Scandal of his life is . . . he rarely fails of being dresst in Women's Cloaths every day, and almost half his time is spent that way, and [he] seldome misses it on a Sacrament day, . . . and this not privately but in face of the Sun and sight of the Town." The most specific accusation came from Elias Neau: "My Lord Cornbury has and dos still make use of an unfortunate Custom of dressing himself in Women's Cloaths and of exposing himself in that Garb upon the Ramparts to the view of the public; in that dress he draws a World of Spectators upon him and consequently as many Censures, especially for exposing himself in such a manner [on] all the great Holy days and even in an hour or two after going to the Communion."

To discredit the charges against Cornbury, Bonomi casts them in the context of his partisan times, when Whigs and Tories battled to control the home government and its patronage plums in the colonies. These struggles were especially rancorous, for neither party regarded the other as a legitimate opposition. Claiming a monopoly on zeal for queen and country, each party regarded opponents as crypto-traitors ready to betray the realm. In their vicious competition, each disseminated scandalous libels, exploiting the lifting of official press censorship in 1695. In London's notorious Grub Street press, anonymous hacks charged great men and women with corruption, adultery, homosexuality, and treason. Not even the sovereign was immune. Mocking King William's failure to sire an heir, a Tory insinuated that the monarch preferred sodomy:

Let's pray for the good of our State and his Soul
That He'd put his Roger into the Right Hold.

Taking cues from the London press, Cornbury's colonial foes aggressively practiced politics by vilification. Seeking Cornbury's recall, colonial Whigs collected compromising evidence and malicious gossip to send to the imperial overlords in London. Eventually, the strategy worked. In 1708, the Lords of Trade replaced the Tory Cornbury with a Whig governor for New York.

Bonomi discounts the evidence against Cornbury as biased and insubstantial. The lone witness to his alleged bribe was a bitter enemy of dubious veracity. The military funds he allegedly embezzled had probably never been collected by the inefficient provincial treasury. The case for Lord Cornbury's transvestism derives from four surviving letters written by three bitter political enemies: Livingston, Morris, and Neau. Conveying hearsay, they did not claim to have seen the governor in drag, nor did they name any actual witnesses.

Bonomi reasons that if Cornbury had been a notorious transvestite, a public uproar would have generated more and better evidence. She observes: "the most intriguing thing is, not the existence of letters from three of Governor Cornbury's most vocal enemies charging him with public cross dressing, but rather the absence of the much larger volume of noise such behavior would have aroused had it actually been observed." Because no charges of transvestism appeared during Cornbury's longer life in England, the accusations derive exclusively from political foes during his contentious nine years in the colonies.

But what about the scandalous painting in the New York Historical Society? Although the portrait probably dates, on stylistic grounds, to Cornbury's generation, it lacks the right provenance. Instead of descending within the Hyde family of Oxfordshire, the portrait belonged to the Pakingtons of Worcestershire, a family without marital or blood ties to the Hydes. And the earliest known assignment of the portrait to Cornbury dates to 1796, seventy-three years after his death. Moreover, Bonomi finds no resemblance between that portrait and two surviving depictions that more certainly represent Cornbury (and do so in male attire). Bonomi plausibly argues that the controversial portrait originally depicted a woman, now unknown, who lived in Cornbury's time. For unknown reasons, the portrait later became confused with the myth of the cross-dressing lord. Bonomi concludes that the portrait as "evidence for the charge that Cornbury was a transvestite must be declared factitious." She may be right, but a nagging question persists: Why would the Pakingtons of the 1790s insist that their painting represented a dead and obscure colonial governor? If Bonomi is right that charges against Cornbury had no substance, why did the cross-dressing story show such staying power and become attached to this picture?

Bonomi demonstrates that the case against the governor as cross-dresser remains unproved. But she cannot prove the negative: that the governor never did appear in public in women's attire. Not proven is not quite the same as not guilty. Indeed, the very oddness of the charge challenges Bonomi's preference to declare the case closed. Eighteenth-century political scurrility dealt in charges of corruption, treason, sexual promiscuity, adultery, and homosexuality—rather than transvestism. If

Cornbury's colonial enemies entirely fabricated their slander, they would have tried something more immediately plausible than cross-dressing. To sustain their public honor as gentlemen, Lewis Morris and Robert Livingston might exaggerate, but they could not afford to advance charges quickly discounted as incredible. They must have believed that they could substantiate their charges on demand—which suggests a germ of truth.

Perhaps, they merely satirized Cornbury's arrogant insistence that his colonial power was monarchical, that he embodied the authority of his sovereign, Queen Anne, his cousin, a woman. To intimidate opponents, Cornbury figuratively clothed himself in the queen's authority. But perhaps on some ceremonial occasion he also literally clothed himself as the queen to make his point visually. Such a miscalculation would help make sense of the private obituary penned by his aunt on the flyleaf of her Bible: "By the blessed passion sweet Jesu[s] I beseech thee to look on the sincerity of his heart and his great charity. Lay not his follies to his charge, but have mercy on his poor soul." What "follies" did she mean?

Discounting all the negative evidence, Bonomi blames the governor's enduring bad reputation on the Whig (or "Country") tradition that predominates in both American and English history-writing. This tradition tells a liberal story of progress from the bad old days of aristocratic privilege and monarchical power onward and upward toward enlightenment, egalitarianism, and democracy. This progressive story offers a moral polarity that divides historical figures into visionary heroes who advanced the democratic future, and reactionary villains who retarded it. Latter-day Whig historians celebrate at face value the libertarian rhetoric of eighteenth-century Whig politicians. The political passion play casts them as proto-patriots anticipating our republican revolution of 1776. But historical woe to any governor who pressed the imperial agenda. Cornbury's predecessor as New York's royal governor, the Earl of Bellomont, and his successor, Robert Hunter, both generated political controversy and suffered fiscal crisis. As Whigs, however, they have reaped celebration rather than the denunciation heaped on the Tory Cornbury.

Inverting the Whig history of colonial America, Bonomi vindicates Cornbury for effectively promoting imperial power over the colonies. She also casts his Whig enemies as small-minded, mendacious, and reckless hypocrites. Her interpretation belongs to a scholarly trend known as the "new imperial history," which breaks with the Whig tradition by taking more seriously, and treating more sympathetically, the administrators of the colonial empire. She observes: "Considerable evidence suggests that the royal governors often responsibly administered their colonies to serve what they reasonably believed was the greater good of the empire." Bonomi argues that, as a royal governor, Lord Cornbury was one of the best of a good breed—and not the worst of a bad lot, as Whig history long has had it.

Although Bonomi does not press the case so far, other new imperial historians imply that "the greater good of the empire" was better for the colonists than they recognized. British imperialism was, of necessity, more inclusive, cosmopolitan, and tolerant of ethnic, racial, and religious diversity than was the provincialism of white colonists. Indeed, their subsequent revolutionary violence and majoritarian nationalism suppressed or exploited racial minorities. This scholarly empathy for empire resonates with a strand in the contemporary discourse of international politics. For example, the ethnic conflicts in the Balkans inspire some intellectual nostalgia for the imperial Hapsburgs, who united diverse groups in mutual subordination. Lord Cornbury has found an effective champion in Patricia Bonomi in part because empire currently enjoys a new respectability among public intellectuals and historical scholars.

In undermining the case against Cornbury, Bonomi wants more than an acquittal. Seeking his complete vindication, she depicts Cornbury as an especially conscientious and effective colonial governor. But that interpretation suffers from the contradictions in her eclectic arguments. She depicts Cornbury as the victim of an especially vicious politics, but she also writes: "One of Cornbury's achievements, often overlooked, is that he actually managed to lower the temperature in politically feverish New York." She initially represents Cornbury as a diligent champion of imperial efficiency and responsibility, a cosmopolitan who irritated provincials by promoting a more rationalized and regularized empire. Later, however, she depicts him as the victim of that bureaucratic drive for centralized power. She insists that treasury audits faulted Cornbury's fiscal management only because the Lord Treasurer had imposed new, higher standards on colonial record-keeping.

Relentless in her celebration, Bonomi neglects the most sordid aspect of Cornbury's administration: his notoriety for exploiting his land-granting power. To enrich himself with fees and his political cronies with massive tracts of frontier land, he sacrificed the interests of Indians and common settlers—and violated instructions from the Crown to limit each new land grant to 1,000 acres. For example, he granted an 800,000-acre tract, known as the Kayaderosseras Patent. Located between the Hudson and the Mohawk rivers, Kayaderosseras relied on a patently fraudulent deed that infuriated and dispossessed the Mohawk Indians. As British allies, the Mohawks were critical to the colony's frontier defense against French attack. By alienating them to reap lucrative fees for this land grant, Cornbury heeded his self-interest rather than the public interest of his colony and empire.

The safest verdict is that Cornbury was a royal governor of mediocre talents and morality. He was neither the paragon of imperial duty depicted by Bonomi nor the utter blackguard of his enemies' accusations. He ultimately failed to resolve the tensions of an impossible office. Every colonial governor struggled to balance the pursuit of private fortune and the cultivation of support among a colonial elite. And every governor struggled to reconcile his royal instructions with the pursuit of popular support in an elected assembly. Almost every governor inevitably fell victim to these political contradictions. Sooner rather than later, they were discredited by colonial criticism and recalled by their imperial superiors, who sent out a newcomer to start the cycle anew. Later in the century, when the lords of empire did, at last, stick by their beleaguered governors, they alienated most of the colonial elite and provoked our revolution.

To defend Lord Cornbury, Bonomi casts his generation's political culture as peculiarly irresponsible, salacious, and paranoid. In the early eighteenth century, she finds "a world steamy with intrigue, gossip, and rumormongering—all part of an early modern political style. . . . In short, a climate of conspiracy, slander, and general foul play pervaded the public life of the Anglo-American world." Casting our own politics as relatively polite and sedate, she observes: "The modern reader—though no stranger to rough political practices—is scarcely equipped to grasp the intense ardor, the unbounded ferocity of politics in the time of Cornbury." Her suggestion of our superior civility, of our progress from the bad old ways, sounds surprisingly Whiggish. In fact, the saga of Cornbury's sexual vilification appears all too contemporary, rather than peculiar to the Whigs and the Tories of another century.

*13*

# The Bad Birds

*August 9, 1999*

Shortly before dawn on a snowy December 14, 1763, fifty armed and mounted Pennsylvania colonists approached the small Indian village at Conestoga. Despite the war raging on the colony's northern and western frontiers, the local Indians slumbered in false security, for they had long submitted to the settler majority surrounding them. Rather than fight, the Conestoga Indians had surrendered almost all of their land, accepting a small reservation of a few hundred acres and occasional government handouts of food and clothing. They lived by raising hogs, hunting deer, tending gardens, and making brooms and baskets for peddling to their settler neighbors.

In their ragged clothing, the Conestogas resembled poor colonists rather than the free and militant Indians dwelling farther up the Susquehanna River. But in the minds of the approaching vigilantes, known as the "Paxton Boys," the Conestogas were simply Indians, and all Indians were their enemies. Unable to come to grips with the frontier Indians, whose raids massacred farm families, the Paxton Boys turned their attention to the nearby sleeping Conestogas. Smashing open cabin doors, the vigilantes butchered the Indian families, then plundered and set ablaze their homes.

Later that day, colonists rummaged through the smoldering ashes and the scorched bones to find a bag containing the Conestogas' most precious possessions: two wampum belts and six old documents, produced at past treaty councils to certify the Indians' status as allies of Pennsylvania. The longest and oldest document was a cherished copy of their treaty made in 1701 with William Penn, the colony's Quaker founder. By the terms of that treaty, the Indians and the colonists pledged "that they shall forever hereafter be as one Head & One Heart, & live in true Friendship & Amity as one People."

In his provocative and eloquent book, James Merrell investigates the

*Into the American Woods: Negotiators on the Pennsylvania Frontier,* by James H. Merrell (Norton, 1999)

history framed between William Penn's optimistic treaty in 1701 and the bloody business at Conestoga in 1763. At first, Pennsylvania's colonists enjoyed unusually harmonious relations with their Indian neighbors, and they long avoided the warfare that racked (and nearly wrecked) the other British colonies founded in the seventeenth century. By the late 1760s, however, no other large colony had fewer Indians or a more remorseless settler determination to kill all the natives who lingered. Merrell sets out to explain this tragic passage from William Penn to the Paxton Boys. Why did the dream of becoming one people living in true friendship fail so brutally?

Merrell has helped lead the "new Indian history" practiced by the present generation of scholars. They break with their predecessors, the so-called old Indian historians, who told a simple story of continuous Indian decline due to virtual annihilation; a story cast almost exclusively in military terms of heroic but futile confrontation; a story that assumed a fundamental incompatibility between the native and the colonial ways of life. Unable to adapt, Indian leaders fought to the end. This military story of inevitable conflict and defeat dismays the new Indian historians, who instead deemphasize incompatibility and war in favor of close attention to Indians' creative ability to adapt to the colonial invasion. By this new standard, a tribe's persistence as a distinct ethnic group becomes a cultural victory—despite diminished numbers and land.

In 1989, Merrell published *The Indians' New World: Catawbas and Their Neighbors from European Contact through the Era of Removal,* one of the finest and most influential works of the new Indian history. In the Carolinas, the Catawbas suffered their share of the post-1492 catastrophes heaped on native peoples: depopulation by devastating new diseases introduced from Europe; economic dependence on new trade goods (including alcohol); dispossession by a growing horde of new settlers; and the cultural intrusion of Christian missionaries determined to save Indian souls by altering their minds. Yet Merrell narrates the Catawba endurance of their travails as, fundamentally, a success story. He details their sufferings and losses, not to highlight the colonists' power but to emphasize the Catawba achievement as survivors. By 1849, they had dwindled to about 110 persons living on a 630-acre reservation, but Merrell emphasizes that the survivors "lived out their lives in ways that, though by no means identical to those of a century or two before, were nonetheless their own." Persistence as Indians was victory.

A more consistently pessimistic tone pervades Merrell's new book, which bears some resemblance to the old Indian history. From the beginning, he argues, in Pennsylvania any middle ground of mutual accommodation was no more than a dangerous illusion. Penn's treaty led inexorably to the Paxton Boys. "There was, after all, a deep fissure between Indian and colonial worlds," Merrell concludes. This conclusion breaks with his peers who produce histories in which an early regime of mutual adjustment and mixed culture gave way as the colonists grew in power and asserted a rigid racial divide that exterminated, confined, or exiled the last of the natives. Richard White's *The Middle Ground* (1991) and Jill Lepore's *The Name of War* (1998) are especially influential examples of this type of work.

Merrell, however, finds no early alternative of cultural syncretism, no mixing of colonial and native ways that might have provided a happier ending. In Pennsylvania, the Conestogas tried to play the Catawba role: they sought security by making themselves poor, obsequious, and useful to the invaders. For this, they became easy victims, thereby terminating their culture. In Pennsylvania, the only measure of safety for an Indian lay in warfare and flight westward. Merrell insists that the brutal conflict of the 1750s and the 1760s was the inevitable ripening of a fundamental incompatibility.

To tell this story, Merrell focuses on the "go-betweens" of the colonial relationship: on the very few men—some Indians and others colonists—who learned enough of the other culture to act as official mediators, messengers, interpreters, and consultants. Although essential to the intercultural diplomacy of the colonial era, these intermediaries ordinarily lurk on the fringes of more conventional histories, which dwell, instead, on the political and military leaders of the colonies and the tribes.

Only a few people possessed the qualities of a proper go-between: patient endurance of hardship; self-possession in danger; and resourcefulness under pressure. The skilled intermediary preferred suasion to threat, smooth words to bullying. He needed a keen memory for past proceedings and a careful regard for, and mastery of, the metaphors and gestures of Indian diplomacy: wiping the eyes and clearing the throats of the bereaved or weary; burying the hatchet to stem violence; delivering a wampum belt to close and certify a speech; and covering a grave with presents for grieving relatives. The go-between could readily and imaginatively dissemble without sacrificing a general reputation for trust. "Disguise and honesty were in constant tension," Merrell observes.

During the early eighteenth century, go-betweens worked primarily to keep the peace by containing the violence unleashed by the drunken murder of an Indian or a colonist by the other. News of a murder spawned alarming rumors of impending war, of a conspiracy by Indians to destroy the settlements, or of a determination by the colonists to kill all natives. These alarms threatened to become self-fulfilling prophecies as frightened people lashed out in preemptive strikes. To stifle the momentum of rumor, Indian chiefs and colonial magistrates mobilized their go-betweens to seek each other out for reassurance. Together, they ceremonially buried the murder by delivering gifts to the grieving relatives, thereby assuring both sides that there would be no revenge killings.

Two intermediaries especially stand out in Merrell's cast: Shickellamy and Conrad Weiser. "Each in his own right a gifted woodsman, together—and they usually *were* together—they possessed unmatched skill, subtlety, and power." Shickellamy was an Oneida (one of the Iroquois Six Nations dwelling to the north in New York) who had been sent south to oversee Shamokin, a multiethnic Indian village on the Susquehanna River. The powerful Six Nations meant to dominate the diverse Pennsylvania Indians (a mix of Conestoga, Conoy, Mohican, Delaware, Shawnee, Tutelo, and some Iroquois). To that end, Shickellamy collaborated with Pennsylvania's leaders to keep the local Indians at peace, despite the occasional cross-cultural murder and the colonial taking of Indian lands in one-sided bargains. Keeping the peace brought Shickellamy into frequent contact with Weiser, a German immigrant who had learned enough Indian protocol and language to make his living as a trader and land speculator and as an interpreter and diplomat for Pennsylvania.

Although sharing the pursuit of immediate peace, these two go-betweens were very different men from alien cultures. Indian negotiators tended to be high-status chiefs, arrogant in the assertion of their superior culture. They were determined neither to emulate, nor even to know much about, the ways of the invaders. They clung to their own language and insisted that diplomacy precisely follow Indian protocol—even when the business of a parley was to dispossess natives of their lands. Owing to the chosen limits on his knowledge, an Indian go-between usually needed a colonial interpreter familiar with native languages and protocol. Shickellamy needed Weiser to complete the connection.

By learning about Indian ways and words, colonial go-betweens lowered their status in their own society, which suspected their association with savages. A colonial emissary "had a menial job and his own people's contempt."

By concentrating on the official few empowered by the colonial government to deliver formal messages, Merrell neglects the more numerous, if even less reputable, unofficial intermediaries. An array of traders and adventurers, both Indian and colonist, women as well as men, regularly crossed the frontier to exchange goods, news, and propositions. Merrell dismisses their effectiveness: traders were too disreputable as cunning cheats and drunken womanizers; missionaries were too pious for the equivocations of forest diplomacy; and Christianized Indians were too poor and too demoralized to enjoy the respect or trust of either side. And yet, there were major exceptions to Merrell's carefully drawn exclusions. Prominent official go-betweens included the trader George Croghan, the Moravian missionary Christian Frederick Post, and the Christian Delaware Moses Tatamy.

Moreover, the many unofficial go-betweens played an important role in the bicultural relationship, a role that warrants more attention. Much of what the Indians and colonists thought about one another derived from more routine encounters at taverns, stores, and paths through the woods. In the official discourse, these unregulated conversations appear as the central problem—as the songs of "Bad Birds" spreading irresponsible alarm. Seeking power by controlling the exchange of information, Iroquois chiefs and Pennsylvania officials collaborated to discredit all common news-bearers. In 1757, an Iroquois chief told the colonists not to "believe every old woman that comes down and brings you news." As alternative sources of information, however, the old women and the Bad Birds checked and challenged the power of the official go-betweens—who found their options constrained by what the other side already knew.

Instead of following the lead of the official discourse by dismissing the Bad Birds, Merrell might have located them at one end of a broad spectrum of contacts that collectively generated the web of information and misinformation that shaped the bicultural relationship. Given that the Bad Birds usually warned of colonial chicanery and Indian attacks, they ultimately told a truer story than did the official intermediaries—who spoke so smoothly, but so duplicitously, of enduring friendship. In 1758, colonial officials assured Indians that, if they deserted the French cause, the advancing English and colonial army would destroy Fort Duquesne in western Pennsylvania and then withdraw eastward. Bad Birds warned the Indians that the promise was a lie. Heeding their hopes rather than their fears, the Indians deserted the French, allowing the fort to fall. Of course, the English and the colonists stayed, rebuilt and renamed the fort, and invited a steady stream of settlers who dispossessed Indians. The natives should have heeded the Bad Birds and the old women.

Sometimes Merrell confines his analysis too narrowly within the bounds of Pennsylvania—a foreshortening of an Indian diplomacy that, in fact, extended deep into the neighboring colonies and far beyond them. Other polities—French Canada, the Six Nations, New York, Virginia, and the larger British Empire—appear in passing, without a full explanation of the conflict between their goals and those of Pennsylvania. The focus on one colony skews the perspective, as relatively obscure Pennsylvanians like Conrad Weiser loom larger than major imperial players like Sir William Johnson, the Crown's superintendent of Indian affairs, who dwelled in New York (but who exercised great influence, through the Six Nations, in Pennsylvania).

Determined to tell a Pennsylvania story, Merrell obscures the larger context of imperial contest between the British and the French empires for mastery over the native peoples and their lands. The French appear as a vague, external menace rather than as equal participants in an overlapping and contested discourse of power that reached into Pennsylvania. In 1755, an Oneida chief rebuked the Pennsylvanians for miserliness by invoking the French contrast: "They never employ an Indian on any Business, but they give him fine Cloathes, besides other Presents, and this makes the Indians their hearty Friends." Was he right? Attention to the French go-betweens at Fort Duquesne would have provided an invaluable standard for comparison.

While too narrow in political geography, Merrell's book compensates with a deep analysis of the words and deeds of the official intermediaries in Pennsylvania. He brilliantly teases rich insights from especially difficult documents, each layered with complexity, evasion, and confusion. Because so few Indians were literate, almost all the surviving documents were produced by colonial writers for colonial readers who shared their prejudices. In the voluminous records of their negotiations with Indians, the colonists included translated transcriptions of lengthy speeches by leading Indians. But Merrell demonstrates that the public council records were selectively crafted to minimize Indian expressions of discontent and to maximize colonial participants' apparent mastery. Much was also lost in translation because Indian languages differed so radically from English—and because so many interpreters were incompetent, corrupt, or both. "Intercultural communication was plagued by ignorance and folly, fraud and mistrust, cupidity and arrogance; indeed, as time wore on, the interference got worse rather than better," Merrell notes. The marvel is that, by careful and critical winnowing, he succeeds in drawing a fascinating and coherent story out of such treacherous sources.

Merrell vividly takes his readers deep into a harsh, demanding, and often violent land. No romantic, he refers to "the frontier, where chaos was king," as a borderland of "endemic confusion and contention." Reaching an Indian village required long, hard travel along narrow, crooked paths through briars, thorns, and swamps, across raging rivers and over stony ridges. Travelers swatted mosquitoes in summer, suffered frostbite in winter, and went hungry in all seasons. Arrival did not always end an ordeal for the colonists, whose expectations of diet, cleanliness, and quiet usually jarred with the dirt, vermin, scarcity, and din of a native village. If a trader had recently introduced a keg of rum, the frolic could roil a village in deadly, disturbing violence. For their part, Indians who reached Philadelphia found the crowds distressing; the inhabitants rude, mean, and stingy; and the pathogens deadly. In 1749, twenty unlucky Oneidas died of smallpox during their brief visit to that city.

Instead of mixing the two cultures, the small cadre of go-betweens permitted the great majority of Indians and colonists to persist in their cherished difference from one another. In 1745, Shickellamy warned a missionary to back off: "We are Indians and don't wish to be transformed into white men. The English are our Brethren, but we never promised to become what they are." Both cultures left to a few experts the distasteful business of dealing with the other to keep the peace.

Nor did the go-betweens themselves converge in their beliefs and expectations to create a shared understanding. Quite the contrary, familiarity with the other only deepened each side's certitude of cultural superiority. In contrast to other historians, who emphasize the bicultural nature of frontier intermediaries, Merrell insists that, with but one tragic exception, named Andrew Montour, the go-betweens remained firmly rooted in one culture and not the other. "While all sought harmony, while they played up similarities, they could not, they did not want to, erase the differences they saw between colonist and Indian." Although Weiser had Indian friends and was adopted into one of their tribes, he never thought of himself as an Indian in any sense. Indeed, over time, he grew increasingly contemptuous of native beliefs and ever readier to manipulate Indians to enrich himself with their land.

The reliance on a few official go-betweens especially hurt the Indians, as they lagged behind the colonists in numbers and power. Because so few Indians understood much English or could read or write, they became increasingly vulnerable to deception and manipulation as colonial interpreters distorted their words and forged documents for their marks. Often, what the Indians took to be a statement of mutual friendship turned out to be a deed passing their lands to colonists, including the interpreter.

As the proponents of a gradual and peaceful process of parting Indians from their lands, Weiser and the other colonial go-betweens compared well only with the genocidal Paxton Boys. Although their means differed radically, they shared the goal of Indian dispossession. When Weiser died, Shickellamy's son denounced him as "one of the greatest thieves in the World for Lands." Merrell explains: "Weiser and other colonial mediators, never shedding prejudices that Europeans brought to America, embraced the idea that getting along with Indians was only a necessary step on the road to a brighter future, a time when those Indians would follow the forest into oblivion."

Even the shared hardships and danger of frontier journeys tended to divide, rather than unite, the colonial and Indian go-betweens. Merrell notes: "Men sharing the rigors of the paths, wearing the same sorts of clothes, eating from the same pot, puffing on the same pipe, nonetheless did not shake their different ways of thinking about the landscape and the people who traveled across it." Thrown together and placed under stress, they became more keenly aware of those differences, more prone to gripe and to draw invidious comparisons. Indians cast the colonial travelers as obtuse bunglers and chronic complainers who disturbed the forest spirits and coveted native lands. Colonial go-betweens increasingly dismissed their Indian guides as naïve and superstitious, as overgrown children given, in Weiser's words, to "silly fancies about spirits, about their dreams, and their sorceries." Merrell concludes: "As it turned out, the greatest obstacles in the way of intercultural understanding were not swollen streams, steep hills, or rotten weather but deeply-rooted perceptions that passage through the woods exposed rather than effaced."

Merrell brilliantly evokes the clashing cultures' discordant ways of marking and perceiving the landscape. The Indians filled their forest with emblems of victories and markers of loss: trees carved with pictographs; abandoned villages; skulls on posts. They sensed that the land was filled with a spiritual power that had to be propitiated and conversed with for safe passage. Despite the discomforts and dangers of the forest, a journey beyond it and into the colonial towns unnerved Indians. The settled landscape of cleared and ploughed fields and of building-clogged towns was eerily mute, disenchanted of its spirits and rendered strange by the obliteration of Indian monuments. For their part, the colonists treated the forest as just so much inert matter, a set of obstacles that should be cleared away for their ease and profit—as they had already done around Philadelphia.

The colonists and the Indians discovered that they had fundamentally antithetical visions of Pennsylvania's future. Indians hoped to remain Indians—politically autonomous, culturally distinct, militarily powerful, and secure in their mastery over most of the landscape. Colonists, however, eagerly anticipated dispossessing the Indians, disenchanting their landscape, and reaping profits from the sale and cultivation of a forest remade into real estate. Colonists grew in arrogance, and Indians grew in alarm, as both noted the swelling colonial population, which threatened to overwhelm the dwindling number of natives. From twenty thousand in 1701, Pennsylvania's population doubled by 1740 and then doubled again by 1760.

No matter of misunderstanding, the wars of the 1750s and the 1760s resulted from both sides' improved understanding of each other. Discovering their incompatible goals hardened their hearts, making atrocities easier to inflict. Colonists concluded that Indians could not be converted until they had been conquered. Indians recognized that the colonists came to conquer and not to coexist. Familiarity bred fear, which provoked war.

After 1754, Pennsylvania's go-betweens operated in a land drenched in the blood of men, women, and children as merciless war became the norm rather than the exception. Go-betweens tried, largely in vain, to restore contact and comity. When they did succeed, peace cost the Indians dearly, for they had to make reparations in the form of sweeping land cessions to the colonial victors. The colonial go-betweens mastered the art of manipulating the natives out of their remaining lands, by plying their skills to bribe, cajole, deceive, and intimidate. "Intended to bring people together, treaties ended up driving them apart," Merrell explains. Worse still for the Indians, the cessions bought them no peace, for during the 1760s, the Paxton Boys and their ilk routinely killed any Indian, no matter how peaceable, who ventured near the colonial settlements.

As Pennsylvania became a white man's country, Andrew Montour became a lost soul. He is the lone figure in this story who, for a time, suggested the possibility of a different ending: cultural fusion. Among the go-betweens, he alone fell in the middle. He was the son of an Oneida chief, Currundawah, and a Canadian mixed-blood. Truly bicultural and multilingual, Andrew Montour became the preeminent interpreter at Pennsylvania's Indian councils during the mid-eighteenth century. But he frustrated both colonial authorities and Iroquois chiefs because neither group could racially categorize him from the cues of his dress, language, or manner. He wore both European clothing and Indian face paint. Increasingly, his uncertain identity rendered Montour suspect by both Indians and colonists.

When Montour proposed his own mixed settlement of colonial tenants and Indian landlords, the leaders of both Pennsylvania and the Iroquois recoiled in horror—and they combined to stifle the scheme. The Indian chiefs wanted mixture no more than did the rulers of Pennsylvania. Merrell concludes: "America was to be a land of lines dividing Indians from Europeans, not a place where lines blurred and people came together." Betrayed by his former employers, Montour lapsed into heavy drinking and disarray in his last years, which terminated in 1772 with his murder by an Indian. Merrell concludes: "Trying to be both Indian and European, Montour ended up being neither. The life that he made for himself, the path he traveled, turned out to be a dead end in English America, not an avenue to some new social order."

*14*

# The Forgotten War

*August 14, 2000*

Fred Anderson hopes to rescue the greatest colonial war from obscurity. "The most important event to occur in eighteenth-century North America, the Seven Years War (or as the colonists called it, the French and Indian War) figures in most Americans' consciousness of the past as a kind of hazy backdrop to the Revolution." Fought between 1754 and 1763 by European empires and their native allies, the war was unprecedented in its global scale, financial cost, and geopolitical consequences. But today few historians and fewer citizens give it much thought. We're not even sure what to call it. "The French and Indian War," the traditional American name, is a bit misleading, for the British colonists fought three previous wars, between 1689 and 1748, against the French in Canada and their Indian allies. "The French and Indian War" also seems parochial, obscuring the campaigns in Europe as well as the global reach across the oceans to the West Indies, West Africa, and India. And the name "French and Indian War" is out of fashion for apparently casting blame on one side, summoning up images of rampaging savages egged on by French priests and fur traders to destroy innocent American colonists. That partisan version of the conflict is now associated with the once-celebrated but now-notorious nineteenth-century historian, the great master of narrative, Francis Parkman. Europeans (and Anderson) prefer the alternative name, the "Seven Years' War," which better fits Europe, where the conflict erupted belatedly in 1756, than North America, where it began in 1754 and endured for nine years. But at least the "Seven Years' War" offers a neutral title that, for want of geographic specificity, can stretch to cover the vast range of the conflict without seeming to blame anyone.

The name, however, only begins the identity problem. In Anderson's view, the Seven Years' War will never receive its due until historians and the public begin to think less of, and about, the American Revolution.

*Crucible of War: The Seven Years' War and the Fate of Empire in British North America, 1754–1766,* by Fred Anderson (Alfred A. Knopf, 2000)

In his introduction, Anderson insists that our preoccupation with the Revolution obscures the greater importance of the Seven Years' War: "For indeed, if viewed not from the perspective of Boston or Philadelphia, but from Montreal or Vincennes, St. Augustine or Havana, Paris or Madrid—or, for that matter Calcutta or Berlin—the Seven Years' War was far more significant than the War of American Independence." Like so many other historians these days, Anderson imagines scholarship as a zero-sum game, where his favored topic cannot receive its due because people pay too much attention to some less-worthy subject.

To pump up the Seven Years' War to epic proportions, Anderson adopts a kind of Rube Goldberg reasoning. If no Seven Years' War, he insists, then no American Revolution, no French Revolution, no Napoleon, no Latin American independence, and no westward expansion by the Americans. But such after-the-fact reasoning can be stretched infinitely backward to rob every subsequent event of its "importance." If there had been no War of the Austrian Succession between 1744 and 1748, there would have been no Seven Years' War during the 1750s. Does that make the former war more important than the latter?

Because the importance of events lies in their subsequent implications, the best case for the Seven Years' War lies in the trajectory it gave to events that fed into the American Revolution. Most members of the generation that led the Revolution (or who fought against it) began their political and military careers during the previous conflict, which shaped their expectations as it tested their abilities. And the Seven Years' War created grave new problems that roiled the relationship of the Atlantic seaboard colonies and Great Britain. Overtly, Anderson rejects that linkage for casting a shadow backward, obscuring the greater significance of the Seven Years' War, and robbing the story of "contingency"—the openness of the past to multiple possibilities. Embracing contingency against the teleology of hindsight, Anderson promises "a story of violent imperial competition that resulted first in a decisive victory and then in a troubled attempt by metropolitan authorities to construct a new British empire along lines that would permit them to exercise effective control over colonies and conquests. It is not, therefore, a story that has the birth of an American republic anywhere in view." And yet, readers may rightly suspect that the "troubled attempt by metropolitan authorities to construct a new British empire" had *everything* to do with the birth of the American republic. Were it not for that connection, would Anderson devote so much loving detail to exploring the strains in the empire?

In addition to honoring contingency, historians inevitably employ hindsight to detect patterns of development over time. In fact, Anderson is too fine a narrative historian not to exploit the revolutionary connections of the Seven Years' War. Once safely beyond his tendentious introduction and launched into his vivid story, he freely associates events and people with their coming celebrity in the American Revolution. To explain the origins and the stakes of the war, for example, he dwells at great length on the Ohio valley of western Pennsylvania during the early 1750s. He lavishes particular detail on a small skirmish fought by a (then) obscure Virginia officer, George Washington. Surely this narrative prominence depends on the officer's later fame as the revolution's miltary leader. In explaining the origins of the war, a purer devotion to contingency would have given equal weight to Nova Scotia, where new French forts offended the British as much as French activity in the Ohio valley did. For want of George Washington's presence, however, Nova Scotia receives less than a tenth of the coverage that Anderson lavishes on the Ohio Valley.

Dispensing with hindsight is more easily asserted than practiced. Defying his opening injunctions, Anderson crafts a narrative haunted by anticipation of the coming revolution. He emphasizes the emerging animosities between the British and their colonists—in sharp contrast to most recent scholarship, which emphasizes their common culture, identity, and interests until the eve of the Revolution. Anderson early and often identifies the diverse and contentious colonists as "Americans" united in a shared identity against their British overlords: "No matter how much zeal he might profess for the common cause, you could still scratch a colonist and, beneath his patriotic veneer, find only—an American."

Writing in the nationalist tradition spawned by the America Revolution, Anderson depicts almost all of the British officers and officials as arrogant and aristocratic twits determined to bully the colonists. King George III appears as the caricature of pop history: a "thick-headed adolescent" with a "callow soul." (A more even-handed portrait would concede his conscientious sense of duty.) Of the Britons, only William Pitt, the great political architect of the war effort, appears in a positive light, primarily because he gave the colonists what they wanted: financial reimbursement for their military expenditures.

In his introduction, Anderson also promises to reveal the war from a global perspective that affords Montréal, Havana, Paris, and Madrid as much weight as London and Philadelphia. He does consider other theaters of the war, principally, the campaigns in Germany and along the French coast, but Anderson still devotes disproportionate attention to British operations on the mainland of North America. Throughout, Britain's foes appear as vague and reactive foils in a war shaped by Anglo-American initiative. Anderson covers the political jockeying in London in excruciating detail, but he neglects comparable attention to the French court of Louis XV. Similarly, the domestic strains within New

France get nothing like the loving attention to the political squabbles within the British colonies. Indeed, Anderson gives less consideration to the French Canadian side of the story than did Francis Parkman in his classic nineteenth-century account of the war, *Montcalm and Wolfe.* Preoccupied with the Anglo-American perspective, Anderson cannot deliver on his promise to reveal the multilateral complexity of the Seven Years' War.

Within his limited framework, Anderson rewards the reader with his special flair for narrating dramatic events and describing vivid characters. And he has a great, sprawling tale to tell, a story that reveals the central importance of Indians and high finance to the contest of empires. Writing for a our antiheroic time, Anderson narrates the military campaigns with far more irony and far less grandeur than did Parkman. For Anderson, victories bring more complications than benefits, while defeats offer silver linings for the losers. In the end, Britain is the biggest loser for winning too much in a war that masked the true limitations of imperial power, provoking a hubris fatal to the union of the empire.

Unlike previous imperial wars, the Seven Years' War began in North America rather than Europe. By 1750, the 1,500,000 British colonists immensely outnumbered the 70,000 French. And while the British were concentrated along the Atlantic seaboard east of the Appalachians, the French scattered through the interior over immense distances, from the mouth of the St. Lawrence to the Gulf of Mexico. Yet, the British colonists dissipated the advantage of concentrated numbers by their political divisions into thirteen bickering colonies, each eager to shunt the costs of frontier defense onto the others. The large and growing British colonial population also alarmed the Indians, who tilted in favor of the French.

To counter the British numerical superiority, the French needed Indian allies. Consequently, they treated most natives with diplomatic respect, generous presents, and ready hospitality. French traders more readily learned Indian ways and languages. By marrying native women, the traders procured the kinship connections that facilitated alliance and commerce. Making a virtue of their small colonial population, the French could keep promises not to intrude new settlements on Indian lands. Instead, they built a long string of small forts and trading posts that stretched along the Great Lakes and down the Mississippi River. Lightly built and garrisoned and located among superior numbers of Indians, the posts depended on the local natives for protection. Reaping trade and presents, most Indians welcomed the French posts as assets, instead of resenting them as threats.

The ultimate colonial war erupted in 1754, as French and British officials jockeyed for advantage along the vague and contested frontiers of their colonies. During the early 1750s, Anglo-American settlers, land speculators, and traders pressed northward and westward into the lands of France's Indian allies. Alarmed, the French built new forts in the Ohio valley of western Pennsylvania and at the head of the Bay of Fundy on the margins of Nova Scotia. Naturally, the British and their colonial officials regarded the new French forts as intrusions, as a French plot to confine and strangle the Atlantic seaboard colonies.

Affiliated with land speculators eager to get rid of the Indians and to develop the Ohio Valley, Gov. Robert Dinwiddie of Virginia sent troops to oust the French from Fort Duquesne at the Forks of the Ohio (now Pittsburgh). He entrusted the command to his land-speculating partner, the young but ambitious George Washington, who promptly displayed his inexperience. Despite the superior French numbers at the Forks of the Ohio, he foolishly surprised, attacked, and destroyed a small French patrol. Outraged, the main French force counterattacked. Surrounding Washington's camp, the French compelled his surrender (on July 4). Hoping to avoid a full-scale war, the French commander allowed Washington and his men to limp back to Virginia.

Informed of Washington's defeat, the British government resolved to send unprecedented sums of money and numbers of troops to help the colonists seize control of their frontier from the French. In the previous imperial wars, the British had neglected the colonies, preferring, instead, to invest their money and soldiers on the nearby European continent and to employ their warships along the coasts of France and Spain. But in the new conflict, the British made North America their highest priority, by mobilizing, equipping, and paying thousands of soldiers, both colonial volunteers and British regulars, to attack and conquer French Canada.

At first, the British reaped scant returns on their large new military investment in North America. In 1755, the stubborn Gen. James Braddock botched a large, new thrust to seize the Forks of the Ohio. Near that goal, he marched his army into an ambush by French soldiers and Indian warriors. Although the French and the Indians had only half as many men, they exploited the forest, firing from behind trees and rocks into the massed and exposed British and colonial ranks. The dead included Braddock.

The British debacle had one silver lining: Washington redeemed his military reputation by bravely and resourcefully conducting the retreat that saved part of the army. Braddock had blundered into the ambush because he lacked the Indian allies needed to supply scouts and partisans for forest warfare. Only eight natives accompanied his army, and Braddock ignored their advice. One of them recalled: "he looked upon us as dogs and would never hear anything [we] said to him."

Braddock's defeat emboldened the Indians to attack and devastate the hated frontier settlements in Virginia, Maryland, and Pennsylvania. The raids pinned down colonial troops, which enabled the French to take the offensive in 1756 and 1757, under the able (but contentious) leadership of Gov. Pierre de Rigaud de Vaudreuil and Gen. Louis-Joseph de Montcalm. They mustered small but effective forces that combined French regulars, Canadian militia, and Indian warriors to capture British forts on Lake Ontario in 1756 and on Lake George in 1757.

But Montcalm spoiled his victories by alienating many of his Indian allies. A regular officer trained in Europe, he despised the disorder and atrocities of frontier raiding—a mode of war that the Canadian-born Vaudreuil championed as essential to the defense of undermanned New France. Montcalm's well-intentioned but shortsighted attempts to deny prisoners to Indians only enraged them. Rather than give up prisoners, the captors killed them and returned home with the scalps. Feeling insulted by the French commander, many Indians declined to assist the French in the subsequent defense of New France. For the Indian desertions, Vaudreuil blamed Montcalm, igniting a bitter feud that ruined their cooperation—with fatal consequences for New France.

In Britain, the embarrassing military setbacks of 1755–57 brought to power a new and more competent administration headed by William Pitt, an acerbic man whose ability matched his towering ego. Despite the escalation of the war in 1756 to include Europe, Pitt clung to the America-first policy, investing even more British troops and money in North America. He also defused the crippling tensions between colonial governments and British commanders over requisitions of men and supplies. Instead of ordering colonial cooperation, Pitt bought it by reimbursing the colonists' costs for men and munitions. Previously reluctant to obey the directives of overbearing British commanders, the colonists enthusiastically helped the war effort once it became a paying proposition. Although politically expedient (and celebrated by Anderson), Pitt's policy was financially reckless. By augmenting the monstrous public debt, it saddled the colonists and Britons with a burden that would violently disrupt the empire after the war.

For the North American campaign of 1758, the British raised some 45,000 troops, about half British regulars and half colonial volunteers. Against such large numbers, New France could muster only 6,800 regulars and 2,700 provincials—supplemented by volatile Indian warriors and drafted Canadian militiamen. Winning command of the Atlantic in 1758, the British Royal Navy isolated New France from European reinforcements and supplies. Putting a higher priority on operations in Europe, the French government virtually wrote off Canada, leaving Vaudreuil and Montcalm to muddle and squabble through with their shrinking forces. The British command of the high seas rendered trade goods scarce at French trading posts in the forest. Dependent on guns, gunpowder, and shot for hunting and warfare, many Indians grudgingly turned to the British traders for an alternative supply. Deserted by the local Indians, in 1758, the French blew up their fort at the Forks of the Ohio and fled northward, leaving the region in British hands.

Pitt also appointed more competent generals to command the growing forces deployed against New France. In 1758, a British army and fleet commanded by Gen. Jeffrey Amherst captured Louisbourg, a fortified city on Cape Breton Island in the Gulf of St. Lawrence. The victory cleared the way for Gen. James Wolfe to lead a difficult but ultimately victorious assault on Québec in 1759. Taking command in New York, Amherst advanced up the Hudson Valley to capture Fort Carillon beside Lake Champlain, the gateway to Montréal. To the west, Gen. Sir William Johnson shrewdly managed a mixed force of Indians, colonists, and British regulars to capture Fort Niagara at the head of Lake Ontario. In 1760, the British mopped up the remaining French forces in Canada. At Montréal in early September, Vaudreuil surrendered to Amherst, submitting all of New France, including the remaining forts around the Great Lakes, to the British victors.

In retelling these battles, Anderson covers ground made famous by Francis Parkman in *Montcalm and Wolfe,* and yet, Anderson is at pains never to mention his predecessor. Formerly celebrated as our greatest narrative historian, Parkman has fallen into scholarly disrepute for so vividly expressing the elitist, racist, and nationalist opinions of his class and century. According to Parkman, Montcalm valiantly defended the glorious lost cause of decaying French absolutism and Catholic superstition (and was uncomfortably saddled with the justly doomed savagery of the Indians). In stark contrast, Parkman presents Wolfe as the great romantic hero of Anglo-American nationalism: a brilliant general who selflessly sacrificed his life so that a Protestant, libertarian, and commercial civilization could triumph in North America.

With the bath water of Parkman's values, recent scholars have generally thrown out his baby: a flair for assembling telling details and revealing character-sketches into a coherent and dramatic story with epic consequences. In recapturing many of these qualities in a book on Parkman's greatest subject, Anderson owes far more than he is prepared to acknowledge. Parkman's legacy is especially evident in the prominence that Anderson affords to retelling the dramatic battle on the Plains of Abraham before the walls of Québec, the climactic episode of *Montcalm and Wolfe.* In a perverse and silent tribute, Anderson inverts Parkman's account to suit our more skeptical time. In Anderson's version, Montcalm and Wolfe represent nothing more than their own follies, which proved unnecessarily deadly to their unfortunate soldiers.

Anderson portrays Wolfe as blessed with more dumb luck than military ability. A self-centered fool, Wolfe alienated his subordinates and insulted colonial troops as filthy and cowardly. The author describes Wolfe's decisive night landing and ascent of the cliffs to the Plains of Abraham as, literally, a suicide mission that succeeded despite the general's hopes for a glorious failure. Racked by a wasting illness and determined not to survive in disgrace his botched siege of the city, Wolfe wanted to die in violent glory, apparently callous to the deaths of the others whom he led into futile battle. As Anderson tells it, Wolfe was confused by his army's surprising success in scaling the cliffs to appear in ranks before the fortified city:

> James Wolfe now stood a fair chance of sacrificing twelve superb battalions to no larger purpose than gratifying his desire for a heroic death. We cannot know whether he worried, in the last moments of his life, over the consequences of his actions, or whether he even fully understood them. But his men, lying face-down in the mud while cannon shot ricocheted through their ranks and musket balls whistled overhead, could hardly have relished the position into which their commander, ardent for any desperate glory and maudlin in his attachment to Gray's *Elegy* had thrust them.

Wolfe probably did prefer a quick and glorious death in battle to a lingering sickness, but that he cared neither to win nor to preserve his troops is pretty implausible. In the obscurity of an endnote Anderson concedes: "There is obviously a substantial degree of speculation in this, for we cannot know Wolfe's state of mind or his plans for the assault." The chief evidence for the suicidal interpretation comes from his partisan reading of the after-the-fact griping by Wolfe's alienated brigadier generals, who bitterly resented the glorious reputation that their commander reaped for dying while winning. No one paid their carping much heed until Anderson needed Wolfe to appear as a selfish and callous fool, the complete inversion of Parkman's self-sacrificing hero-genius.

If Wolfe was incompetent, how did his army win the most important battle of the war? Anderson answers that Montcalm threw away the advantages of the city walls to march out for battle on the Plains of Abraham: "Now for the first time in the war, Montcalm found himself out-generaled, and it rattled him out of his wits." Out-generaled? A few paragraphs earlier, Wolfe's ascent appears as suicidal folly, but for the climactic battle, Anderson needs Montcalm to appear even more foolhardy and defeatist than Wolfe. Cooler under fire, the British regulars won the day as the French broke and ran back into the city, leaving Wolfe dead on the field and bearing Montcalm back to die within the walls. A few days later, the city leaders surrendered Québec to Wolfe's successor.

A more plausible reading of the decisions by Montcalm and Wolfe would dispense with both romantic fancy and psychological speculation. They were veteran commanders trained according to conventions appropriate to northwestern Europe's broad and open fields. In North America, to their deep frustration, they had to adapt to irregular warfare in a wooded landscape. Longing for a good, old-fashioned European battle by massed ranks in an open field, neither could resist the temptation presented by the Plains of Abraham.

Throughout the empire, Britons effusively celebrated the triumphs of 1759 and 1760, and especially Wolfe's dramatic victory at Québec. After so many failed attempts in former wars, the colonists and the British felt giddy with relief and delight. They danced around bonfires, fired volleys of cannon, rang church bells for days, lit up the sky with fireworks, and consumed massive quantities of alcohol toasting Pitt, the king, the empire, the Royal Navy, the Royal Army, and the colonial volunteers. Horace Walpole facetiously lamented: "our bells are worn threadbare with ringing for victories." Wolfe's death in battle as an apparent martyr to the empire added a note of romantic pathos to the celebrations. In death, he became larger than life. Walpole saw an infusion of nationalism as the "whole people . . . triumphed—and they wept—for Wolfe had fallen in the hour of victory!"

The British won by overwhelming the colonial French with sheer numbers of soldiers and sailors. The superior ability of the British to project power across the Atlantic and into North America depended not on numbers alone (for France had a much larger population in Europe) but on the British superiority in shipping, finance, and military organization. And that superiority reflected the more advanced nature of Britain as a capitalist society endowed with far more liquid capital and financial acumen. The British had far more money to spend, spent it with wild abandon, and concentrated their expenditures in North America. The conquest of Canada cost the British Empire about four million pounds, more than ten times what the French spent to defend it. Never before had any empire lavished so much money to wage war on a transoceanic scale.

The conquest of Canada, however, remained provisional until confirmed by a peace treaty. With victories in Europe, the French might still recoup their position in North America. In early 1762, such a recovery seemed likely when Spain belatedly entered the war as France's ally. Instead, the Spanish provided expanded horizons for more British victories. British forces captured Manila and Havana, where the Spanish had stored much of their bullion, which enriched the captors as plunder. Another British fleet and army seized the sugar-rich French West Indian islands. These victories embarrassed British diplomats striving to draw the proud French and Spanish into peace negotiations.

At last, in 1763, the British made peace with the French and the Spanish in the Treaty of Paris. The French conceded Canada and all of their claims east of the Mississippi, including the Ohio Valley. The British also retained the lesser of their French West Indian conquests: Dominica, Grenada, St. Vincent, and Tobago. To mollify the French, the British returned the major islands of Guadeloupe, Martinique, and St. Lucia. The victors also restored French access to the valuable fishing waters off Newfoundland by conceding two small, unfortified islands in the Gulf of St. Lawrence. As a sop to their defeated allies, the French gave New Orleans and Louisiana, lying west of the Mississippi, to the Spanish. To secure the return of coveted Havana, the Spanish ceded Florida to the British. The various swaps made the Mississippi the boundary between the British and the Spanish claims in North America. Of course, most of the interior remained in the possession of many Indian peoples, who denied that the European powers could dispose of their lands.

The collapse of the French Empire in North America came as dreadful news to the Indians. No longer could they play the French and the British off against one another to maintain their own independence. British traders cheated and abused Indians in pursuit of immediate profit rather than cultivate long-term relationships, as the French had done. Colonial governors no longer made any serious effort to restrain the settlers who flocked westward into the Ohio valley. Grown arrogant and obtuse from too many victories, the British commander, General Amherst, cavalierly curtailed the gifts of guns, gunpowder, and shot that the French and the British had given to secure Indian goodwill. What Amherst considered a rational measure of economy, the Indians took as a grievous insult. Setting aside their linguistic differences and traditional animosities, multiple Indian nations prepared to seek a common redress.

During the spring of 1763, far-flung native peoples rose up to surprise and capture most of the British forts around the Great Lakes and in the Ohio Valley. Through the summer and fall, the Indians also raided the settlements of western Pennsylvania, Maryland, and Virginia, killing or capturing about two thousand colonists. But the rebels failed to take the three largest and strongest British posts: at Detroit, Niagara, and Fort Pitt. Preferring to blame Indian uprisings on a single mastermind, the British called the conflict "Pontiac's Rebellion," after an Ottawa chief prominent in the siege of Detroit. Although more influential than most chiefs, Pontiac could not command the diverse and scattered Indian peoples. For their own shared reasons and under their own chiefs, the natives rose up in a rebellion that had no central command.

By the summer of 1764, the Indian rebels were suffering shortages of gunpowder, shot, and guns. Without a European supplier, they could not maintain their resistance for long. Unable to take the major forts, most of the Indians longed to resume peaceful trade. At the same time, the British government eagerly sought to end the expensive and frustrating war by recalling Amherst in disgrace. The new and more pragmatic commander, Thomas Gage, recognized that presents and respect for Indians were far cheaper than military expeditions against them. Gradually, the various Indian villages made peace, allowing the British to reoccupy the captured forts in return for more respectful and generous treatment from the post commanders. Sufficiently mollified, most of the Indians would assist the British against their rebellious colonists in the next great conflict in North America: the War of the American Revolution.

The conquest of Canada, which made the Indians so anxious, delighted the colonists of British America by offering a vast and fertile continent for their settlement. The colonists also felt proud of their contributions to the war effort, and of their membership in such a powerful, prosperous, and relatively free empire. Within thirteen years, however, the thirteen Atlantic seaboard colonies would revolt and wage a long war for their independence from that empire.

As Anderson shows, the imperial crisis and the Revolution ripened from strains initiated by winning the Seven Years' War. During the war, British authorities began to pay closer attention to the colonies and to rethink how best to administer them. After making such a major investment of money and lives in North America, the British were not about to resume the prewar policy of benign neglect. Impressed by the widespread prosperity of the colonists, British observers concluded that they should pay higher taxes to support the empire that benefited them so greatly. This seemed only just and fair to the British, who were overtaxed and had just spent so much blood and treasure making North America safe for the prospering colonists.

During the war, British officers and officials were also appalled to discover that the colonists routinely ignored imperial regulations that hurt their economic interests. In particular, New English shippers continued to trade with the French West Indies, prolonging the war to the detriment of the empire and the death of many British soldiers and sailors. Members of Parliament and the imperial cabinet concluded that the empire was too weak and the colonists were too insubordinate. The British vowed to teach them discipline, and to reap greater revenue for the empire.

Victory had not come cheap, doubling the British debt from a prewar 73 million pounds to a postwar 137 million pounds. During the mid-1760s, interest payments on that debt consumed more than 60 percent of Great Britain's annual budget. Moreover, the expanded empire in

North America was more expensive to garrison and to administer. Before the Seven Years' War, the British had posted only a few hundred troops in North America. In 1763, the Crown decided to maintain ten thousand soldiers in the colonies, primarily in Canada and the Great Lakes country. With the British people already taxed to the limit, Parliament hoped to pay for the new army by taxing the colonists.

Of course, the colonists balked at the new taxes, detecting a dangerous precedent ominous for their prosperity and their liberty. Paradoxically, by protesting British taxation, the colonists affirmed their cherished identity as liberty-loving Britons. They rallied behind the most cherished proposition of their shared political culture: that a free man paid no tax unless it was levied by his own political representatives. The colonists devoutly believed that, without such protection from arbitrary taxation, a people inevitably would become enslaved by domineering rulers. Consequently, they would pay taxes imposed by their own assemblies but not by the distant Parliament, where no colonist sat.

Instead of seeing the British army in North America as a source of protection, the mainland colonial leaders felt threatened as those troops became both the pretext for raising new taxes and the means of enforcing them. After the British made peace with the Indians, moreover, the colonists concluded that the army served to assist the natives—rather than to help the colonists dispossess and kill the Indians. In sum, rather than preserving the North American empire, the new postwar garrisons (and their associated taxes) provoked the crisis which soon lost most of that empire to revolution.

We can explain the blowup as the structural consequences of the Seven Years' War, and therefore beyond the capacity of even the most able leaders to avert; or we can blame the particular politicians of the postwar era for ruining a still-viable empire. Anderson wants it both ways. In narrating the war years, he depicts the emerging preconditions for revolution, as a united and self-conscious American people resented their ties to a bullying and obtuse British elite (with Pitt as a glorious exception). When he turns to the postwar era, however, Anderson insists that capable British leaders in the Pitt mold could have short-circuited the crisis and averted the Revolution. In fact Pitt had bought temporary colonial cooperation at a very heavy cost that British taxpayers could not, and would not, sustain in peacetime. No basis for imperial stability, his profligate expenditures deepened the national debt, provoking a crisis that no latter-day Pitt could solve.

Anderson argues that in 1763 the British could have, and should have, dispensed with both an army and taxes in North America. Of course, he concedes, such a solution would have drenched the frontier in the blood of Indians and settlers as the colonies dictated their terms of conquest.

In other words, Anderson insists that the British should have saved a shadow empire by unilaterally surrendering its substance in order to avoid the bother of a revolution. Given that the British eventually lost the colonies, at a still-greater expense in lives and treasure, hindsight insists that they should have folded sooner rather than later. But the British elite lacked that luxury of hindsight and could not, after investing so much to conquer New France, walk away from their expanded empire. Nor could they have anticipated losing a war to colonists after so thoroughly trouncing the combined empires of France and Spain. For better and certainly for worse, the British felt obligated to enforce their notions of order and justice on restive colonists who, instead, wanted the freedom to conquer and to develop the continent as their own empire.

*15*

# Power Shopping

*March 1, 2004*

Hindsight assumes that Americans naturally and easily united to revolt against British rule in 1775–76. In fact, American revolution and union astonished contemporaries as sudden and unprecedented, a break with a long history of chronic dissension between the thirteen colonies of the Atlantic seaboard. John Adams marveled that "thirteen clocks were made to strike together." Prior to the 1770s, few colonists considered themselves "Americans." Instead, their particular colony or region commanded greater loyalty. Carolinians distrusted Virginians; Marylanders wrangled with Pennsylvanians; and the Yorkers of New York despised the Yankees of New England. Boundary disputes and regional rancor undercut intercolonial cooperation, even during the desperate wars with the French and their Indian allies. Only a massive infusion of British men and money secured the colonists by conquering French Canada in 1759–60. An English traveler observed that "fire and water are not more heterogeneous than the different colonies in North America." Colonial unity and independence seemed impossible because, without the subordinating control of the British Empire, "there would soon be a civil war from one end of the continent to the other."

So how was the extraordinary unity of revolutionary America achieved? T. H. Breen, an especially accomplished historian, offers an innovative explanation: "What gave the American Revolution distinctive shape was an earlier transformation of the Anglo-American consumer marketplace." Before Americans could resist the awesome might of the British Empire, they needed to develop sufficient trust in one another, despite their differences and distance. "Unless unhappy people develop the capacity to trust other unhappy people," he reasons, "protest remains a local affair easily silenced by traditional authority."

According to Breen, that trust developed during the 1760s and the early 1770s, when colonists crafted a novel strategy: a massive consumer

*The Marketplace of Revolution: How Consumer Politics Shaped American Independence,* by T. H. Breen (Oxford University Press, 2004)

boycott of British goods to pressure Parliament into rescinding provocative new taxes imposed without colonial consent. The colonists began to think of themselves as Americans as they read newspapers, broadsides, and pamphlets that reported widespread protests and boycotts. That strategy and literature ultimately depended on the prior proliferation of British goods in colonial markets, creating a unifying empire of consumer goods that eroded colonial parochialism. As consumers, diverse colonists could "communicate with each other about a common experience." According to Breen, consumer goods provided the essential and "powerful link between everyday life and political mobilization."

During the early decades of the eighteenth century, a swelling volume of shipping carried information, goods, and people more frequently across the Atlantic, producing economic growth and a greater integration of the British Empire. Consumer goods proliferated, declining in price and expanding the options of common people. During the early 1750s, an immigrant marveled that "it is really possible to obtain all the things one can get in Europe in Pennsylvania, since so many merchant ships arrive there every year." Between 1720 and 1770, per capita colonial imports increased by 50 percent.

A romantic mythology has miscast the common colonists as self-sufficient yeomen who produced all that they needed or wanted. Although most colonists did live on farms that produced most of their food and fuel and some homespun cloth, no household could produce everything that a family needed. And by no means did mere subsistence satisfy colonial desire. Consequently, colonial farms and plantations produced crops both for household use and for the external market. The colonists needed to sell produce so that they might purchase imported consumer goods beyond their own ability to make. Some derived from another climate, such as West Indian sugar and Asian tea, but the colonists also imported metal and cloth goods produced by the workshops of Britain. In the production of manufactures, which required abundant capital and cheap labor, relatively crowded Britain had an advantage over the land-rich but thinly populated colonies. In addition to such necessities as plows, hoes, axes, knives, and hammers, colonists sought the pleasures and the comforts of pewter knives and forks, bed and table linens, ceramic cups and saucers, drinking glasses and windowpanes, metal buttons and silver buckles, and finished cloth and clothing. Drawing astutely on museum collections, newspaper advertising, merchants' correspondence, probate inventories, field archaeology, and customs records, Breen demonstrates the rapid and voluminous spread of consumer goods into every colonial corner, rural as well as urban.

Lacking cash, colonists relied on credit offered with increasing generosity by manufacturers to London exporters and on to the wholesale importers of colonial seaports, the far-flung stores of country towns, and, ultimately, to thousands of common farmers and artisans. He concludes that the consumer revolution "depended ultimately on an extraordinary expansion of credit throughout the entire Atlantic world." In 1754, a colonist observed: "Trade, we know, is supported by Credit; and Credit is to Trade, what the Blood is to the Body; If credit fails, Trade stagnates." This he knew all too well, for this colonist wrote from a debtor's cell in an age that imprisoned the bankrupt.

Because Britain's economy and public revenues increasingly relied on exporting manufactured goods, the growing colonial market became ever more valuable. In 1773, the American colonies consumed about 26 percent of British exports, up from 6 percent in 1700. On both sides of the Atlantic, writers effusively celebrated the mutual benefits of maritime commerce in consumer goods. Defined by the flow of goods, the British Empire seemed natural, rational, and perfectly balanced: "a splendidly ordered Newtonian system." Of course, the empire especially benefited by legislating, in the Navigation Acts, that colonists could purchase their manufactured goods only from Great Britain. Fortunately for the colonists, British manufactories led the world in producing the best goods at the lowest prices. By making so much of the colonial market, British writers encouraged colonists to consider their consumption as essential to the empire. This conclusion later led colonists to boycott British goods, thereby expressing a conviction that the empire could not survive without their purchases.

While trumpeting the aggregate growth of commerce in Panglossian terms, colonial writers harshly criticized the consumer revolution at the personal level, especially when the purchasers were poor. Buying on credit beyond their means to dress far beyond their humble class, such common consumers allegedly imperiled social stability as well as their own souls. Tradition insisted that social harmony required a distinct, stable, and visible hierarchy of status and wealth. Conservative moralists doubted that a genteel elite could enjoy its just deserts of public deference if laborers walked the streets in silk clothing or sipped tea from porcelain cups. In 1744, the wealthy and genteel Dr. Alexander Hamilton (no relation to the later and more famous revolutionary) delighted in his own consumption but denounced that of common colonists. He concluded that, "if Luxury was to be confined to the Rich alone, it might prove a great national good." Touring the colonies, Hamilton expressed horror at the fine goods displayed in otherwise common dwellings. At one farm, he found "superfluous things which showed an inclination to finery . . . such as a looking glass with a painted frame, half a dozen pewter spoons and as many plates . . . a set of stone tea dishes, and a teapot." Far better, he thought, for farmers to make do with "wooden plates and spoons," and "a little water in a wooden pail might serve for a looking glass." Hamilton despised what the farmers cherished most about consumer goods: the opportunity to express aspiration.

Genteel moralists especially disliked the leading role of women in the consumer revolution. Women of middling means had the most to gain from increased consumption, for imported goods reduced their long and arduous labor, especially the making of candles and soap or the spinning and weaving of cloth. By accumulating and displaying fashionable goods, these women also obtained a new vehicle for self-expression and self-assertion. Astute storekeepers appealed to the growing influence of women over household consumption. In 1748, a Maryland merchant wrote to an associate: "You know the influence of the Wives upon their Husbands, & it is but a trifle that wins 'em over, [and] they must be taken notice of or there will be nothing with them." But genteel moralizers detected and denounced an erosion of patriarchal power that allegedly left men emasculated and financially ruined by their newly aggressive wives.

Breen dismisses the genteel moralizers as conservative cranks threatened by social changes that liberated common men and women. He also disavows those scholars and commentators in our own day who depict consumption, past and present, as "a vacuous, wasteful activity that somehow embodies the most objectionable features of modern capitalism." Instead, he dwells on "the comforts and pleasures of consumption," particularly for ordinary people of modest means. He describes stores as "sites of imagination" and shopping as "a moment of excitement and entertainment, a gathering of humble neighbors in their capacity as consumers of British manufactured goods." Consumer goods liberated colonists from the drab seventeenth-century: "By introducing vibrant colors into the poorly illuminated rooms of colonial houses, imported manufactures made the world of ordinary men and women come alive . . . imported goods transformed monochrome spaces into Technicolor." Thus colonial Dorothys attained their Land of Oz in eighteenth-century consumption.

Breen invests consumer goods with a power to liberate the minds of common people and to weaken colonial inequality. The new goods "brought them warmth, beauty, color, comfort, sanitation, leisure, and a heady sense of self-worth." British imports "invited colonists to fashion themselves in bold new ways . . . to appear prettier, or more successful." Looking good and feeling better about themselves, ordinary people could think in more egalitarian terms: "the act of choosing could be liberating, even empowering, for it allowed them to determine for themselves what the process of self-fashioning was all about." He credits the consumer revolution with spawning a liberal society premised on "the ability of ordinary men and women to establish a meaningful and distinct sense of self through the exercise of individual choice, a process of ever more egalitarian self-fashioning."

In his enthusiasm for colonial consumption, Breen gets a little carried away. In the eighteenth century, he asserts, "free Americans entered a new era, a distinct colonial period as different in terms of material culture from the [seventeenth-century] years of initial conquest as our times are from the late nineteenth century." In fact, the eighteenth century offered nothing like the technological breakthroughs and proliferation of vast new categories of consumer goods produced in the twentieth century by the internal-combustion engine, plastics, electronics, and the microchip. Instead, eighteenth-century goods simply offered cheaper, more colorful, and more diverse variations of long-familiar objects: clothing, dishes, carpets, wines, and mirrors.

By emphasizing the egalitarian consequences of consumption, Breen vividly tells half the story, obscuring the equal role of inequality in the consumer revolution. In the new and fluid societies of colonial America, the display of fine consumer goods laid claim to enhanced social status. Colonists wished to see themselves, and to be seen by others, as something more than rude rustics. Such claims were particularly important to wealthier colonists, especially those of new fortunes without the pedigree of birth into a prestigious family. Emulating the English gentry, the wealthier colonists cultivated "gentility": a conspicuous and self-conscious style that emphasized personal displays of harmony, grace, delicacy, and refinement. Imported goods provided essential props for the performance of gentility.

By perfecting a genteel style, colonial elites sought common cause with one another and with the gentry of the mother country. Yet that goal defined sharper boundaries within colonial communities by distinguishing the polite and refined from fellow colonists disdained as rude and common. Throughout the British Empire, traveling ladies and gentlemen felt a greater solidarity with one another at a distance than with their cruder neighbors. Claiming superior morals, taste, talents, and possessions, gentlemen and ladies looked down on the common farmers and artisans as obtuse and mean—as Dr. Hamilton did on his tour.

Common folk, however, aspired to gentility by stretching their budgets to buy some of its associated goods. Artisan and farm families wanted to sip tea from ceramic teacups—because the elite did so. Such emulation tried to erase the insulting line between gentility and commonality that the elite worked so hard to construct and maintain. In 1749, a genteel essayist warned against "an Emulation most dangerous to the Community when every one beholding the *Finery* of his Neighbours pines to see himself outdone—burns with Envy—Or perhaps ruins his own Fortune and Credit to keep with him in those things that excite his Envy."

Ultimately, the envious and aspiring fell short because the wealthy constantly renewed their superiority by cultivating more expensive tastes in the most current fashions. In 1771, an Englishman in Maryland reported: "The quick importation of fashions from the mother country is really astonishing. I am almost inclined to believe that a new fashion is adopted earlier by the polished and affluent American than by many opulent persons in the great metropolis. . . . In short, very little difference is, in reality, observable in the manners of the wealthy colonist and the wealthy Briton." Fashionable goods, and their proper uses, became both the exclusionary symbols of social superiority and the inclusive currency of social emulation. In that social tension lay the energy behind the consumer revolution.

Breen aptly and vividly tells the story of common aspiration—but to the relative neglect of inequality's persistent power. To stress the accessibility of genteel things for common people, he dwells on the cheaper, more ubiquitous goods within middle-class reach, especially tea and teacups. He pays scant attention to the more expensive goods that purchased genteel distance, such as gilded carriages, fine furniture, and grand mansions. We can detect how distant and elusive true wealth and power remained in colonial society in John Adams's reaction to the mansion of a merchant grandee in Boston. The furniture alone, he remarked, "cost a thousand Pounds sterling. . . . the Turkey Carpets, the painted Hangings, the Marble Table, the rich Beds with crimson Damask Curtains and Counterpanes, the beautiful Chimney Clock, the Spacious Garden, are the most magnificent of any Thing I have ever seen." Although the consumer revolution gave expression to common aspirations and aroused dread in the elite, at the end of the day, it did not affect the increasingly unequal distribution of wealth. According to tax records, in 1771, the wealthiest tenth of Bostonians owned over 60 percent of the urban wealth, while the bottom three tenths owned virtually nothing.

Compelled to engage in a status competition that few could win, many common colonists felt uneasy in the face of genteel superiority. The well-trained eyes and ears of gentility scrutinized every detail of manners and possession for the proper nuances of fashion. A faulty performance damned the unfortunate as imposters deserving of ridicule. Pity the poor common man invited to eat and drink at the table of Robert Carter, a great planter in Virginia. The family tutor dismissed the guest as dull and vulgar because "he held the Glass of Porter fast with both his Hands, and then gave an insignificant nod to each one at the Table, in hast[e], & with fear, & then drank like an Ox." His awkwardness expressed the insecurity that common people often felt in the presence of gentility, no matter how many teacups they had bought.

A desperate defensiveness often characterized the efforts of common men and women to claim an enhanced and elusive status. At a Maryland inn, Dr. Hamilton encountered a common traveler, William Morison, and described him as "a very rough spun, forward, clownish blade, much addicted to swearing, [and] at the same time desirous to pass for a gentleman." Disdaining Morison as a common "ploughman," the innkeeper offered him only "scraps of cold veal" in contrast to Hamilton's finer fare. The insulted Morison angrily threatened to smash the table. Claiming a decent meal equal to Hamilton's, Morison boasted "that tho' he seemed to be but a plain, homely fellow, yet he would have us know that he was able to afford better than many that went finer; He had good linnen in his bags, a pair of silver buckles, silver clasps, and gold sleeve buttons, two Holland shirts, and some neat nightcaps." Pulling them out and putting them on, he asserted a superficial gentility, which only deepened Hamilton's ridicule. Morison's manic "self-fashioning" bought him neither respectability nor peace of mind. Clothes did not suffice to make the gentleman. In Hamilton's ridicule and Morison's anger we may measure the invidious pressure of status competition in a (partially) fluid society.

As contemporaries often noted, the competition for status drove colonists to buy more than they could well afford. Consumption embroiled thousands in debt, litigation, bankruptcy, and imprisonment, casting a pall on many a tea party. The consumer dynamic also created an economic problem, as the colonies imported more than they exported, generating a chronic trade imbalance, rather like our own day. In 1750, a colonist lamented: "In Debt we are and in Debt we must be, for those vast Importations from *Europe*, and as we increase, so will our Debts, without, from the present Prospect of things, ever being able to make suitable Returns." In 1762, a New Yorker conceded: "Our importation of dry goods from England is so vastly great, that we are obliged to betake ourselves to all possible arts to make remittances to the British merchants. . . . and yet it drains us of all the silver and gold we can collect." The pervasive shortage of cash, mounting debts, and the trade deficit fed a nagging unease at odds with the overt colonial prosperity and general contentment with the empire. In colonial minds, that unease surged to the fore when the British began to tighten their imperial control after 1760.

Anxiety about the future—rather than egalitarian confidence—was the primary engine of resistance to British taxes and, ultimately, to British rule. The celebrated empire of commerce suddenly appeared more troubling during the 1760s, when British officials began taxing consumer goods shipped to the colonies. Affirming their cherished identity as freeborn Britons, the colonists rallied behind the core proposition of their political culture: that a free man should pay no tax unless levied by his own representatives. They would pay taxes levied by their own provincial assemblies but not by the distant Parliament, where no colonist sat. Without any sense of irony or proportion, the colonists fiercely asserted that, if taxed without representation, they would become "slaves" to British masters. Long-cherished consumer goods suddenly appeared in a harsh new light as pernicious bait to establish parliamentary taxation and to deepen colonial dependence. Far from offering mutual benefit, the empire of goods began to seem like a British plot to exploit and impoverish their captive customers, the American colonists.

The Stamp Act of 1765 inspired the first, massive wave of colonial protests: a mix of mob violence against tax collectors, intellectual arguments for colonial rights, and local agreements to cease importing British goods. Boycotts demanded considerable sacrifice because imported consumer goods had become so essential to colonial social life. Crude American substitutes, such as homespun clothing, were a hard sell in such a competitive society, where aspiration daily confronted inequality (and vice versa). A Connecticut woman explained that social compulsion obliged aspiring young women to wear fancy, imported clothing to please men, for if women "appeared in Home Spun dress, we should have been treated as kitchen maids by you." George Washington similarly blanched at wearing homespun, lest it "create suspicions of a decay in my fortune, & such a thought the World must not harbour." If seen as downwardly mobile, a gentleman lost public respect and might face ruinous lawsuits from nervous creditors calling in debts—which few colonists could afford to pay on short notice. Although the Boston radical Samuel Adams championed the boycotts, he had to don fashionable new clothes on joining the First Continental Congress at Philadelphia, lest the more genteel delegates dismiss him as a rogue. Striking a rare dark note, Breen observes: "Like addicts, the colonists looked to someone else to protect them from their own dangerous habits, in this case, purchasing British goods whose price tag was political dependence."

Calls for patriotic sacrifice to defend liberty contradicted the definition of freedom promoted by the consumer revolution. During the eighteenth century, colonists began to speak of their access to abundant, inexpensive, and high-quality consumer goods as a right—rather like contemporary Americans devoted to gasoline. One colonist wrote: "I, for myself, choose that there should be many Stores filled with every Kind of thing that is convenient and useful, that I might have my choices of Goods, upon the most reasonable or agreeable Terms; whether foreign or homemade; I would have Liberty of either, and to Deal as I judge best for myself. And I wish the same Privilege to all my Friends and Neighbors." If free consumption was an inalienable right, how could Patriots justly constrain the purchases of neighbors who wanted no part of a boycott? Picking up on that contradiction, Loyalists denounced the Patriots as hypocrites for harassing consumers in the name of liberty. Championing the tyranny of the majority, the Patriots countered that "the public" could suppress any behavior deemed antithetical to their definition of liberty.

Initially, the boycotts depended on the seaport merchants, who held meetings and organized committees to define the local rules. But, as secretive competitors, the merchants failed as enforcers. Unable to trust one another for very long, the merchants of one seaport soon began evading their own boycott in the conviction that others were already cheating. Nor did the celebrated Founding Fathers—the politicians who led colonial assemblies and congresses—distinguish themselves with self-discipline. Despite the boycott, John Adams persisted in drinking tea until he was upbraided by a common innkeeper. Thomas Jefferson imported British window glass for his new mansion at Monticello until publicity threatened to discredit his patriotism. "It is not from a love of the English, but a love of myself that I sometimes find myself obliged to buy their manufactures," Jefferson later confessed.

Conceding that the initial boycotts were economically disappointing, producing minimal disruptions in British exports, Breen locates their greatest significance in their cultural work. Although they put surprisingly little real pressure on the British, the boycotts of the 1760s did help to make the colonists into Americans. By reading in newspapers about patriotic meetings, resolutions, and boycotts in distant colonies, the diverse colonists slowly built a new identity: as more than mere inhabitants of a single colony, as fellow citizens of a new nation. The continental communication of shared sentiments and consumer sacrifices created the "larger imagined community" of America, rendering independence and union possible.

That process accelerated in 1774, when local committees of middle-class men took enforcement of the ultimate boycott away from the merchants, transforming a weak nonimportation into a coercive nonconsumption. Empowered by the Continental Association adopted by the First Continental Congress, local committeemen went door to door with subscription lists. Signers promised to restrict their consumption and to identify as enemies any neighbors who refused to comply. Denounced in newspapers and public meetings, holdouts lost business, suffered social ostracism, and risked mob violence, including a painful coat of hot tar topped by a humiliating veneer of feathers. Today we tend to forget how divisive and violent our Revolution became. Denouncing

Loyalists in 1774, a Patriot writer accurately predicted a day "when the Sons of Liberty will be bound by Duty, both to God and themselves, to hang, drown, or otherwise demolish these execrable Villains from the Face of the Earth, that Posterity may enjoy a peaceful and happy Land, preserv'd from utter Ruin, by the Noble Efforts of Freedom's Sons."

To build a majority committed to confronting Britain, the Patriots engaged a broader spectrum of colonial society—including women and poor laborers—in political activity. By forsaking, albeit temporarily, coveted consumer goods, distant colonists made significant sacrifices that persuaded them to trust in their mutual commitment. Without a prior consumer revolution, colonists would have had nothing significant to give up to prove their virtue and unity as Americans.

Although brilliantly suggestive, Breen's presentation ultimately seems incomplete in three ways: geographic, political, and temporal. First, he retains the standard but restrictive definition of colonial America as confined to the thirteen provinces that rebelled to form the United States in 1776. This narrow definition omits the other nine colonies that composed British America, including Nova Scotia, Québec, Jamaica, and Barbados. Their colonists also avidly participated in the empire's consumer revolution. Why, then, did they fail to develop a solidarity as consumers with their fellow American colonists? A satisfactory interpretation of the Revolution needs to assess all of British America, explaining the persistence as well as the rejection of empire.

Breen similarly retains the conventional rhetoric that implies virtual unanimity by Americans (of the thirteen colonies) in support of the political revolution. By casually equating "colonists" and "Americans" with revolutionary patriotism, he erases the approximately one fifth of the people who remained loyal to the empire. Taking his cues from Patriot discourse, Breen mentions Loyalists only in passing and in the pejorative guise of "Tory sympathizers"—a quaint term of historical partisanship. Loyalists poorly fit the book's central argument: that a unifying political identity as Americans emerged from a standardization of colonial material culture wrought by a ubiquitous consumer revolution.

But Loyalists properly belong in a history that concludes with enforcement of the Continental Association by an array of local committees. Breen quite rightly credits those local extralegal committees with crafting and cajoling a strong majority in favor of armed resistance and violent revolution. But those unconstitutional and menacing committees also activated hitherto passive Loyalists. Embittered by harassment, they rallied to the British Empire as the lesser of evils. Contrary to their stereotype as out-of-touch elitists, most Loyalists were common farmers and artisans—similar in class to most Patriots—and they often acted in resentment against the wealthy elites who led the Revolution in their counties. Is there any reason to believe that common Loyalists were any less avid consumers than their Patriot counterparts?

In fact, regional variation in support for the political revolution works against regarding the consumer revolution as the essential prerequisite for Patriotism. Within the thirteen colonies, Loyalism was strongest in the Middle Colonies and the Carolinas, which is precisely where Breen finds the greatest per capita growth in consumption during the mid-eighteenth century. Conversely, Patriotism overwhelmingly prevailed in New England, where consumption had increased at the slowest rate. Should we, then, instead look to the consumer revolution to explain opposition to the Revolution? After all, the Loyalists explicitly defended their precious rights as consumers to buy whatever they wanted without having to answer to an upstart committee or to a violent mob. In defending free consumption, the Loyalists claimed best to defend true American liberty. Now they seem prescient for asserting the most popular definition of freedom in our own America. Imagine, for example, the impossibility today of an attempt by revolutionary committees to humiliate with tar and feathers those enemies of American energy independence, the owners of Hummers.

Breen abruptly concludes in 1774 with the Continental Association, depicted as the consummation of a political revolution premised on the negative exercise of consumer power and the positive expression of American nationalism. This ending seems premature when Breen credits the Americans with "repudiating the empire of goods" and with having "destroyed a vital cultural bond with the mother country." Quite the contrary. In 1775, the revolutionary war introduced a mania for privateering—or licensed piracy—to acquire by violence the "baubles of Britain." And avid consumer demand for a limited supply of captured goods combined with a reckless monetary policy to drive an inflationary spiral that nearly destroyed the fragile new nation. The postwar 1780s brought not only a resumption but also an intensification of consumer imports from Britain, with a consequent trade deficit. The consumer "repudiation" of 1774 was brief indeed.

Economic and cultural dependency on Britain endured for decades after political independence, precisely because Americans remained unequal and continued to consume in competition for status. But national independence did generate powerful myths of revolutionary unanimity, and of British vulnerability to consumer pressure. In 1807–9 those myths inspired Pres. Thomas Jefferson's foolish "Embargo," which tried to coerce British policy by suspending our maritime commerce. Inflicting more misery on Americans than on Britons, the abortive Embargo revealed how little the political revolution had altered American patterns of trade and consumption.

Today, we import relatively little from Britain, relying, instead, on the eastern half of the Pacific rim for our baubles and on the Persian Gulf to fuel them. Although our trading partners have shifted, we persist as debtors—both individually and nationally—because consumption on credit remains essential to American competition, American culture, and American identity. We can tell the social winners by the Hummers they drive.

In the end, Breen vaguely hopes that a history of the revolutionary boycotts will somehow inspire contemporary Americans "to cooperate effectively for the general political welfare." We can once again make our goods "speak to power. The choice is ours to make." At present, however, few Americans seem willing to compromise their standard of living as individuals to achieve collective goals such as energy independence or environmental protection. In our own time, the perpetual consumer revolution has trumped even the American Revolution as our most cherished legacy from the eighteenth century.

# Part IV
# Founders

*16*

# For the Benefit of Mr. Kite

*March 19, 2001*

Today we know Benjamin Franklin mainly from an advertising image: an elderly man in knickers, long coat, and spectacles, with a bald crown and long side hair—a zealot foolishly determined to fly a kite during a thunderstorm. This Franklin seems eccentric, comic, antiquated, and harmless (except to himself). This Franklin no longer matters and no longer arouses either controversy or adulation—merely laughter. We only dimly sense his importance in the nineteenth and the early twentieth centuries as the paragon of, and the pattern for, American middle-class values. Former generations of striving Americans sought the keys to social mobility in the aphorisms of Franklin's *Poor Richard's Almanac*—such as "Early to bed and early to rise, makes a man healthy and wealthy and wise." And they admired his autobiography, which reiterated the rewards of thrift, labor, moderation, and reason.

Of course, that influence provoked critics, who blamed Franklin for the materialism of American culture. Having now lost his moral model, we find it hard to comprehend D. H. Lawrence's rage at Franklin as the original self-repressed and self-satisfied philistine, pinching spontaneity as well as pennies—the very font of American Babbitry. Modern readers also do not get the joke in Mark Twain's satire of Franklin as a pedagogical killjoy imposed by stern fathers on "boys who might otherwise have been happy." Twain mused: "He had a fashion of living wholly on bread and water, and studying astronomy at mealtimes—a thing which has brought affliction to millions of boys since, whose fathers had read Franklin's pernicious [auto]biography." Rarely read by children (or parents), the autobiography now belongs to college students, assigned as a way into a lost culture rather than as a guide for contemporary life.

Having reduced Franklin to a kite-flying fool, we are ill-prepared to see that the moralizing Franklin of past centuries was already a truncation

*The First American: The Life and Times of Benjamin Franklin,* by H. W. Brands (Doubleday, 2000)

of a complex, contradictory, and controversial genius. In a clear and sprightly biography, H. W. Brands partially recovers the Franklin who lived before he became a bourgeois icon and long before we trivialized him. Dispensing with scholarly debates, Brands practices popular history: light on analysis but rich in the description of settings, personalities, and action. Consider this example of his breezy style, a summary of the 1730s: "Meanwhile an insidious rationalism—the work of Newton and the other apostles of the Enlightenment—had driven the center of religious gravity from the bowels of believers up toward their brains."

Brands offers an affectionate—indeed, an indulgent—portrait of a great and good man. He observes: "Franklin's story is the story of a man—an exceedingly gifted man and a most engaging one. It is also the story of the birth of American—an America this man discovered in himself, then helped create in the world at large." Depicted as consistently sunny and considerate, Brands's Franklin is superficial: "While others agonized upon life's deep issues, Franklin contented himself with incomplete answers, maintaining an open mind and seeming to skate upon life's surfaces." So, too, does Brands, who rarely attends to the inner contradictions, conflicts, or repressions that might have driven Franklin and perhaps earned him at least a few of his enemies.

Brands advances a double definition of Franklin as "the First American." He was both the foremost colonist of his generation and the earliest to embrace a national identity distinct from Europe's and a politics independent of the British Empire. Brands has far the stronger case for his first sense of Franklin's priority. Until eclipsed by Washington after 1776, no American achieved greater renown and influence. A self-educated polymath endowed with formidable charm and true genius, Franklin became the leading figure in colonial politics, literature, science, and social reform. Born in 1706 into the modest circumstances of an artisanal family in the stagnating seaport of Boston, Franklin soon ran away from his indenture as an apprentice to his brother's newspaper. With impeccable timing, he moved south to Philadelphia, which was just then becoming the most dynamic seaport city in the colonies. By dint of hard work, keen intelligence, and useful friends, Franklin developed a lucrative newspaper and an almanac that combined wit and moralism (no easy task). His impact on American culture was immense and long-lasting. Franklin's greatest creation was his own persona, crafting the first self-made man as public celebrity—a still-powerful and pivotal type in our culture.

Although a religious skeptic, Franklin admired the promotional talents and moral impact of the great revivalist George Whitefield. By publicizing Whitefield's sensational tour and by publishing his sermons and journals, Franklin helped spread the revivals of the Great Awakening through the northern and middle colonies. Of course, he profited handsomely from selling Whitefield's works.

A clever writer as well as an astute businessman, Franklin also developed a cast of comic characters that opened an enduring vein for American humor. Silence Dogood, Poor Richard Saunders, and Polly Baker appear as disarmingly plain folk, the better to convey wicked insights into the follies of social conventions and the pretensions of the pompous elite. Facing her fifth conviction for bearing an illegitimate child, Polly Baker challenged the double standard that allowed her first seducer to escape punishment and to become her judge. Citing her biblical duty to increase and multiply, she concluded: "for its sake, I have hazarded the loss of the public esteem, and have frequently endured public disgrace and punishment; and therefore ought, in my humble opinion, instead of a whipping, to have a statue erected to my memory." A long line of American humorists—from Davy Crockett and Mark Twain to Garrison Keilor—still rework the prototypes created by Franklin.

Once enriched, Franklin gradually retired from business, entrusting his press to a junior partner. Freed from daily commerce, he remade himself again, this time as a public-spirited gentleman. Brands observes: "In the two centuries after his death Franklin would be cited—in praise by some, in scorn by others—as a prototype of the American capitalist. The citation was misleading. Had Franklin possessed the soul of a true capitalist, he would have devoted the time he saved from printing to making money somewhere else. But he did not. For Franklin the getting of money was always a means to an end, never the end itself."

During the 1730s and the 1740s, Franklin helped to found and to lead an array of cultural and philanthropic institutions: the Library Company, the American Philosophical Society, an academy (which later became the University of Pennsylvania), and a network of volunteer fire companies. Within the British Empire, these institutions rendered Philadelphia third only to London and Edinburgh in cultural activity.

Franklin also conducted his celebrated scientific experiments, primarily with electricity, demonstrating that it comprised lightning and could be harnessed to electrocute chickens and turkeys. Published in London and Paris, his scientific reports dazzled European intellectuals, rendering Franklin the most famous of British colonists. A utilitarian at heart, Franklin also applied science to craft inventions meant to improve common life: a lightning rod to protect buildings and a stove to heat them.

Franklin also became Pennsylvania's preeminent politician. Although a weak orator, he could mesmerize individuals and small gatherings with amusing conversation and insightful stories. A fellow politician later remarked: "He is no speaker. . . . He is, however, a most extraordinary man, and tells a story in a style more engaging than anything I ever heard."

In his skill at telling stories to make a political point lightly, Franklin anticipated the art of Abraham Lincoln.

By energizing the Pennsylvania Assembly, Franklin antagonized the colony's English proprietor—Thomas Penn, the choleric son of the saintly founder, William Penn. Determined to protect his vast landholdings from assembly taxation, Thomas Penn directed his appointed governor to veto tax bills that funded frontier defenses. The assembly then sent Franklin to London to lobby Penn. When that failed, Franklin lingered, pressing the imperial bureaucracy to repossess Pennsylvania as a royal colony with a Crown-appointed governor. Foiled a second time, Franklin stayed on to represent the assemblies of Pennsylvania, Georgia, and Massachusetts in arguing against the new British program of colonial taxes and stricter regulations. Frustrated yet again, Franklin returned to Philadelphia, arriving in early 1775, ready to assist the armed revolution against British rule.

Joining the Continental Congress, Franklin took the lead in framing the rebels' foreign-policy initiatives. In 1777, he left for Paris to seek France's military assistance and alliance against their common enemy, the British Empire. Persistent, tactful, and engaging, Franklin dazzled French high society and won the alliance that proved essential to the Americans' military victory. Then, in 1782–83, Franklin led the American commission that negotiated an extraordinarily favorable peace treaty with the British.

In 1785, Franklin returned home in triumph, but he did not accept the quiet retirement that he claimed to covet. Instead, he won election and reelection as the "president" of Pennsylvania's Executive Council (the closest thing to a governor under the state's revolutionary constitution). In 1787, Franklin also represented his state in the convention that met in Philadelphia to draft a new national constitution for the American union. Slowed by age, Franklin played only a minimal role, but he did suggest the pivotal compromise that gave the small states equal representation in the Senate while awarding larger delegations in the House of Representatives to the more populous states.

Retiring from politics in 1788, the increasingly infirm Franklin died two years later, at the age of eighty-four. Even in death, he created a legacy, for his will established a fund to capitalize young and single artisans starting out in business. Having become more legalistic in his old age, Franklin limited the borrowers to those who had "faithfully fulfilled the duties required in their indentures"—something he had evaded as his brother's apprentice. Through repayment with interest, the loans kept the fund growing over the decades. When it matured in 1990, the bicentennial of his death, the fund bestowed $4.5 million on Boston and $2.0 million on Philadelphia (which had less successfully managed its half of the legacy).

Given Franklin's multiple talents and prodigious accomplishments, Brands aptly depicts him as the foremost American of his generation. But the biographer is far less effective at establishing his second sense of Franklin as the "first American": as the earliest to reject British rule. In fact, Franklin was a belated convert to the radical cause of American independence.

Until 1774, Franklin sought a more integrated and more equal empire that invited colonial leaders into new institutions of imperial rule. Beginning in the late 1730s, he cultivated a political expertise and influence beyond Pennsylvania through his appointment as the empire's postmaster for the American colonies. He developed a cosmopolitan perspective transcending the parochialism that limited the politicians of the individual colonies. During the early 1750s, Franklin urged an intercolonial union under British auspices, the better to conquer the French in Canada and the Indians in the Ohio Valley. In Albany in 1754, a convention of colonial delegates endorsed Franklin's plan of union, but their assemblies rejected it, jealously guarding the petty autonomy of the individual colonies.

By strengthening transatlantic, as well as intercolonial, bonds, Franklin meant to render the empire more powerful and permanent. "I should hope too," he wrote, "that by such an union, the people of Great Britain and the people of the Colonies would learn to consider themselves, not as belonging to different communities with different interests, but to one community with one interest." Practicing what he preached, Franklin exulted in the British conquest of Canada "not merely as I am a colonist, but as I am a Briton."

Noting the more rapid population growth of the colonies, Franklin expected that an integrated empire of political equals would gradually and peacefully shift the center of imperial gravity across the Atlantic to America. In 1760, he explained: "I have long been of opinions that the foundations of the future grandeur and stability of the British Empire lie in America; and though, like other foundations, they are low and little seen, they are nevertheless broad and strong enough to support the greatest political structure human wisdom ever yet erected." But this imperial vision appealed neither to most colonists, who increasingly coveted autonomy, nor to the British, who aspired to tighter control over their empire.

Between 1757 and 1774, Franklin spent all but three years in England, making more friends than he retained in the colonies. Smitten by London's sophistication, Franklin delayed returning home and contemplated remaining permanently. He also learned how to play the London game of patronage politics. Pride in himself and in the empire reached new heights in 1762, when he secured the appointment of his son William as royal governor of New Jersey. Franklin also contemplated accepting a rumored position in the imperial bureaucracy as an undersecretary of state for the colonies. And father and son assembled a cartel of colonial and English grandees with political clout to lobby the Crown for a massive land grant involving twenty million acres of fertile land in the Illinois country, then an Indian domain.

Although he opposed the Stamp Tax levied on the colonists in 1765, Franklin scrambled to secure for a political ally, John Hughes, the potentially lucrative post as Pennsylvania's collector. Hughes soon regretted that friendship when a protest mob threatened to dismantle his house and his body. From a safe distance in London, Franklin urged Hughes to hang tough: "a firm loyalty to the Crown and faithful adherence to the government of this nation, which is the safety as well as the honour of the colonies to be connected with, will always be the wisest course for you and I to take, whatever may be the madness of the populace or their blind leaders, who can only bring themselves and country into trouble, and draw on greater burthens by acts of rebellious tendency." In 1765, Franklin lagged far behind the first Americans.

During the imperial crisis of the 1760s and the early 1770s, Franklin undertook an impossible balancing act as a colonial agent seeking favors and concessions from Parliament and the Crown. He needed to represent his constituents, who were increasingly restive under British control, yet not alienate the imperial officials who could deliver redress. Preferring compromise to violence, Franklin opposed both the British taxes and the colonial mobs that violently shut down ports and courts and silenced the champions of law and order. Radical violence alienated British public opinion, complicating his efforts to persuade Parliament that the colonists remained loyal subjects warranting concessions rather than punishment.

While radicals at home pushed for virtual autonomy, Franklin fell a beat behind. Late into the 1760s, he continued to press for Pennsylvania's reconstitution as a royal colony more fully integrated into the empire. Although he opposed the Stamp Tax as provocatively "internal," Franklin suggested that the colonists would accept Parliament's constitutional right to levy "external" taxes, those on imports and exports. Seizing on that artificial distinction, Parliament replaced the Stamp Tax with new duties on commerce, only to discover that, in fact, the colonists did not accept Franklin's formula. Thereafter, both colonial radicals and imperial officials accused Franklin of bad faith. He was suspected, Franklin sighed, "in England of being too much an American, and in

America of being too much an Englishman." Only in January 1774, when the British elite decisively refuted his imperial vision and publicly humiliated him, did Franklin embrace uncompromising resistance to British rule.

At least four years earlier, the radicals had decided that a rupture was unavoidable and better provoked than delayed. In this sense, the title of "first American" better fits the Massachusetts cousins Samuel and John Adams, or the Virginia brothers Arthur and Richard Henry Lee. Impatient with Franklin's temporizing, the Adamses and the Lees regarded Franklin's conversion as opportunistic and insincere. That his son and protégé William Franklin remained loyal to the empire compounded their doubts.

During the revolutionary war, many congressmen felt ambivalent toward Benjamin Franklin. On the one hand, they desperately needed his transatlantic expertise and influence to decipher British politics and to seek a French alliance. On the other hand, they worried that he might sell out their new country to either the British or the French. Only by seeing Franklin as a "late American" rather than the "first American" can we understand the persistent controversies that swirled around his conduct in London and Paris.

Accounting for Franklin's enemies is the least of Brands's concerns. He dismisses them as a few cranks oddly immune to Franklin's charm. In his prologue, he announces: "Franklin's self-effacing style succeeded remarkably; at sixty-eight he had almost no personal enemies and comparatively few political enemies for a man of public affairs." And yet Brands's subsequent pages reveal a steady succession of foes, who often expressed a peculiarly intense detestation.

As an adolescent in Boston, Franklin began to accumulate both admirers and critics. In satirical essays for his brother's newspaper, he ridiculed the town's leading ministers, riling the celebrated Cotton Mather. Appealing to popular prejudices, the Franklin brothers denounced Mather's enlightened attempt to protect Bostonians from deadly smallpox by introducing the new technique of inoculation. For that satire, Benjamin paid a heavy atonement in 1736, when his son Francis died of smallpox. As an old man, Franklin remarked: "I long regretted bitterly, and still regret, that I had not given [smallpox] to him by inoculation."

Franklin's departure from his brother's print shop was abrupt, acrimonious, and illegal. Only eighteen years old, Franklin still had three years to serve on his contract as an apprentice. Fed up with taking orders from his brother and father, he fled to Philadelphia. There he easily made new friends, but he also readily discarded those who became inconvenient. In 1724, he violently quarreled and permanently broke with John Collins, his closest friend, who drank and gambled excessively. The eccentric printer Samuel Keimer hired Franklin, but soon developed a deep distrust that provoked a sudden and contentious discharge. Franklin went into business with a partner, Hugh Meredith, who provided more capital than ability. Their ending was predictable: once their newspaper prospered, Franklin found new investors to oust the disgruntled Meredith. To sell copies of his new almanac, Franklin predicted in print that his chief rival, Titan Leeds, would soon die. When the outraged Leeds refused to cooperate, Franklin depicted him as an imposter masking the real man's death. The gambit (appropriated from Jonathan Swift) was far more amusing to readers than to Leeds.

In 1737, Franklin helped set up a cruel practical joke that victimized Daniel Rees, "a gullible and perhaps mentally impaired apprentice." Exploiting Rees's longing to become a Freemason, some of Franklin's friends staged a phony ceremony meant to mock him. Accidentally doused in flaming brandy during the ceremony, Rees died in agony two days later. Although Franklin did not attend the initiation and was not prosecuted, he reaped heavy criticism for facilitating and encouraging the dangerous charade. "It was hardly Franklin's finest hour," Brands concedes, "and he knew it."

Moving into politics, Franklin accumulated more—and more intense—enemies. In Pennsylvania he feuded with the governors appointed by Thomas Penn. One governor reported: "I really believe there never will be any prospect of ease or happiness here, while that villain has the liberty of spreading about the poison of that inveterate malice and ill nature, which is so deeply implanted in his own black heart." Moving to London, Franklin tangled directly with Thomas Penn. After one especially acrimonious exchange, Penn denounced Franklin for "vile misrepresentation" and refused any further contact. Franklin also offended prominent Crown ministers, principally George Grenville, the First Lord of the Treasury, and Lord Hillsborough, the Secretary of State for the colonies. The latter killed Franklin's bid for a vast land grant in the Illinois country.

In late 1773 and early 1774, Franklin antagonized the British elite by sending stolen letters to the Massachusetts radicals to bolster their waning confidence in his allegiance. Written primarily by Thomas Hutchinson, the royal governor of Massachusetts, the letters urged tighter British restrictions on colonial liberties. Franklin exhorted his correspondent, Thomas Cushing, to show the letters only to trusted associates and, by all means, to keep them out of the press. But Cushing shared the letters with Samuel Adams, who promptly had them published. That publication created an uproar, in Massachusetts against Hutchinson and in Britain against Franklin. By dealing in purloined letters, Franklin had violated the code of honor expected of gentlemen. The royal Privy Council summoned Franklin to a hearing, where the acerbic prosecutor, Alexander Wedderburn, subjected him to an hour of invective and diatribe, to the great applause and amusement of the lords and a gallery of spectators. Two days later, the Crown summarily dismissed Franklin from his office as postmaster general for the colonies. The British newspapers celebrated Wedderburn and denounced Franklin. From this, Brands concludes that the British were "an arrogant people maliciously led."

In May 1775, Franklin returned to an America at war with the British Empire. Two years later, Congress sent Franklin to Paris as a diplomatic commissioner, but provided two fellow commissioners, one the notoriously suspicious Arthur Lee. His complaints and harsh reports to Congress drove Franklin to despair. At last he drafted (but did not send) a rebuke of Lee, expressing "pity for your sick mind, which is forever tormenting itself with jealousies, suspicions and fancies that others mean you ill, wrong you or fail in respect for you. If you do not cure your self of this temper, it will end in insanity." In particular, Franklin abruptly dismissed Lee's suspicions that their secretary, Edward Bancroft, was a British spy. In fact, Bancroft *was* on the British payroll. In 1778, Congress sent to Paris another commissioner, John Adams, who soon came to share Lee's suspicions and added a few of his own. Regarding Franklin as lazy, dissipated, devious, and too accommodating to French interests, Adams blamed him for the many disputes in the American delegation: "Franklin's cunning will be to divide us. To this end, he will provoke, he will insinuate, he will intrigue, he will maneuvre."

Ambitious and powerful men invariably make enemies, but *how* he made his share of enemies warrants more attention. A few aroused Franklin's ire by frustrating his plans and his hard work. Here Thomas Penn was conspicuous, consistently outmaneuvering Franklin in London politics. That Penn was arrogant, callous, and insulting rubbed salt in Franklin's wounds. Not used to losing, Franklin lashed out with an intemperate rage, in stark contrast to the studied moderation that he usually displayed. After 1775, he lavished similar anger on his own son, treating William's loyalty to the empire as a personal betrayal. Despite having defied his own father, Benjamin Franklin pulled patriarchal rank to demand that his son defer to him in politics. He pointedly instructed his son: "*there are natural duties which precede political ones, and cannot be extinguished by them.*" When William refused to obey, Franklin wrote his son off with a complete and stony rejection and did nothing when the rebels arrested and imprisoned him. Instead, he took in William's son—William Temple Franklin—and taught him to despise his father and Britain. After the war, Benjamin rebuffed William's earnest attempts at reconciliation. When denied mastery and control, Benjamin Franklin's equanimity could dissolve into a cold, unforgiving fury.

Most of Franklin's enemies were colleagues who concluded that he was a bit too clever, sly, secretive, flexible, and manipulative. The Philadelphia lawyer John Webbe was typical. In 1740, Franklin approached Webbe to become his partner in a new magazine. Webbe declined, preferring to deal with Franklin's competitor, Andrew Bradford. When Franklin insinuated that Webbe had stolen his idea for a magazine, the lawyer bitterly responded that Franklin practiced "the most mischievous kind of lying; for the strokes being oblique and indirect, a man cannot so easily defend himself against them." Brands acknowledges that "Webbe's complaint presaged many Franklin would hear in the future about his style of attack."

Indeed, Franklin took a special pride in masking his plans and hiding his true feelings. In *Poor Richard's Almanac* he advised, "Let all Men know thee, but no man know thee thoroughly; men freely ford that see the shallows." Franklin meant to ford, never to be forded. He studied personalities closely and applied charm and flattery to cultivate allies and to disarm critics. He readily shared, and even deflected, credit—as long as he achieved his goal. Flexible in tactics and allies, Franklin moved indirectly toward his objectives, which offended more forthright colleagues. John Adams was not alone in wondering if Franklin held any principles dearer than self-gratification.

In a place and time that celebrated sincerity while practicing insincerity, Franklin seemed far too accomplished at the latter. Arthur Lee characterized him as a "false friend." His smooth manner and shifting tactics invited a distrust disproportionate even to Franklin's actual ability and intent to trick. Even when frank and honest—indeed, especially when frank and honest—he aroused suspicion that he must be up to something especially devious. In 1771, Lee insisted that Franklin was subservient to Lord Hillsborough as either his "dupe" or his willing "instrument." Considering further, Lee concluded that Franklin could only be an instrument, never a dupe: "notorious as [Hillsborough] is for ill faith and fraud, his duplicity would not impose on one possessed of half Dr. F[ranklin]'s sagacity." In sum, Franklin paid a price for being so conspicuously clever—and for trying, sometimes, to mask it.

It attests to the power of Franklin's compelling personality that, more than two centuries after his death, his charm still takes captives. Dazzled by Franklin's gifts and usual good humor, Brands cannot bring himself to analyze his subject's darker moments. After reviewing Franklin's clever and deceptive diplomacy with France and Britain, Brands hastily adds: "his was not a personality that reveled in intrigue and artful maneuvering." If not, he certainly fooled his contemporaries.

*17*

# The Good Father

*January 19, 1998*

To the degree that Americans pay any heed to our national origins, it has been a time for Thomas Jefferson. In a documentary, Ken Burns and George Will assure us that Jefferson was the preeminent American of the revolutionary generation. They promote Jefferson into the "man of the millennium," primarily responsible for the global spread of democracy. And following Joseph Ellis's recent biography, they characterize Jefferson as the "American Sphinx" whose riddles we must explore to know ourselves. In his human contradictions, in the collision of his expressions of principle and his moral evasions, Jefferson seems timely and accessible, our flawed representative among the Founding Fathers.

But it was George Washington who once seemed the supreme Founding Father, the true man of the millennium. In the more confident and dutiful public culture of the nineteenth century, Americans revered Washington as their paragon of virtue and integrity and as the symbol of their national union. In 1844, a biography written for young people insisted that "the first word of infancy should be mother, the second father, the third Washington." Later in the century, when a historical novelist crafted a Washington with a few human foibles, an outraged critic responded: "Why this is the very essence of falsehood. Washington was not like other men; and to bring his lofty character down to the level of the vulgar passions of common life, is to give the lie to the grandest chapter in the . . . annals of the human race."

Of course, such panegyrics leave us cold, rendering Washington alien to our antiheroic sensibility precisely because he was so iconic to our predecessors, who believed in heroes on the grand scale. Some recent screenplays, novels, and revisionist histories try to update Washington by "Jeffersonizing" him with petty passions and moral hypocrisies, but these efforts lack conviction and plausibility. Consequently, our Washington continues to languish behind stone monuments or to wither into trivia about his wooden teeth.

*Writings: George Washington,* edited by John Rhodehamel (Library of America, 1997)

Now the Library of America seeks to revive and rescue Washington by publishing a new edition of his writings. Unfortunately, the bare-bones format compromises that purpose. Readers without an expertise in eighteenth-century American history will often feel lost without an editorial introduction and without fuller notes to place the documents in some context. This austerity can work in the other Library of America volumes, dedicated to previously published and widely known works of fiction, but most of Washington's "Writings" consist of private correspondence replete with references and inferences understood by his friends but lost on us without some expert guidance. Many letters would be more revealing if accompanied by their counterparts written to Washington. Readers will often feel frustrated as they follow half of a cryptic dialogue.

Yet the patient reader will find here the materials to reconstruct Washington's remarkable story. With enormous pains and internal struggle, he developed a public persona dedicated to consolidating an imperial union and power in North America. Our national prowess and "imperial presidency" began in George Washington's expansive vision of his own and our potential. In the volume's first document, an adolescent Washington obsessively copied a detailed list of 110 rules of civility: "Let thy carriage be such as becomes a Man Grave, Settled, and attentive to that which is spoken"; "Labour to keep alive in your Breast that Little Spark of Celestial Fire called Conscience." And over the subsequent half-century, Washington mastered himself into an almost perfect presentation of gravity, dignity, and integrity—all despite recurrent battles with despair at his own limitations and frustrations. No American of his century created a greater public reputation or labored more to bear up under its accumulating weight.

As an ambitious young man, Washington linked his personal development and his growing reputation with his understanding of a larger destiny for the colonies. Far earlier and far more consistently than any other colonist, Washington came to think of himself as more than a Virginian. He precociously defined himself as an American; and he imagined a national union on a continental scale and with imperial potential. He hoped that the diverse and fractious colonists could find a common purpose in a shared expansion westward.

In the late 1740s, as a boyish land surveyor on the frontier, and later, during the 1750s, as an army officer, Washington became a staunch advocate of American expansion beyond the Appalachian Mountains into the Ohio valley. Entrusted with Virginia's frontier defense against devastating French and Indian raids, Washington struggled with civilian panic, mutinous soldiers, inept subordinates, inadequate supplies, rampant desertion, and bickering colonies. In 1756, he insisted that "nothing

I more sincerely wish than a union to the Colonys in this time of Eminent danger." Frustrated by colonial pettiness, Washington looked to British military aid and commanders to rescue the colonists from their own shortsighted selfishness. Early in his career, he hoped to pursue his own, and America's, greatness within the British Empire.

In 1759–60, the British, with colonial assistance, conquered Canada, a triumph that seemed to fulfill Washington's imperial vision. But by subsequently taxing Americans to help administer the expanded empire, Britain alienated most of the colonists. Retired to his Virginia plantation at Mount Vernon, Washington struggled to maintain a genteel way of life while encumbered by mounting debts owed to his mercantile creditors in London. Something seemed chronically wrong with the colonies' terms of trade within the empire. Economic frustration rendered the colonists sensitive to the constitutional innovations of their British overlords. In British taxation, Washington detected a plot to hinder American development, to perpetuate the petty subdivision into thirteen distinct colonies, and to seal off the trans-Appalachian west as a reserve for Indians. He saw a link between the "Invasion of our Rights & Priviledges by the Mother Country—& our lives and properties by the Savages." Yet in the widespread colonial anger, Washington also detected a new potential for an American union that could claim its western destiny by asserting independence from the British Empire.

In the spring of 1775, war erupted, and a Continental Congress of delegates from the thirteen colonies assumed effective government in defiance of British rule. Washington's patriotic sentiments, his political weight as a leading Virginian (the largest and wealthiest colony), his military experience, and his prodigious public dignity combined to secure his appointment to command the rebel army. He characteristically explained: "It was utterly out of my power to refuse this appointment without exposing my Character to such censures as would have reflected dishonour upon myself." Determined to construct an army that would embody a new sense of American nationalism, he announced: "They are now the Troops of the United Provinces of North America; and it is hoped that all Distinctions of Colonies will be laid aside." During the long hard war, Washington saw a dual prospect for America: liberation from British constraints and the construction of a union both republican and imperial. He extolled "this glorious revolution" both for "rescuing millions from the hand of oppression and" for "laying the foundation of a great Empire."

As commander, Washington confronted a nearly fatal contradiction. A revolution in the name of liberty demanded extraordinary unity, discipline, and sacrifice from a people who defined their liberty as the unlimited pursuit of individual opportunity. In taking command,

Washington promised his fellow Americans "a firm belief of the justice of our Cause—close attention in the prosecution of it—and the strictest Integrety." Although he delivered on all three promises, too many Americans minimized their own sacrifices while pursuing private profits. He lamented: "for notwithstanding all the public virtue which is ascribed to these people, there is no nation under the Sun (that I ever came across) [that] pay[s] greater adoration to money than they do."

A bitterly divided and chronically weak Congress could procure little material support for the army from the fractious states and from a public that increasingly hoped that someone else would win the war for them. Despite occasional victories and impressive gains in discipline, the Continental Army remained undermanned, poorly fed, clad in rags, divided by state prejudices, and racked by officers' feuds over promotions. Amid the chaos, the greed, and the bungling, Washington found solace and hope in the persistent endurance by a saving remnant among the common soldiers: "To see Men without Cloathes to cover their nakedness, without Blankets to lay on, without Shoes, by which their Marches might be traced by the Blood from their feet, and almost as often without Provisions as with; Marching through frost and Snow . . . and submitting to it without a murmur, is a mark of patience and obedience which in my opinion can scarce be parallel'd."

Washington often blundered as a battlefield tactician, but he mastered the strategic and political essence of his difficult command. Above all, he had to secure respect for himself and the American cause by consistently presenting, in orders, letters, speech, and posture, a persona of utter dignity and self-assurance—no easy task, given his ramshackle army, divided country, and powerful enemy. Washington exhorted his soldiers that "the Eyes of all our Countrymen are now upon us, and we shall have their blessings, and praises, if happily we are the instruments of saving them from the Tyranny meditated against them. Let us therefore animate and encourage each other, and shew the whole world, that a Freeman contending for Liberty on his own ground is superior to any slavish mercenary on earth."

But behind this bravado, he often felt trapped in a hopeless command that would destroy his cherished reputation. In September 1776, in the midst of defeat, he poured out his soul to a relative: "In short, such is my situation that if I were to wish the bitterest curse to an enemy on this side of the grave, I should put him in my stead with my feelings; and yet I do not know what plan of conduct to pursue. I see the impossibility of serving with reputation, or doing any essential service to the cause by continuing in command, and yet I am told that if I quit the command, inevitable ruin will follow from the distraction that will ensue. In confidence I tell you that I never was in such an unhappy, divided state since I was born. By keeping private his despair, Washington preserved, almost miraculously, an unruffled public demeanor that commanded the respect and sustained the hopes of his people. His greatest service and greatest sacrifice was to endure the psychological and emotional toll of this rigid detachment of his public resolve from his private agony. By sheer force of will and by an extraordinary mastery of appearances, he kept alive a suffering army that sustained the Revolution until the fall of 1781, when French military assistance secured the critical victory at Yorktown.

When the British sued for peace, Washington celebrated the victory of America's "steubendous fabrick of Freedom and Empire." But as British rule faded, American state politicians felt freer to ignore and virtually to dismantle their confederation government. Without a common enemy, most Americans were ready to abandon Washington's dream of consolidating a national union and a national identity. He worried: "I see one head gradually changing into thirteen." In 1783, he calmly cowed a potential military coup by disgruntled officers, peacefully demobilized the army, and retired to his civilian life as a Virginia planter.

Admiring his devotion to the republic, and relieved by his ready relinquishment of power, the people revered Washington as their greatest patriot. Yet he nearly became trapped by the monumental reputation that he had nurtured. During the 1780s, as fellow nationalists contended bitterly with the advocates of state autonomy, Washington wished to remain above the fray, untainted by dispute, compromise, and criticism. Having built up enormous influence and popularity, he dreaded their expenditure, even to strengthen the union. He dithered when chosen by the Virginia state legislature to serve as a delegate to the Federal Convention to meet in Philadelphia in the spring of 1787, to frame a new constitution for the faltering nation. Expressing concern for appearances and reputation, he advanced a ludicrous excuse: that he could not attend because he had already declined an invitation to preside over a meeting in that city of the Society of Cincinnati, a controversial organization of retired army officers. He feared "the disrespect it might seem to offer to that Society, to be there on another occasion."

He begged his correspondents to reveal "what the public expectation is on this head—that is whether I will, or ought to be there?" Fortunately for the nation, Washington's fellow delegates refused to take no for an answer. Fortunately for Washington, he immediately became the convention's presiding officer, and so was elevated above entanglement in the debates.

Ratification of the new Constitution brought the inevitable expectation that Washington must become the first president of the new federal government. Unanimously elected, he accepted, but grimly insisted "that my movements to the chair of Government will be accompanied with feelings not unlike those of a culprit who is going to the place of his execution."

To modern, politically cynical eyes, such protestations seem hollow and self-serving. Yet Washington had good reason to dread his new position as the focus of public attention and as the fount of precedents for the new government. He knew that only domestic seclusion could preserve his most difficult and fondest accomplishment: his almost universal reputation as the disinterested patriot with perfect integrity. Inevitably, political strife would erode popular awe.

As the first president over the empire of liberty, Washington created and mastered an almost impossible role that has consumed most of his successors: somehow to appear always, perfectly, and simultaneously imperial and popular. He worried obsessively about how best "to maintain the dignity of Office, without subjecting himself to the imputation of superciliousness or unnecessary reserve." Should he attend private tea parties? How often should he hold state dinners? How many congressmen could he invite on a given occasion "without exciting clamours in the rest of the community"? He sought that perfect balance that would "support propriety of character without partaking of the follies of luxury and ostentation." As in the war, more was at stake than his personal vanity, for he knew that his performance in the presidential role could build the popular respect desperately needed for the new national government. And he regarded the union's survival as essential to "the preservation of the sacred fire of liberty, and the destiny of the Republican model of Government."

Despite the weakness of the government's means, Washington's administration achieved a stunning succession of triumphs. During his eight-year presidency, the United States secured its western frontiers, funded an immense war debt, located a national capital in the new District of Columbia, and surged in economic and population growth. In 1795, he asked Congress: "Is it too much to say, that our country exhibits a spectacle of national happiness never surpassed if ever before equalled?" If peace with prosperity is the measure of presidential administrations, Washington's was the most successful in our nation's history.

Still Washington felt that his accomplishments were obscured and imperiled as federal politics became shrill and partisan. He despaired that Congress behaved "with a warmth & intemperance; with prolixity & threats; which it is to be feared has lessened the dignity of that body, & decreased that respect which was once entertained for it." The partisan rancor seeped into, and intensified within, the newspapers, much to Washington's dismay: "I have brought on myself a torrent of abuse in the factious papers in this country, and from the enmity of the discontented of all descriptions." Partisanship even divided his own cabinet, as Thomas Jefferson, the more democratic Secretary of State, confronted Alexander Hamilton, the more elitist Secretary of the Treasury. In vain, Washington cautioned both men to show "more charity for the opinions and acts of one another."

During the mid-1790s, as France and Britain resumed warfare, the two eighteenth-century superpowers pressured the weaker United States to choose a side. Solicitous of maritime trade, Hamilton favored Britain. Optimistic about the French Revolution, Jefferson tilted toward the new French republic. Determined to preserve the peace, Washington struggled to keep the country united and neutral, but he alienated Jefferson, who assumed leadership of the opposition in Congress, the states, and the newspapers.

Weary of the conflict, Washington retired in the spring of 1797, returning to Mount Vernon to improve his long-neglected plantation. In retirement, he took pride in inspecting the progress of the new national capital nearby on the Potomac River. But he also remained anxious about the fate of the republic under the stewardship of John Adams, his overmatched successor and fellow Federalist. Washington privately seethed as the Jeffersonians criticized every Federalist measure as an alleged plot "to introduce monarchy." He charged the Jeffersonians with "poisoning the minds of our people and to sow dissentions among them, in order to alienate their affections from the Government of their Choice, thereby endeavoring to dissolve the Union." In particular, he denounced the readiness of Jefferson to champion states' rights by threatening nullification to frustrate federal laws. On December 14, 1799, Washington died, and so was spared the mortification of witnessing Jefferson's election to the presidency in early 1801.

Perhaps Washington's greatest accomplishment came with the execution of his last will and testament, which stipulated freedom for all of his slaves on the demise of his widow. Washington also required his heirs "comfortably" to clothe and to feed the elderly blacks and to provide for the education of the young. Like so many of the Founders, Washington had championed liberty while holding blacks in plantation slavery. But he exceeded most of his contemporaries, notably Jefferson, in developing a revulsion for the system of slavery.

In the early documents from the 1760s, Washington appeared as a conventional planter. Without moral qualms, he advertised a reward for runaways and sought to exchange an especially troublesome slave for a consignment of molasses, rum, limes, tamarinds, and sweetmeats. But the Revolution taught Washington a greater sensitivity to the plights and the rights of the enslaved. Patriot leaders hyperbolically charged the British with a plot to enslave the colonists. Although Washington subscribed to this rhetoric, he recognized the Americans' own tyranny. He feared that continued British rule would render the colonists "as tame & abject Slaves, as the Blacks we Rule over with such arbitrary Sway."

More than most planters, Washington provided generous clothing, housing, and provisions for his slaves. And, beginning in the early 1780s, he would neither sell his slaves nor buy new ones. Owning more than he could profitably employ, Washington suffered a prolonged financial drain as a consequence of his principled determination to avoid selling slaves "as you would do cattle in the market." To sustain his plantation and to keep intact his slave families and community, Washington had to raise funds by selling off most of his frontier lands in the Ohio Valley, lands that he had painstakingly acquired at the Indians' expense during the 1760s. Indian dispossession later helped to fund Washington's attempts to do right by his slaves. Such were the paradoxes of race, property, and conscience in revolutionary America.

Unlike Jefferson, who notoriously asserted black racial inferiority, Washington readily recognized and applauded talents among the enslaved. In 1776, he received a poem from a young woman and, "with a view of doing justice to her great poetical Genius, I had a great Mind to publish the Poem." Grateful for the gift, he invited her to visit his headquarters in Cambridge. The poet was the now-famous Phillis Wheatley. In writing of and to her, Washington made no reference to her race: a remarkable omission by the standards of his day (and of our own). Of course, he especially contrasted with Jefferson, who sought to demonstrate black inferiority by mocking the quality of Wheatley's poetry.

In private correspondence during the 1780s and the 1790s, Washington repeatedly expressed a devout hope that the state governments would legislate "a gradual Abolition of Slavery; It would prevent much future Mischief." Like Jefferson, though, Washington was unwilling to expend his formidable political capital openly to lead so controversial a cause in Virginia. Nor did he advance emancipation in national politics. He detested the interstate and international slave trade, but he supported southern congressmen, who rejected the petitions by Quakers to terminate both immediately. Like other prominent Virginians with misgivings about slavery, Washington preferred to avoid political confrontation by confining emancipation to his own slaves and to the moment of his widow's death.

From our vantage in time, Washington's actions may seem painfully limited; but by the standards of his century and state, he was remarkable for his willingness to subordinate racism and self-interest to a recognition of common humanity. If Jefferson reminds us of the moral contradictions and racial injustice manifest in our national origins, then it is Washington who exemplifies the possibilities that individuals can grow and recognize their own responsibilities to promote racial justice.

*18*

# The Founding Swindlers

*June 26, 2000*

The great planters of eighteenth-century Virginia have long enjoyed a romantic and patriotic allure for living in grand mansions and for leading the American Revolution to victory. Freshly painted and carefully manicured, Monticello, Mount Vernon, and Gunston Hall shimmer in our eyes and our imaginations as pristine stages for the lost world of our moral and political superiors. The heroic version of the Founding Fathers dates to the new generation of the early nineteenth century. In 1817, William Wirt, an ambitious Virginia lawyer, wrote a fawning history of Patrick Henry and his compatriots. Wirt demanded: "Were not these men, giants in mind and heroism? Compared with them, what is the present generation, but a puny race of dwarfs and pigmies?"

We continue to ask the same self-flagellating question. Charles Royster, however, quotes Wirt for ironic effect, because *The Fabulous History of the Dismal Swamp Company* leads us into the private lives and sordid business practices of the Virginia gentry to find an interlocking web of illusions, deceptions, and evasions. Royster depicts the standard great events of eighteenth-century America, including the Seven Years' War, the colonial resistance to British taxes, the War for Independence, and the early republic. But, as if by refocusing our lens, these affairs of state appear diminished because subordinated to the deceptive wheeling and dealing that usually preoccupied the gentry.

Cast in a harsh new light, eighteenth-century Virginia reappears as a tawdry landscape of human folly. Royster describes Norfolk, for example, as the very antithesis of our pristine Colonial Williamsburg: "Flimsy new buildings lined crooked, narrow, dirt streets. . . . New clapboard warehouses among the wharves—some stood three stories high—were bigger than most residences and stores but just as ugly. Construction followed no design, creating a maze of lanes and alleys. Raw sewage ran in open ditches bridged by narrow planks. Near the river a stench hung over the city, especially at low tide."

*The Fabulous History of the Dismal Swamp Company: A Story of George Washington's Times,* by Charles Royster (Alfred A. Knopf, 1999)

A distinguished professor of history at Louisiana State University, Royster has written three prize-winning books, each a profound meditation on the interplay of warfare and the American character. In *The Fabulous History,* he turns from war to land speculation to find a new key to our national origins. George Washington, Patrick Henry, Thomas Jefferson, Benjamin Franklin, Alexander Hamilton, Aaron Burr, James Wilson, and Robert Morris were all avid speculators, but more often than not, their estates eventually collapsed into bankruptcy because of excessive acquisitions in miserable locations—like the Great Dismal Swamp.

Eighteenth-century fortunes rested on shaky foundations of bad debts—both owed to, and owed by, every man of apparent property and probity. Prominent Virginians procrastinated in paying their debts while living far beyond their means. Meanwhile, they kept compulsively adding new debts to build an expanding network of undercapitalized land companies. Robert Beverly explained that his fellow Virginians lived by "being in Debt & making great Promises for the future." Surely, they reasoned, the next, bigger land speculation would recoup every gamble and retire every debt in one colossal score. The grandest speculations involved millions of acres and functioned like pyramid schemes, requiring new marks to invest at a premium before the original debt became due. In the end, almost no one—except the lawyers like Wirt—outran the approaching wave of crushing debt. Eventually, impatient and desperate creditors consigned a surprising number of apparently wealthy gentlemen to a debtors' prison or to a dotage of genteel poverty.

Exploiting their political connections, eighteenth-century gentlemen cheaply purchased government title to thousands of acres of Indian lands. After expelling the natives, the speculators expected to grow rich by retailing land to the common settlers, who would turn the forest into productive farmland. On a vast, fertile continent, with a population doubling every twenty-five years, American land speculation seemed a sure path to riches—provided the locations were good. As a young man, George Washington recognized that "the greatest Estates we have in this Colony were made . . . by taking up & purchasing at very low rates the rich back Lands which were thought nothing of in those days, but are now the most valuable Lands we possess." Resolved to become richer, Washington accumulated political offices and allies, obtaining the leverage to procure an array of lands in the Great Dismal Swamp and the Ohio Valley.

To curry favor with Britain's imperial government, colonial land speculators usually promised that their schemes would lead to the massive cultivation of hemp—which eighteenth-century governments valued to make rope for shipping rather than dreaded as marijuana for smoking. Almost nothing came of these projects, because Russian hemp remained cheaper and better for rope; but the colonial speculators kept patriotically promising to save the Royal Navy from its dependence on a foreign supplier. So characteristic of their age, the hemp projects combined pipe dreams with remarkably detailed (albeit wildly unrealistic) calculations of all the (small) costs and (stupendous) benefits.

The projectors even saw an opportunity in the Great Dismal Swamp, a watery tract of approximately nine hundred square miles located along the Virginia–North Carolina border. The swamp both alarmed and intoxicated visitors. “Moving into the swamp,” Royster writes, “one waded in standing water the color of tea. Farther in, bamboo among the trees grew more thickly. Vines climbed trunks and hung from branches above huge, intricate ferns. Clouds of mosquitoes were so large as to make it hard to guess what kept all of them alive.” The Great Dismal Swamp hosted a complex and intense array of vibrant life and frequent death: “In the night, frogs and bats consumed part of the vast population of insects. In summer, blood-sucking horse flies swarmed. Large mosquitoes hovered in thick clouds. Barred owls preyed on shrews and mice. . . . Dense growths of tall bamboo hung in broad arches. On these, snakes sometimes sunned themselves—copperheads or a water snake exposing its bright red underside. Water snakes consumed fish and fell prey in turn to long king snakes.” In the teeming and predatory swamp, Royster finds a metaphor for the tangled connections and unscrupulous intrigues of the Virginia elite.

With good cause, colonial farmers bypassed the Great Dismal Swamp to settle on drier and more elevated land. But all of that cheap real estate, so conveniently close to the seaport at Norfolk, teased the greedy imaginations of ambitious men, who calculated the profits of draining the swamp to procure fertile farmland for retail sale to farmers. Here, Royster hints, we find the origins of the enduring American talent for selling swampland, bridges, Web sites, and foreign wars to dupes.

During the 1720s, the great planter and writer William Byrd first proposed to drain and clear the swamp by employing enslaved Africans to dig ditches and fell the immense trees, producing boards, shingles, pine tar, hemp, cattle, and more slaves as by-products. Nothing came of this project until 1763—nearly two decades after Byrd’s death—when twelve grandees, including George Washington, founded the Dismal Swamp Company. They promised to raise hemp, persuaded the colony of Virginia to grant them title to the swamp, and assembled fifty slaves to dig and chop amid clouds of voracious insects. Over the next decade, the slaves’ hard labor made barely a dent in the immense and resistant landscape, which consumed slave lives and speculator money. The slaves produced bundles of shingles and clapboards—but almost no hemp and little drained land.

The War of the American Revolution dispersed the slaves and paralyzed the company, as some partners embraced and led the independence movement while others remained loyal to the British Empire. Revived during the late 1780s, the Dismal Swamp Company continued to drain the partners of funds rather than the swamp of water. Fed up, Washington sold his shares, seemingly for a great profit. Of course, the buyer was yet another speculator who never paid his debt, eventually obliging the frustrated Washington to reclaim the shares. By abandoning land draining in favor of timber cutting, the company at last began to turn a profit in 1810—eleven years after Washington's death.

The Dismal Swamp Company, however, is less the subject of Royster's book than an excuse to pursue a kaleidoscopic array of digressions suggested by fortuitous, and often tenuous, connections to the twelve partners—and dozens of their friends, relatives, acquaintances, and enemies. For most of this hefty tome, the swamp and the company recede into the background as hundreds of stray threads become the real fabric of the book. Ranging far beyond the swamp, the company, and Virginia, Royster's narration extends around and across the Atlantic to the West Indies, West Africa, the Gulf of St. Lawrence, London, and the coal mines of Wales.

Francis Farley was a West Indian sugar planter who invested in the Dismal Swamp, which invites Royster to describe, in succession and great detail, the Caribbean island of Antigua, the processes of cultivating cane and making sugar, and Farley's brothers. A decade later, Farley's daughter Eleanor married Capt. John Laforey, of the Royal Navy—which leads Royster to recount the captain's prior naval career, including a long description of the British conquest of the French fortress of Louisburg on Cape Breton Island in 1758. Two other company partners, the merchants Anthony Bacon and Samuel Gist, moved to England—which encourages Royster to explore, at length, insurance underwriting, parliamentary politics, and the London stage. In addition to the melodramatic Sarah Siddons, celebrated London performers included "the Amazing Learned Pig," who used his mouth to arrange cards bearing letters and numbers into apparent answers to questions.

Few of these far-flung people, places, and animals directly bear on Royster's starting point—the Dismal Swamp Company—to which he sporadically returns to start a fresh chain of distant connections. He cleverly entitles one chapter, "The Last Voyage of the Slave Ship *Hope*," but the vessel merely provides a nicely ironic name and a shaggy dog for the chapter's rambling narrative. One third of the way into the chapter, the ship becomes wrecked off the coast of Africa, far short of its Virginia destination. Proceeding without the *Hope,* the chapter discusses a royal governor of Virginia, spring flooding in the colony, the trade in convicted

English felons, a depression in London trade, a hurricane in Antigua, and the provocative British tax on tea shipped to the colonies.

Apparently setting aside no fact and no anecdote, Royster seems to weave every one of his research notes into his book—which turns thick and heavy, given the prodigious dimensions of his learning and research. Readers enter dense thickets of obscure names and extraneous details:

> As Gist grew acquainted with his fellow underwriters, he could survey the room and review any number of stories telling how diverse men had come to Lloyd's: Samuel Chollet, once Bourdieu's clerk, now his partner; Robert Bogle, Sr., in the Virginia trade; Joshua Mendes da Costa, who subscribed policies in the Portuguese trade and others; William Devaynes, newly returned from the Gold Coast and soon to be director of the East India Company; John Nutt, heavily involved in the Georgia and South Carolina trade; John Shoolbred, not yet thirty, like Angerstein a rapidly rising young man, cutting an ever bigger figure in the Canada trade and the African slave trade; a merchant in Mark Lane with Shoolbred, the policy broker Thomas Bell, not to be mistaken for Captain Thomas Bell, a merchant and insurance broker in Aldermanbury near St. Paul's, who "had the Good Luck to be call'd Honest Thom Bell, in Distinction to another who frequented Loyds Coffee House."

Except for Gist, none of these men invested in the Dismal Swamp Company, and few reappear later in *The Fabulous History*. Such paragraphs, replete with asides, compose much of the book.

Confronted with disparate details from the past, historians ordinarily make hard choices: what to omit; what to include; and in what sequence. In these choices, they heed their fundamental assumptions and their governing ideas. But Royster seems to have abandoned selectivity, sequence, and order. Experimenting in a free-form history without an overt argument, he never explains his evidence, methods, and conclusions. With remarkable consistency, he provides no commentary and no analysis, no introduction, and no conclusion to guide the reader.

Writing ominously and allusively, Royster hints and teases without committing himself. On January 1, 1777, William Byrd Jr., a member of the company, died of unknown cause. Many years later, a friend named David Meade vaguely lamented that Byrd's gambling led to "poverty, want, misery and often suicide." Royster cryptically adds: "This was as close as Meade could bring himself to recording that Byrd had killed himself, and Meade came closer than anyone else." And this is as close as Royster comes to telling us whether Byrd committed suicide. Later, in discussing the unpopularity in rural Virginia of the new federal Constitution, Royster remarks: "During the war, the Virginia authorities had thought Nansemond [County] people were Tories, while the British had considered them rebels. Electing delegates to the ratifying convention, they did not expect impending ruin and anarchy in the absence of the new Constitution, or they did not care." Or Royster does not care. Here, as throughout, the style is breezy, evocative, noncommittal, and cynical.

Perhaps Royster's rambling detail is something more than self-indulgence. Apparently by perverse design, he means to force readers to find their own pattern in the welter of particulars. He seems determined to counter the dominant mode of scholarship where a hard and repetitive argument overwhelms the many nuances and crosscurrents in the historical context. Swinging to the other extreme, he abandons structure for a Rabelaisian profusion of detail.

Closely read, the book does imply patterns through the repetition of similar quotations and episodes. The apparently erratic wandering through topics, places, and names implicitly highlights the integration of the eighteenth-century Atlantic world through the nexus of sailing ships and correspondence. The steady circulation of people, news, and goods linked London underwriters, African slave merchants, West Indian sugar planters, Royal Navy captains, and Virginia land speculators in complex webs of credit and debt. The schemes and evasions of Virginians echoed around the Atlantic rim.

Patient readers will also detect the intricate family interconnections of the Virginia gentry through both marriage and investment in interlocking land speculations. Newly arrived in Virginia, a young woman warned her sister: "[The Virginians] are all Brothers, Sisters, or Cousins; so that if you use one person in the Colony ill, you affront all." Marriages built family alliances that encouraged the construction of land companies. Dr. Thomas Walker married a cousin to George Washington, whose sister married Fielding Lewis. All three men became partners in the Dismal Swamp Company. Along with John Robinson and Peter Jefferson (Thomas's father), Dr. Walker also founded the even more ambitious Loyal Company, which meant to monopolize Virginia's western lands, including much of Kentucky. Lewis and Washington invested in the rival Ohio Company with equally colossal ambitions. Royster remarks: "Had Virginia's land companies been a spiderweb, Dr. Walker would have been the spider." And so would John Robinson or George Washington.

Although Royster scrupulously avoids offering editorial comments, he does employ, as a sort of Greek chorus, a succession of quotations that reiterate his apparent themes: nothing was what it seemed; everyone chronically deceived himself and cheated others; and, in the end, only the pursuit of money (and the evasion of creditors) mattered to anyone in eighteenth-century Britain and its colonies. In 1768, a royal official announced: "the Rapacity of the Land Jobbers in Virginia is insatiable." During the 1780s, a traveler insisted that Virginia's frontier settlers were "abused by the dreams of enthusiasts, and the falsehoods of knaves."

In 1789, a Frenchman described Virginians as "indolent, unindustrious, poor credit risks, big gamblers, tricksters." Lamenting corruption in the House of Burgesses, one member assured an outsider: "You know little of the Plots, Schemes, and Contrivances that are carried on there; in short, one holds the Lamb while the other skins; many of the Members are in Places of Trust and Profit, and others want to get in, and they are willing to assist one another in passing their Accounts." With more concise wit, William Byrd observed: "Our land produces all the fine things of Paradise, except innocence."

Royster also conveys his sensibility by narrating with evident delight the disasters reaped by almost all of his characters as the fruits of their delusions. In grim detail, a succession of company partners succumb to drink, insanity, death, and bankruptcy. In 1766, a judgmental bolt of lightning destroyed six warehouses, stuffed with merchandise, all the property of Robert Tucker, a Norfolk merchant and a partner in the Dismal Swamp Company. Shattered, Tucker promptly lost his sanity and dwindled into a death that revealed an insolvency at odds with his conspicuous display of wealth. Conveniently for Royster, another member of the company observed, as Tucker's obituary: "We are often deceived by Appearances."

One of the book's running, sardonic jokes is the naïveté of all its characters. Everybody foolishly assumes that partners, debtors, or marks are solvent—despite the insistent evidence revealed at every death that everyone milked his credit far beyond any sane limit. The most notorious failure was John Robinson, the consummate Virginia politician of the 1750s and the 1760s. As both the speaker of the House of Burgesses and the treasurer of the colonial government, Robinson controlled patronage, funding, and oversight: a reckless combination. In 1766, his death suddenly exposed his estate to a scrutiny that revealed his shocking embezzlement of 100,000 pounds in public funds, which Robinson had lent, usually without security, to his friends. No wonder he had been the most popular politician in the colony.

Almost all of the book's characters belonged to the genteel classes of enhanced status and sufficient credit to live in the grand style. Ordinary folk, including slaves, appear only occasionally and as the objects of elite action or neglect. The few who are named and characterized merely display scruffier versions of the elite vices. In 1764, the individual partners provided slaves to the company: "Robert Burwell offered a couple in their twenties: Jack and his wife, Venus. Jack was tall and slim, Venus short and stout. They had in common a gift for fast, smooth talk. They did not look like people who would devote themselves to draining a swamp; they looked like people Burwell wished to get rid of at his partners' expense." On the one hand, Royster avoids the cant of finding noble resistance in every slave; on the other hand, he never detects it in any slave. Mostly, he just does not bother with them.

As the narrative roams around the Atlantic, Royster finds human nature much the same in all settings and among all peoples, slave or free, African or European. On the west coast of Africa, the native Fante merchants eagerly and shrewdly bartered slaves to the British, often getting the best of the mutual cheating. A British official considered the Fante "the most rapacious set of People on earth," which was quite a compliment, given the competition from London underwriters and Virginia speculators. Another Briton whined that the Fante "think it meritorious to Cheat a White man all that lyes in their power."

In effect, Royster establishes a moral equivalency between every people at the lowest common denominator. Consequently, the great political movements of the eighteenth century appear trivial: mere variations on the theme of universal, immutable human corruption. In Royster's narration, the Revolutionary War was primarily an orgy of plundering, burning, and cheating—an escalation of previous forms of bad behavior. Col. Fielding Lewis complained: "every man now trys to ruen his neighbour." The Revolution's rhetoric of collective self-sacrifice quickly proved a hollow sham. Immediately after the war, Royster notes, "many Virginians resumed the habit of spending more money than they possessed; while others newly experimented with buying more than they could afford."

The Revolution established an independent American republic, which merely enhanced the greedy ambitions of the land speculators and commercial profiteers who dominated both the state and national governments. Royster writes: "Charles William Janson arrived in America from England in the summer of 1793. Thirteen years later, he realized that he had been duped at every turn." Under the new regime, as in the old, elections pivoted on vice rather than virtue. In 1794, Francis Walker, the alcoholic son of Dr. Thomas Walker, ran for Congress from Virginia but lost. Royster wryly observes: "A shrewd candidate kept the voters drunk, not himself."

Robert Morris dominates the last two chapters—although the Dismal Swamp Company was virtually the only speculative venture he did *not* plunge into. A wealthy Philadelphia merchant and a United States senator, Morris pursued riches on a continental scale. During the early 1790s, with two equally reckless partners, he tried to corner the market on real estate in the new national capital, Washington City. The partners also cheaply purchased over six million acres of frontier land—mostly swamps and barren mountains—in scattered tracts from Georgia to New York. Quantity mattered more than quality, for Morris expected to unload his holdings on distant and naïve Europeans, who had never seen the tracts.

Paying little or nothing down, Morris and his partners counted on selling for a profit before their debts became due. When Europeans refused to play the fool, Morris and his partners were ruined. In 1798, he landed in Philadelphia's prison for debtors, where he lived for three years.

Royster has written an often opaque satire on both the artificiality of eighteenth-century life *and* the futility of standard scholarship to capture the delusions of the past. Consider the book's title. *The Fabulous History of the Dismal Swamp Company: A Story of George Washington's Times* cleverly resembles the misleading prospectus of an eighteenth-century land speculation that promised fields of hemp but delivered a swamp. For *The Fabulous History* is only sporadically about the Dismal Swamp Company; Washington looms no larger than another twenty characters; and there is none of the plot structure, building to a transforming climax, that usually characterizes a "story."

In quoting David Hume, Royster comes closest to explaining *The Fabulous History.* Noting the political opportunist John Wilkes, Hume sarcastically observed: "I am delighted to see the daily and hourly Progress of Madness and Folly and Wickedness in England. The Consummation of these Qualities are the true Ingredients for making a fine Narrative in History." Taking Hume literally, Royster presents a catalog of unrelenting human folly. The blizzard of names, places, dates, events, companies, and schemes eventually blurs into a common mass of corruption and waste. Minor variations on the same basic theme, the dozens of characters eventually become a composite: the land speculator as addicted gambler. Robert Morris just happened to live a generation after William Byrd; George Washington was no better than Samuel Gist. Initially amusing, the multiple episodes of deceit eventually become dispiriting, for want of any counterexamples of decency and hope.

Royster's cumulative effect perversely acquits the Virginia elite of moral hypocrisy. If no better than others, they were at least no worse, given the pervasively lousy state of humanity. If the Virginians cannot be awarded extra credit for the Declaration of Independence, they also cannot be faulted for cheating their creditors and keeping slaves—for they were simply acting out their very human nature. In the end, Royster leaves us with an implicit version of the current apology for corrupt or philandering American politicians: that everyone does it.

*19*

# Pluribus

*June 30, 1997*

Patriotism teaches Americans to revere icons detached from their historical content and imbued with a symbolic power far beyond their original significance. In Philadelphia, we throng to see the Liberty Bell as if it played a critical role in the struggle for independence. And in Plymouth, Massachusetts, we admire a nondescript rock enclosed in a pavilion, because a nineteenth-century antiquarian arbitrarily declared that Pilgrims had stepped on it in 1620. And so it is with the parchment called the Declaration of Independence and displayed in the rotunda of the National Archives in a triptych with the Constitution and the Bill of Rights. How many of the millions who visit the shrine have read the entire Declaration?

At best, they know part of one celebrated sentence in the second paragraph: "We hold these truths to be self-evident, that all men are created equal, that they are endowed by their Creator with certain unalienable Rights, that among these are Life, Liberty and the pursuit of Happiness.—That to secure these rights, Governments are instituted among Men, deriving their just powers from the consent of the governed." Mischievous pollsters and sociologists periodically have fun at the public's expense by quizzing citizens to identify a part of that paragraph's conclusion: "when a long train of abuses and usurpations, pursuing invariably the same Object evinces a design to reduce [the people] under absolute Despotism, it is their right, it is their duty, to throw off such Government." Unable to recognize or endorse that sentiment, many Americans erroneously assume the words derive from *The Communist Manifesto.*

In her new book, Pauline Maier argues that our nation's revolutionary documents have been subdued by reverence and spectacle. The Declaration of Independence, the Constitution, and the Bill of Rights "are encased in massive, bronze-framed, bulletproof glass containers filled

*American Scripture: Making the Declaration of Independence,* by Pauline Maier (Alfred A. Knopf, 1997)

with inert helium gas." Although labeled "Charters of Freedom," they have been imprisoned: flanked by day by military guards dressed in black and lowered at night "into a vault of reinforced concrete and steel that . . . is twenty-two feet deep, weighs fifty-five tons, and was built . . . in 1952, when the Cold War was beginning to make bomb shelters something of a fashion."

An astute and accomplished historian, Maier finds the scene disturbing. For a scholar so committed to precision and complexity, what torture could be greater than to wait in line overhearing tourists' reverential misunderstandings of history as they stare raptly at the shrine and its surrounding mural? "To me the vital documents themselves seemed pretty dead. In fact, the spectacle had the air of a state funeral." Maier concludes: "The original, signed texts of the Declaration of Independence and, to a lesser extent, the Constitution have become for the United States what Lenin's body was for the Soviet Union, a tangible remnant of the revolution to which its children can still cling."

With a special tenacity and a thoroughly American optimism, Maier sets out to liberate and to enliven the document by writing an accessible history of its origins and its later transformation. In this carefully researched and thoughtfully written book, she persuasively argues that the Declaration began in 1776 as a revolutionary manifesto, but was reconceived in the mid-nineteenth century as a sanctified foundation document for our empire of liberty. By recovering both the making and the remaking, she means for next year's tourists to understand the complex history behind the glass.

Maier balks at the romantic tradition that highlights an individual genius in both the original drafting (Thomas Jefferson) and the subsequent reinvention (Abraham Lincoln). She deems Jefferson "the most overrated person in American history . . . because of the extraordinary adulation (and, sometimes, execration) he has received and continues to receive." Misled by his exaggerated claims to almost exclusive authorship, many American pundits confuse Jefferson with "an incarnation of the American nation." Viewers who endured Ken Burns's ponderous and hagiographic film will know what she means. Maier has a higher regard for Lincoln, but she does not share Garry Wills's view that Lincoln alone transformed the Declaration of Independence into our sacred text by the great, single act of writing the Gettysburg Address. As a social historian of politics, Maier deemphasizes the lone, great intellectual and, instead, reasserts the collective influence of the "words and thoughts of many people."

To whittle down Jefferson's role to mortal dimensions, Maier reconstructs the complex social and political context of 1775–76, when a civil war erupted within thirteen North American colonies of the British

Empire. The war mobilized thousands of common farmers and mechanics and women—as well as the more famous "Founding Fathers," who, as delegates to the Continental Congress, governed the rebelling colonies. The congressmen faced an almost impossible task: to concoct from scratch a government with an army and navy capable of defending the long seaboard and an equally extended frontier against the world's most powerful empire, which retained the support of about a fifth of the colonists as Loyalists.

War erupted in April 1775, but for the rest of that year most congressmen and their constituents clung to a hope that the British would back down by withdrawing their troops, their taxes, and their commercial restrictions. Had they done so, the colonists could have remained within a commercial empire while enjoying domestic autonomy. But the king and Parliament refused to relent. During the summer and fall of 1775, they rejected the Congress's petition for redress; declared the colonists rebels; dispatched to America thousands of additional troops, including provocative Hessian mercenaries from Germany; blockaded transatlantic commerce; impressed colonial sailors into the Royal Navy; burned three substantial coastal towns; encouraged Virginia's slaves to run away; and recruited Indians to attack frontier settlements.

The British war measures outraged most Americans, undercutting the cautious congressmen and emboldening the radicals who promoted independence. To increase popular pressure on the cautious, in the spring of 1776, congressional radicals encouraged colonies and localities to adopt resolutions endorsing independence. One of Maier's greatest accomplishments is the recovery of some ninety examples of these "other Declarations of Independence" from May and June of 1776. "Most have been forgotten under the influence of our national obsession" with a single, national, and sacred Declaration of Independence. The local declarations include the resolves of New York mechanics, Pennsylvania militiamen, Massachusetts town meetings, Virginia county conventions, and South Carolina grand juries.

In general, these documents express the American cause in concise, clear, and forceful language. New York City's mechanics asked how Americans could remain subject to a monarch "who is deaf to our petitions for interposing his Royal authority in our behalf, and for redressing our grievances, but . . . seems to take pleasure in our destruction." The Boston town meeting asserted that "for the prayer of peace" the king had "tendered the sword; for liberty, chains; and for safety, death." Most of these local declarations anticipated the national Declaration by combining a philosophical preface with a bill of indictment against King George III, concluding with a formal commitment to independence.

By recovering the influence of the earlier local declarations, Maier effects two major shifts in our perspective on the national Declaration. First, she ends its grand isolation by placing it in a thick social context as the culmination of a great popular political movement involving thousands of common Americans, as well as the Founding Fathers. Second, she reasserts the central importance, in both the local and the congressional declarations, of the charges against the king. Although those charges dominate the Declaration of July 4, they have been slighted in twentieth-century scholarship because of a preoccupation with the document's eloquent and philosophical preface. Recent historians of the congressional Declaration have plumbed for the contents of Jefferson's mind, emphasizing his reading in British political philosophy. Then these scholars have split hairs over whether John Locke or Francis Hutcheson had the greater influence on Jefferson.

Maier demonstrates the much more immediate influence of the grassroots declarations on Jefferson's draft. In particular, he admired, and appropriated much from, George Mason's "Declaration of Rights," recently drafted for Virginia and published in a Philadelphia newspaper. Mason wrote: "That all men are born equally free and independant, and have certain inherent natural rights, of which they cannot, by any compact, deprive or divest their posterity; among which are the enjoyment of life and liberty, with the means of acquiring and possessing property, and pursuing and obtaining happiness and safety." In the celebrated second paragraph of the Declaration, Jefferson would express the same cluster of ideas in more concise and forceful clarity. And because the local declarations informed Jefferson's thinking and primed the colonists' expectations, they universally regarded the enumerated charges against the king as the very essence of the Declaration. In 1776, both Patriots and Loyalists said little about the preface because they considered it commonplace rhetoric.

The local declarations strengthened the hand of the radicals, who pressed Congress to act. Led by John Adams of Massachusetts, Congress took a giant step toward independence on May 15, by authorizing and encouraging the colonies individually to draft and adopt republican constitutions, thus effectively rejecting the authority of the British Empire. In a second great leap forward, on June 7, Richard Henry Lee of Virginia introduced a resolution that Congress declare independence, seek foreign allies, and form a permanent confederacy of the new states. Congress put off a decision until the end of the month, but, in the interim, it appointed a five-man committee headed by Adams to draft a declaration of independence.

Four of the committee members, including Adams, possessed such daunting executive responsibilities for conducting the critical war effort that they had no time to write a declaration. Deeming the task relatively insignificant, they assigned the drafting to their most junior and most silent colleague, the shy and defensive Thomas Jefferson. He had the further recommendations of being their best political writer and of hailing from Virginia, the most important colony.

Historians have generally followed Jefferson's self-serving, late-life reminiscences in reconstructing the poorly documented process of drafting the Declaration. He claimed to have created the document virtually alone, with only token contributions from the rest of his committee. He also insisted that when congressmen got hold of his draft on July 3 and 4, they "mangled" it, lopping off the best quarter of his words. Maier challenges Jefferson's claims by recovering the important contributions of the other committee members, especially the astute Benjamin Franklin, and by demonstrating the constructive editing role performed by Congress as a whole.

Jefferson was not the lone, creative author that he later claimed to be. As was the common practice of eighteenth-century writers, especially those pressed for time, he freely appropriated ideas and language from other texts, including his own pamphlet, *A Summary View of the Rights of British America* (1774) and, especially, George Mason's recent "Declaration of Rights" for Virginia. Eighteenth-century intellectuals cherished clever reworking rather than the spontaneous invention subsequently celebrated by nineteenth-century romanticism's cult of the original genius.

Jefferson's draft was of mixed quality: an eloquent preface and a spirited concluding sentence braced a long, turgid, and vague litany of supposed grievances against the king. Maier observes that much of Jefferson's draft "left observers, then and now, scrambling to figure out what it was talking about." Especially implausible was his diatribe entirely blaming the slave trade on the British king. This was a rather odd argument for a Virginia slaveholder to press, but it is Jefferson's longest, most impassioned, and ultimate charge in his twenty-one count indictment. Maier notes that he "meant it to be the emotional climax of his case against the King." Instead, it embarrassed his colleagues, most of whom either owned slaves or came from colonies that profited from their commerce. They had the good sense to drop Jefferson's final charge rather than call attention to the contradiction of preaching liberty while practicing slaveholding. In sum, Maier finds Jefferson's draft inferior to its shorter and more direct local prototypes: "From a comparative perspective, it is difficult to avoid the conclusion that the states and localities had offered a more effective case for Independence."

On June 28, the committee reported Jefferson's draft to Congress, which, on July 1, took up the business of declaring independence. Maier carefully distinguishes Congress's votes to declare independence on July 1 and 2 from its authorization on July 4 of the document known as the Declaration of Independence. By restoring the chaotic drama of Congress in 1776, she corrects the legendary depictions of magisterial dignity, solemnity, and patience. During the first week of July, Congress was in ominous suspense over a deteriorating military situation. The disease-ridden northern army had been routed in Canada, and British armadas had recently appeared off Charleston and New York City. Given the power gathering against the Americans' weak defenses, it was a most inauspicious moment to declare independence. Indeed, the congressmen were desperate gamblers; for, if Britain ultimately prevailed, their declaration would mark them as traitors deserving execution. Meanwhile, the immense difficulties and the innumerable details of military and political administration demanded most of their time, exhausting them with interminable hours of committee work. They were hard-pressed to find the time to declare independence. On July 3, Congress could not take up the draft declaration until it had first established the wage scale and benefits for military shipwrights.

Having cast the crucial votes for independence, congressmen had no time to send the promising but flawed draft back to the committee for revision. Instead, as a committee of the whole, members had to edit the text in open meeting during parts of just two days, July 3 and 4. Given the usual camels produced by committees meant to design horses, the result is miraculous: as Maier rightly puts it, "an act of group editing that has to be one of the great marvels of history." Collectively, the congressmen rescued the potential in Jefferson's draft by tightening his language and by reducing or eliminating his most forced and rambling accusations.

They discarded one quarter of Jefferson's words while clarifying the rest with judicious insertions. The changes infuriated the hypersensitive Jefferson, who, for the rest of his life, insisted on the utter superiority of his original draft. Maier corrects Jefferson by displaying, in an appendix, his draft with Congress's modifications. Every change improves the whole, to the immense benefit of the ingrate's enduring reputation. Maier explains: "What generations of Americans came to revere was not Jefferson's but Congress's Declaration, the work not of a single man, or even a committee, but of a larger body of men with the good sense to recognize a 'pretty good' draft when they saw it, and who were able to identify and eliminate Jefferson's more outlandish assertions and unnecessary words." Yet Jefferson has subsequently reaped all of the credit.

Congress designed the Declaration primarily for domestic consumption, as propaganda to stiffen the flagging morale of exhausted soldiers and anxious citizens. The vote and the Declaration clarified what Americans were fighting for: a crusade to protect liberty by securing nationhood from a grasping, foreign tyrant. After a flurry of public readings and newspaper publications in the summer of 1776, the Declaration quickly dropped from sight, little recalled in subsequent celebrations of the Fourth of July. "Independence was new," Maier explains, "the rest of the Declaration seemed all too familiar, a restatement of what had already been said time and again."

During the 1790s, the Declaration reemerged from obscurity as Jefferson became the national leader of the Republican Party (not to be confused with today's very different Republican Party). Committed to democracy, the Jeffersonian Republicans challenged their more elitist rivals, the Federalists, who dominated both the federal government and most local celebrations of the Fourth of July. The Republicans staged countercelebrations, which culminated in reverential public readings of the Declaration. These partisan celebrations began the dual process of sacralizing the document while treating Jefferson as its exclusive author—and, therefore, as the very incarnation of American republicanism. In vain, the Federalists struggled to discredit Jefferson's role in writing the Declaration. As Federalism collapsed in electoral politics, beginning with Jefferson's election to the presidency in 1801, the Jeffersonian mode of celebrating the Fourth triumphed.

During the 1820s, a new generation of Americans began to heroicize the dead and dying leaders of the Revolution and began to treat both the Declaration and its republic as divinely inspired works of universal truth. "In the course of recalling and recording the events of the Revolution, Americans of the 1820s remembered the revolutionaries as mighty fathers whose greatness threw into relief the ordinariness of their descendants," Maier observes. As two of the longest-lived revolutionaries, Jefferson and Adams were best positioned to claim most of the credit for Congress's 1776 vote for, and declaration of, independence. Few of their peers were alive to contest their claims.

In a revived correspondence, friendly and spirited, the two former colleagues and rivals bolstered their joint claims to greatness, above all the other Founders. At the same time, of course, each jockeyed for advantage over the other. Adams insisted on the superior significance of the congressional vote of July 2, a vote that he had primarily engineered. In response, Jefferson reiterated the transcendent importance of the written Declaration of July 4. Because Jefferson was by far the more popular of the two former presidents, the public continued to endorse his claim and to adore the Declaration. The adulation was a mixed blessing. Uninvited visitors flocked to Monticello, taxing Jefferson's time, larder, and patience. One woman "even smashed a window with her parasol to improve her view of the old man."

Both Jefferson and Adams had the exquisite timing to die on July 4, 1826—the fiftieth anniversary of the Declaration. Public commentators took that apparently providential conjunction as "proof that the United States had a special place in His plans and affections."

As a new generation of Americans exalted Jefferson and his Declaration, they began to focus on its eloquent preface, especially the egalitarian second paragraph. This refocusing occurred as Americans became polarized over the persistence of slavery in the South and its westward expansion into new territories. Slavery's foes highlighted Jefferson's insistence "that all men are created equal." Recognizing the public power of reverence for the Declaration, slavery's apologists scrambled to deny that Jefferson's words applied to black Americans. As early as 1789, a South Carolina politician had warned against a federal Bill of Rights because, like the Declaration of Independence, such documents "generally began with a statement that all men are born free and equal, which was not the case in South Carolina."

The southern defenders of inequality were historically correct. Jefferson's egalitarian rhetoric properly described the theoretical and prepolitical state of nature. According to eighteenth-century Anglo-American political philosophy, men accepted gradations of inequality when they established society—which was essential, in theory, to securing property and civilized order. But that philosophical distinction between the state of nature and the state of society eluded almost everyone in the nineteenth century. During the 1850s and the 1860s, antislavery politicians took Jefferson's words out of context to exalt them as a universal truth that Americans consistently must seek if their republic was to survive. Maier notes that the antislavery "version of what the founders meant was full of wishful supposition." But their bad history made for an inspiring creed that won the Civil War and subsequently empowered the civil rights movement. Lincoln's understanding of the Declaration "became in time that of the nation."

Maier is uncomfortably aware of the paradox that Lincoln helped create a liberalizing creed by distorting the national memory of Jefferson's intent. A scrupulous scholar, she cannot endorse Lincoln's historical sleight of hand; a committed liberal, she cannot wish that he had been a more precise historian. This tension makes for an awkward ending for an otherwise profound and eloquent book. In the epilogue, she insists that knowing the full, clumsy truth about our national origins will revitalize our currently apathetic civic culture. Although I hope that she is right, I fear that Maier exaggerates the redemptive power of a complicated historical understanding.

Indeed, her demonstration of how Lincoln and others reinvented a mythic Declaration suggests that our republic cannot do without a set of noble fictions. Historians find it reassuring that our nation's public life apparently requires some sense of connection with a powerful past, with the founding and refounding acts of Adams, Jefferson, and Lincoln. Alas, of necessity, the public and its pundits invariably rework that past into a convenient shorthand that mixes half-truths with reassuring fictions. Despite Maier's powerful book, reverential visitors will continue to flock to see the enshrined Declaration, thinking of it in Lincoln's terms while giving Jefferson all the credit.

*20*

# Clintonism

*February 22, 1999*

At the end of the eighteenth century, the new American republic teetered between the danger of collapse and the promise of greatness. By expanding westward to occupy most of North America, the United States might develop into imperial wealth and power—if the nation could survive its first, vulnerable decades. The great paradox of the new nation was that its short-term prospects appeared dire, and yet, its long-term potential seemed limitless. This paradox derived from the immense size and great resources of the continent—a scale and riches that could either pull apart or pull together the people striving to possess them.

The continental scale immediately threatened to overwhelm and fracture the new union of states sprawled along the Atlantic seaboard from Maine to Georgia. In 1791, the secretary of war warned the president: "The United States have come into existence as a nation, embarrassed with a frontier of immense extent." Expansion westward might weaken the coastal states by creating new, independent, and hostile settler states in the interior; and those new polities might gravitate into the rival empires of Spain to the south or Britain to the north.

The new nation's republican gamble enhanced the prospects of such a centrifugal dissipation into collapse. Reliant on popular consent, republics had been historically few, inherently weak, chronically unstable, and usually short-lived, especially when they expanded to absorb a large and diverse population. Most past republics had been riven with violent factionalism and had quickly collapsed into anarchy before settling for the oppressive order of a military tyranny. Only small, homogeneous, and antiquated polities—ancient city-states or medieval cantons—had sustained a republic for multiple generations. The nations and empires of eighteenth-century Europe relied on coercive and centralized power exercised by a monarch, assisted by an aristocracy, to dominate far-flung and variegated peoples. To expand into an empire, Americans feared that they might have to forsake their republican liberty.

*The Birth of Empire: DeWitt Clinton and the American Experience, 1769–1828,* by Evan Cornog (Oxford University Press, 1998)

The initial years of the American republic seemed to confirm this conventional political wisdom. After staggering through a long and debilitating war for independence from Britain, the United States nearly dissolved during the mid-1780s—as western settlers plotted secession with covert encouragement from Spanish and British agents. The federal Constitution framed in 1787 and ratified in 1788 represented a last-gasp bid to unify the thirteen republican states—a final, desperate formula for combining imperial scale with republican principles. From our own retrospect of American global domination, the new administration of George Washington seems the predetermined foundation for an inevitable superpower, but his contemporaries could not be so sure.

The republic's leaders derived both inspiration and anxiety from their republican predecessors, the ancient Romans. From a republican base, the Romans had achieved a great empire, but at a great cost, as imperialism consumed their republic, substituting a military despotism. As Rome became imperial, Caesar supplanted Cicero. Americans could only hope that they might succeed where the Romans had failed—that they might sustain an expanding, imperial republic.

DeWitt Clinton of New York considered himself (and impressed his contemporaries) as a latter-day Roman, an American incarnation of Cicero, or perhaps of Caesar. Tall, handsome, strong, keenly intelligent, and conspicuously learned, Clinton spoke and carried himself with a complete self-assurance that seemed to mark a great historical figure, a true classical statesman. He cultivated the multiple expertise of the neoclassical tradition, presenting himself simultaneously as a patrician politician, a cultural patron, an antiquarian scholar, and an amateur scientist. Hiding behind a pseudonym, he praised himself to the reading public: "Mr. Clinton, among his other great qualifications, is distinguished for a marked devotion to science; few men have read more and few men can claim more various and extensive knowledge; and the bounties of nature have been improved by his persevering and unremitting industry."

By exposing Clinton's identity behind the pseudonym, his enemies gleefully compounded his legendary reputation for overweening egotism. To mock his combination of stature and hauteur, his enemies dubbed him "Magnus Apollo"—but the gibe redounded against them, for it suggested that Clinton did, indeed, live and think on a grander scale than ordinary mortals. Unintentionally, the sobriquet diminished its inventors. If he was Magnus Apollo, they were mere pedestrian office-seekers.

Like his fellow New Yorkers and early political rivals, Alexander Hamilton and Aaron Burr, DeWitt Clinton was a complex compound of republican rhetoric and imperial opportunism. He embodied a protean energy that could either sustain or explode the growing, vulnerable republic. Observers were divided over the national implications of his drive to enhance the economic wealth and political power of New York. Would that state's success benefit the nation or blow it apart? Would an imperial state become virtually autonomous, or would it serve as a model for national growth and integration? Would Clinton's phenomenal career hasten or postpone a collapse of the union into civil war (a prospect that recurrently haunted the republic's leaders)?

DeWitt Clinton inherited an imperial vision of New York's prospects from his father, James Clinton, and from his formidable uncle George Clinton. Both had helped to lead the American Revolution in New York. As a Continental Army general, James Clinton commanded the invasion that destroyed the Indian villages of central and western New York, turning the Iroquois inhabitants into demoralized refugees and opening the region's fertile lands to rapid postwar settlement by the victors. In 1777, George Clinton became New York's first elected governor, and, in five successive reelection victories, he consolidated power as the state's preeminent politician. Determined to enrich and empower New York, Clinton often defied the Continental Congress during the 1780s.

In microcosm, New York reflected the national paradox of immediate weakness and immense potential. Long hemmed in by the Iroquois and recently devastated by war, New York was a middle-tier state in terms of population and prosperity. Among the initial thirteen states, it ranked sixth in population in 1790, lagging behind even Connecticut. New York's authority and inhabitants were both largely confined to its eastern quarter: Long Island and the Hudson Valley. To the west stretched immense tracts of fertile but heavily forested land, recently wrested from the Iroquois but not yet secured to New York by settlement. As in the nation at large, those potential western riches threatened to attract the designs of rival states, unruly squatters, and the jealousy of the British Empire in adjoining Canada.

Yet geography favored George Clinton's vision of an empire state. New York combined the nation's most promising seaport city with the best route westward—through the Appalachian Mountains by way of the Mohawk Valley and the Finger Lakes—to the potential riches of the continent. New York could become the great conduit for settlers to emigrate deep into the interior to secure farms, and for their produce to flow eastward through New York City into the transatlantic market.

During the 1780s, George Clinton's zealous pursuit of power for himself and for his state threatened to unravel the tenuous American confederation. As New York transformed its interior from unsettled menace to settled asset, the state seemed to grow too powerful for the confederation to control. By becoming imperial, New York imperiled the federal bid to achieve the same objective on a national scale. Determined to preserve his state's primacy in collecting import taxes from New York

City's swelling international commerce, George Clinton worked to keep the confederacy weak and to prevent ratification of the federal Constitution. His nephew, protégé, and secretary assisted by writing anonymous newspaper essays that attacked the Federalist supporters of the Constitution as antidemocratic elitists.

Despite the Clintons' best efforts, the Federalists ratified the Constitution in New York, as in the other states. Ever resourceful and adaptable, George Clinton intrigued to become the first vice president of the new government he had so vigorously and so recently opposed. He lost out to John Adams, but he established the precedent that the Clintons would pursue state power by keeping a hand in the national politics of making presidents and vice presidents.

DeWitt Clinton was born and bred to pursue his uncle's vision in the next generation. Raised in comfort and exquisitely well educated, he was an arrogant but talented young man in a hurry to enjoy power. He attended a private academy, graduated first in his class at Columbia University in 1786, and studied law in the office of the city's preeminent trial attorney. Along with Uncle George, during the early 1790s, he gravitated to the Republican Party, nationally led by Virginians Thomas Jefferson and James Madison. After losing two races to Federalists, Clinton won a seat in the state legislature in 1797, and a year later he advanced to the state senate, where he became, by 1801, at the age of thirty-one, the dominant power broker in the legislature.

Evan Cornog's book displays both the strengths and the limitations of a conventional political biography. He creates a forceful and colorful portrait of his vital and powerful subject, but he tends to reduce politics to the interaction of a few leading men acting out the strengths and weaknesses of their personalities. This biographical approach makes for a lucid story that lingers on the personal and contingent. Sticking to the surface of New York's politics, Cornog fails to plumb the depths to define the larger structures of power. He attributes too much to the vagaries of Clinton's personality and too little to the political culture that defined his options.

Cornog depicts his protagonist as mercurial and erratic—when, in fact, more should be credited to the peculiar dictates of New York's chronically unstable politics. Clinton rose so far and so fast by mastering the factional intricacies of New York, but he could ascend no farther, to national power, because that state's political culture was so vicious and so mysterious. Although Oliver Wolcott had previously excelled at politics in neighboring Connecticut, he later lamented that, "after living a dozen years in New York, I don't pretend to comprehend their politics. It is a labyrinth of wheels within wheels, and it is understood only by the managers."

As the consummate political manager, DeWitt Clinton understood New York politics all too well. The state puzzled outsiders, who took too seriously the identity and the rhetoric of the political parties. Lacking in formal apparatus, those parties were convenient fronts claimed by shifting coalitions of "interests." In New York parlance, an "interest" was an unstable cluster of ambitious men and the voters they could influence, all mustered under the leadership of the preeminent man of an especially powerful family. In New York during the 1780s and the 1790s, the leading interests were those of the Clinton, Livingston, Schuyler, and Van Rensselaer families—as well as the personal following of the charismatic and cunning Aaron Burr. No single interest could gain and hold state power without framing an alliance with another interest or two. George Clinton clung to power from 1777 to 1795 by sharing state patronage with the Livingston clan and with Burr, all united by little more than the Republican name and a determination to hold at bay the Schuylers and the Van Rensselaers, who called themselves Federalists.

Pragmatic rather than ideological, the interests sought state power less to promote policy than to reap patronage: government contracts, bank charters, and salaried positions. The great prize of power was the Council of Appointment—a constitutional feature peculiar to New York. The council consisted of the governor and four state senators chosen by the state assembly. The council exercised the power to appoint and to replace almost every public officeholder in New York at the city, county, and state levels. Every local justice of the peace, militia officer, county judge and clerk, city mayor, and state-level department head obtained and held office at the sufferance of the Council of Appointment.

To seek or to keep public office, aspiring men enlisted in an interest that entered a coalition intent on capturing the governorship and the state legislature so that they might control the council. The victors swept the losers from office. Consequently, New York pioneered and perfected the infamous "spoils system" of nineteenth-century American politics. In combination with the political framework of family interests, the Council of Appointment rendered politics more overtly crass and ruthless in New York than in the other states, where abstract principles seemed more apparent and more real.

Because there were always many more ambitious men than offices to satisfy them, even victory generated discontent. In search of their just deserts, the underappreciated scrambled into another interest to work for electoral triumph. Consequently, interests were volatile and ever-shifting, requiring constant attention by vigilant leaders. None were better at this than the Clintons, George and DeWitt. In the end, however, even they could not transcend the constraints that New York's political culture placed on the pursuit of national power.

One of the political mysteries of the early republic was the failure of New York's leaders to win the presidency by capitalizing on their state's growing power. By 1810, New York had outstripped Virginia to become the wealthiest and most populous state in the union. Yet the state's national power lagged. The first ten terms of the presidency went to Virginians (Washington, Jefferson, Madison, and Monroe) or to an Adams from Massachusetts (John and his son John Quincy). Although New York's electoral votes were critical to presidential victory, the state's political leaders were repeatedly trapped in the hollow honor of the impotent vice presidency. Aaron Burr, George Clinton, and Daniel D. Tompkins learned the hard way that the office was a political graveyard rather than a springboard to the presidency. It was a mark of ultimate futility that no other state produced so many vice presidents during the nation's first half-century.

New York's politicians fell short less because of their personal failings than because their political base at home remained so chronically unstable. Their rivals from Virginia and Massachusetts enjoyed more-secure home fronts and could always find in New York some aspiring politician eager to betray that state's presidential contender. Cornog argues that DeWitt Clinton failed to develop a national network because he preferred holding city and state office to pursuing a career in Congress. Clinton did win a seat in the United States Senate in 1802, but, less than two years later, he resigned and returned home to become mayor of New York City and, at the same time, to win a seat in New York's senate. Cornog presents this choice as shortsighted and self-indulgent.

But Clinton needed to come home, to tend the city and state supply of patronage, lest rival interests secure control of the Council of Appointment in his prolonged absence. In the politics of his state and his day, a mayoralty and a state senate post were better bases of power than a United States Senate seat, which drew its holder away from the essential contest for patronage at home. For this reason, few New Yorkers served out a full term in the senate, and New York exercised less power in that body than the state's growth should have warranted.

In 1800, the interests of Aaron Burr, the Livingstons, and the Clintons cooperated to win New York's electoral votes, securing the presidency for Jefferson and the vice presidency for Burr. When the latter tried to exploit a constitutional loophole (since closed) to steal the presidency, Jefferson recruited the other New York Republicans to destroy Burr. While Jefferson denied him federal patronage, the Clintonians and Livingstonians did the same at the state level. Like a canary deprived of oxygen, an interest died without patronage for its followers.

Driven to the wall by his former allies-turned-enemies, Burr fled from the vice presidency to run for the governorship of New York in 1804.

This time, the Clintonians rallied behind a Livingston as their candidate for governor. Although an intellectual mediocrity, Morgan Lewis had the good fortune to marry a Livingston. If the marriage recommended Lewis to that clan, his mediocrity attracted DeWitt Clinton, who meant to exercise real power through a weak and dependent governor. To win, Burr needed Federalist support to add to his own faction of Republicans. But Lewis prevailed, due in part to Clinton's shrewd electoral management and, in part, to Alexander Hamilton's sabotage of Federalist support for his longtime enemy Burr. Furious at defeat, he provoked a duel that killed Hamilton's body and Burr's career.

It seemed that nobody remained to challenge DeWitt Clinton's standing as New York's power broker. To his astonishment, however, the new governor chafed at subordination and sought true power at Clinton's expense. In 1805, Lewis supported a legislative charter for a new bank in New York City that threatened the profits of an older bank controlled by Clinton and his political friends. Enraged, Clinton struck back through his control of the Council of Appointment, sacking Lewis's supporters throughout the state. A year later, the Livingston interest, in alliance with Federalists, captured the state legislature. Seizing control of the Council of Appointment, they promptly ousted DeWitt Clinton as mayor of New York.

Like Burr before him, Clinton needed to win back a share in the executive power, lest his interest dissipate as ambitious followers sought out a new leader. Too controversial to run himself, Clinton again sought a front man popular enough to win but weak enough to take orders. In 1807, he settled on Daniel D. Tompkins, a handsome, charming, and apparently innocuous state judge. Tompkins's rural and modest origins could be attractively packaged for sale to the electorate as the "Farmer's Boy" made good, as an appealing contrast to the wellborn and aristocratic Morgan Lewis. After an especially bitter and hard-fought campaign, Tompkins prevailed, and the legislature became Clintonian. The new Council of Appointment restored DeWitt Clinton as mayor of New York City.

Confident that he had at last secured his base in New York state, DeWitt Clinton sought the presidency in 1812, seizing on an emerging sectionalism, as northern leaders increasingly resented the national power of Virginia. That tension increased in 1808, as the Jefferson administration enforced an embargo that closed American seaports to international commerce. Meant to pressure Great Britain, the embargo instead brought financial ruin to much of the Northeast. Federalist merchants and politicians suspected a plot by jealous southern planters to undermine northern commerce. Recognizing the failure, Jefferson's successor, James Madison, lifted the embargo, but in 1812, he substituted a declaration of war against Britain, a war that further imperiled northeastern seaports by exposing them to attack by the British fleet.

To win the presidency, Clinton needed Federalist votes to add to disgruntled northern Republican votes. But that bid for Federalist support proved as ruinous to Clinton as it had been to Burr and Lewis. In previous campaigns, Clinton had all too effectively demonized the Federalists as aristocrats and crypto-monarchists determined to betray the republic. Persuaded by two decades of political rhetoric, a strong majority of the New York electorate would never trust a politician who flirted with the Federalist minority. At the same time, Federalist voters did not trust the sincerity of a new friend who had so long and so effectively insulted them.

Moreover, Daniel D. Tompkins seized the opportunity to escape the role of puppet. Casting his lot with Madison, Tompkins reaped the national patronage in New York State, the better to build his own interest at Clinton's expense. Forced to expend too much political capital in his home state, DeWitt Clinton lost his bid for the presidency. Worse still, when the war ended in early 1815, with an appearance of American victory (after a long string of real but soon-forgotten defeats), Clinton paid dearly for his association with the antiwar Federalists. The victorious Republicans depicted the Federalists and Clinton as defeatists who had nearly betrayed the nation to the British enemy. In 1815, Tompkins had the Council of Appointment sack Clinton as mayor of New York. For the first time since 1797, DeWitt Clinton was out of public office (except for an apparently innocuous seat on the state's Canal Board). His political career seemed to be as dead as Aaron Burr's.

But it was in that seat on the moribund Canal Board that DeWitt Clinton saw an opportunity to revitalize his political power by renewing his uncle's imperial vision of western development. Defeated at the old politics of interest, DeWitt Clinton reinvented himself as the champion of a new politics of policy. For once, he would run by advancing a visionary issue. He called on the state legislature to fund an immense, costly, and risky public works project—construction of a 363-mile-long canal extending across upstate New York to link Lake Erie in the west with the Hudson River in the east. In an era of limited government and hand labor, such a mammoth public project was unprecedented. No state government had dug a canal, and the nation's longest extended a mere twenty-seven miles and had yet to turn a profit. Clinton's enemies scoffed that an Erie Canal was "so visionary and absurd that no rational man for one moment could seriously entertain it."

With promotional flair and organizational genius, Clinton mounted a publicity campaign to pressure the state legislature. "If it be important," he preached, "that the inhabitants of the same country should be bound together by a community of interests, and a reciprocation of benefits; that agriculture should find a sale for its commodities; manufacturers a vent for their fabrics; and commerce a market for its commodities: it is your incumbent duty, to open, facilitate, and improve internal navigation." Governor Tompkins balked for fear of reviving Clinton's political influence, but that very opposition backfired as the public rallied to Clinton's vision of boundless wealth generated by a great canal. In 1817, after Tompkins left New York to become vice president in Washington, Clinton captured the governor's seat in a landslide. Giving way, the legislature passed the Erie Canal bill just before the new governor took office.

Although Clinton won a remarkable 97 percent of the vote in 1817, he proved remarkably ineffectual in office. His landslide had secured legislative passage of the canal bill, but Clinton had surprisingly little to do with the subsequent administration of the project. The canal bill was passed by his chief opponent in the state legislature, Martin Van Buren, who proceeded to pack the Canal Board with his own supporters. Construction contractors recognized that they needed to curry favor with Van Buren rather than Clinton. A political friend of Clinton despaired that, "however noble and magnificent were his ends, he failed in providing the means for their accomplishment." All vision, he lacked attention to detail.

Cornog depicts DeWitt Clinton as a statesman who cared too much about governance and too little for politics: "Government, in his view, was a noble career, one that a man of his attainments owed it to the people to pursue. Politics, in contrast, was a tawdry struggle for office, a sacrifice of principles to expediency." In that tawdry business, Clinton was simply no match for the wily Van Buren. Cornog is half right: Clinton did divide politics and government, and as governor he was inept at the former. But that dichotomy underestimates Clinton's prowess during elections as it overestimates his commitment to good government.

In fact, Clinton was far better at winning elections than at running a government. He won four of the last five New York gubernatorial elections held during his lifetime; the lone exception came in 1822, when he chose not to run. Van Buren was the superior legislative politician, but Clinton repeatedly bested the electoral candidates chosen by his rival's formidable political machine. Despite those victories, Clinton achieved remarkably little as governor. The energy of his campaigns dissipated in his administrations. He knew how to ride policy positions into office, but he never learned how to employ an office to effect policy. Feeling vindicated and vindictive after each electoral triumph, Clinton squandered his political capital on foolhardy feuds with his rivals. A friend sadly observed that it was Clinton's nature to "listen to no overtures until he himself, or his opponent, was completely conquered." Since electoral victories were always partial and provisional, complete conquest remained elusive, stalling governance.

Completed in the fall of 1825, the Erie Canal became fabulously successful, generating immense profits and escalating the already impressive growth of western New York and of the metropolis of New York City. By 1828, the year of Clinton's death, his city had become the commercial and financial capital of the continent. Nearly half the nation's imports and almost a third of its exports flowed through its port. The combination of grand canal and great city made New York the wealthiest and the most integrated state economy in the nation.

In the boisterous celebrations of 1825, Governor Clinton reaped more than his share of the credit for the Erie Canal. Joining the celebration, Cornog concludes that, "had [Clinton] not given the project all his energies, the moment might have passed and a different America might have emerged." In his more restrained passages, Cornog acknowledges the ambivalence of Clinton's legacy for the expanding nation. The Erie Canal did enrich and strengthen New York, but the phenomenal success of the empire state complicated the nation's political bonds. After financing their own expensive, but profitable canal, New York's politicians vigorously and effectively fought a federal program of internal improvements to benefit the other states. And when some of those states, principally Pennsylvania, proceeded with their own more-expensive and ill-conceived canal programs, they reaped financial woes that, for the rest of the century, discredited government activism.

The Erie Canal helped to unite the Midwest with the Northeast, and that integration alleviated the great anxiety of the revolutionary generation: that the West would secede from the East. But that economic and political alliance of Midwest and Northeast tended to isolate and alienate the South, which came to feel impotent and insulted. When the Union collapsed in the long-dreaded Civil War, the polarity pitted North against South instead of East against West. DeWitt Clinton had helped to make New York into the empire state and to create a northern political identity, but those victories altered without alleviating the uncertainties that clouded the national prospects for sustaining a continental empire of liberty.

# Part V
# Historians

21

# The Exceptionalist

*June 9, 2003*

During the mid-1980s, at a national convention of historians early in my career, I first saw Bernard Bailyn, a legendary figure in my chosen field of colonial and revolutionary America. I stood waiting, with several colleagues of equally modest status, for a glass elevator to descend to the open lobby of the convention hotel. Out of the corner of an eye, I noted the famous—and famously aloof—Professor Bailyn looming behind us alone and at a discreet distance. From a conspicuous array of seven (or so) elevator pods, my group had gambled on the one most likely to reach bottom most quickly—or so it seemed, until that elevator stopped short. Instead, far to our left, another glassy pod surprisingly and suddenly dropped multiple floors to our level. Quicker than thought, Bailyn dashed across the lobby into the elevator and quickly pressed the buttons, shutting the door to ascend in splendid isolation, looking down on the gaping, excluded throng. The tableau seemed perfectly to represent his lofty professional standing and reputation: smarter than others and rising above the fray.

Bernard Bailyn has been, at once, the most influential and one of the most controversial American historians of the past half century. Born in 1922 in Hartford, Connecticut, Bailyn graduated from Williams College in 1945, and served in the Army at the end of World War II. He subsequently studied American history at Harvard, receiving his doctorate in 1953. Oscar Handlin, then the nation's premier social historian, trained Bailyn to apply the questions of social science to the patterns of ordinary life—a daring approach that transcended the profession's traditional preoccupation with statesmen and generals. Infamous for eating its young, the Harvard history department made a singular exception for Bailyn, who never had to endure exile to a provincial university, much less to some rustic teachers' college. Instead, in 1953, he joined the faculty and flourished until his retirement at the end of the 1980s. Along

*To Begin the World Anew: The Genius and Ambiguities of the American Founders,* by Bernard Bailyn (Alfred A. Knopf, 2003)

the way, he won the annual presidency of the American Historical Association, two Pulitzer Prizes, and a National Book Award. He also trained nearly seventy doctoral students, including such luminaries as Richard D. Brown, Richard L. Bushman, Michael Kammen, Pauline R. Maier, Mary Beth Norton, Jack N. Rakove, and Gordon S. Wood. Dazzled by Bailyn's "charismatic yet enigmatic" example, those protégés have disseminated and ramified his influence in research universities throughout the land. Most entered the profession at an especially auspicious moment, during the 1960s and the early 1970s, a boom time for academia, in general, and for the writing of early American history, in particular.

Initially, Bailyn practiced social history in the Handlin mode, publishing his first book, *The New England Merchants in the Seventeenth Century,* in 1955. By examining relatively worldly men, Bailyn gently diverged from the usual treatment of Puritan New England as exclusively inhabited by the religiously profound and driven. Bringing a social perspective to economic development, he wrote: "Trade was the creation of men and . . . the bonds that kept its parts together were the personal relationships existing among them." In 1959, Bailyn and his wife, Lotte Bailyn, produced *Massachusetts Shipping, 1697–1714: A Statistical Study,* a pioneering application of the computer to statistical data, which revealed the broad distribution of investment in mercantile shipping, thereby democratizing our view of commercial enterprise in colonial New England.

Beginning with an influential essay, "Politics and Social Structure in Virginia," in 1959, and a concise book, *Education in the Forming of American Society,* a year later, Bailyn's social history took a political turn by focusing on the social origins of elites and the modes of distributing and validating power. He emphasized the increasing divergence of colonial society from Great Britain, necessitating new American ways of thinking about the relationship of government to the governed.

Early and often, Bailyn endorsed the metanarrative known as "American exceptionalism": a celebration of American deviation from Old World tradition. This was the reigning orthodoxy of the 1950s, and it still pervades popular history and our political culture—think, for example, of Donald Rumsfeld's disdain for the "old Europe." American exceptionalism insists that an abundant new world liberated talented and ambitious colonial emigrants from aristocratic Europe, where birth assigned privilege and limited mobility. Abundance and opportunity created the American character—optimistic, individualistic, materialistic, innovative, and democratic—in sharp contrast to those hide-bound, uptight European pessimists, so perversely conformed to the absence of social mobility. Deeply rooted in our national identity, American exceptionalism suffuses the writings of J. Hector St. John de Crevecoeur during the 1770s; the late nineteenth-century frontier thesis of Frederick Jackson

Turner; and the mid-twentieth-century historical work of David Potter, Oscar Handlin, and many others.

During the late 1960s, in two remarkable, celebrated, and overlapping books—*The Ideological Origins of the American Revolution* (1967) and *The Origins of American Politics* (1968)—Bailyn applied American exceptionalism to explain the coming of the American Revolution. These books delineate a paradigmatic change during the mid-to-late eighteenth century, as old habits of British thought, increasingly out of touch with American social realities, gave way to radical new ways of perceiving and thinking about society and politics, ways better attuned to American needs. Eighteenth-century Britons celebrated their constitutional stability, which was premised on counterpoising the commons with an aristocracy and a monarch. The stabilizing power of the monarch depended on an abundant patronage to buy members of Parliament; on an electorate restricted by a daunting property requirement; and on an unequal mode of representation that favored aristocratic estates over the urban masses. But none of those conditions prevailed in colonial America, where abundant land elevated most white men into the electorate; where the sojourning royal governors possessed little patronage and less security; and where ambitious men of commercial means dominated the elected colonial assemblies that filled the power vacuum left by the weak governors.

As a consequence, colonial politics was especially petty, fractious, and inconsequential—generating much anxiety that something was amiss. Early in the eighteenth century, most leading colonists blamed themselves, casting their political deviations from the British norm as marks of provincial inferiority. At mid-century, however, American leaders felt compelled, as never before, to justify their distinctive society and its political implications. Confronted by new British demands for taxes and greater imperial control, the colonists mobilized a body of alarmist ideas originating in England and known to scholars as "Country," "Commonwealth," or "Opposition" thought. During the late seventeenth and early eighteenth century, several embittered English political writers—principally, John Trenchard and Thomas Gordon (the coauthors of *Cato's Letters*)—excoriated Parliament and the king's ministers as thoroughly corrupt and power mad, driven by greed and ambition to conspire against the traditional liberties of Englishmen. Marginalized in Britain, these Country ideas became pervasive and persuasive in the thirteen colonies, where the colonists needed a political vocabulary to vindicate their social order and to justify their resistance to British authority.

With Country thought as their prism, the leaders of colonial resistance detected nothing but malice, corruption, and conspiracy in even the most innocuous of British initiatives. In 1775 and 1776, those convictions impelled most colonists to revolt, securing both independence and a republican form of government shorn of aristocracy and monarchy. Republicanism brought the American polity into line with the relatively egalitarian society, abating the anxieties generated by the colonial contradiction between political beliefs and social realities. Endowed with a republic, Americans could sustain and even improve that society in subsequent generations, gradually extending liberty and opportunity to slaves and women.

Lyrically expressed and brilliantly framed, Bailyn's interpretation concisely explains both the coming of the Revolution and its republican legacy. In reward, *The Ideological Origins of the American Revolution* and *The Origins of American Politics* reaped critical acclaim, scholarly prizes, and a surprisingly large readership for such academic tomes. But Bailyn's work on the Revolution also evoked a backlash from many historians, who felt either conned by rhetorical sleight-of-hand or scorned by Bailyn's abrupt dismissal of other interpretations.

Bailyn's writing magically combines vivid imagery with rhetorical escape hatches. Depending on their sensibility, readers can find in his prose either multiple layers of sophisticated meaning or a self-serving ambiguity and internal contradiction. Consider, for example, this controversial passage, from *The Ideological Origins of the American Revolution,* about Country thought's power over the revolutionaries: "This peculiar configuration of ideas constituted in effect an intellectual switchboard wired so that certain combinations of events would activate a distinct set of signals—danger signals, indicating hidden impulses and the likely trajectory of events impelled by them. Well before 1776 the signals registered on this switchboard led to a single, unmistakable conclusion—a conclusion that had long been feared and to which there could be only one rational response." Here Bailyn initially indicts the Patriots as mechanistically trapped by their alarmist ideology into overreacting to British initiatives as a conscious plot to enslave white Americans. At passage's end, however, he adroitly retreats by characterizing the Revolution as the one and only "rational response." If the revolutionaries were constrained by their psychological "switchboard" to detect only some stimuli, and those in the most fearful manner, why categorize their response as "rational"?

In sharp contrast to the evocative and allusive ambivalence of his own formulations, Bailyn turns definitive and categorical to reject alternatives offered by other scholars. Insistent on the binding and blinding power of Country thought, he is quick to dismiss—rather than careful to explore—the other ideologies that circulated in revolutionary America. What about the liberalism associated with John Locke or the utopian rationalism of Enlightenment philosophers? Overrated, Bailyn declares.

How about the plebeian traditions of radical protest in the colonial seaports and the tenant-farm districts? Insignificant, Bailyn maintains. Perhaps the egalitarian evangelicalism promoted by Protestant revivalists contributed to the republican revolution? Of no political consequence, Bailyn counters. There was, he insists, just one mobilizing ideology, and it could be found exclusively in pamphlets and newspapers expressing the dread-filled Country thought. If this is so, revolutionary America had a surprisingly simple and homogeneous political culture.

By reducing the Revolution to a forensic debate conducted by well-educated pamphleteers, Bailyn also slights the economic distress, urban rioting, rural uprisings, and slave agitation that preoccupy other historians committed to the rival "Progressive interpretation," which emphasizes class and racial conflict. In the negative, Bailyn waxes explicit, declaring in 1973 that "the Revolution was not the result of social discontent, or of economic disturbances, or of rising misery, or of those mysterious social strains that seem to beguile the imaginations of historians straining to find peculiar predispositions to upheaval." He deemed no evidence necessary to support these negatives, satisfied that his own asserted authority sufficed. By casting his "ideological interpretation" as purely political, and diametrically opposed to any social interpretation, Bailyn retreated into a more traditional, elitist mode of intellectual history at surprising odds with the innovative social perspective of his early scholarship.

By insisting on a homogeneous American commitment to Country thought, Bailyn also neglected the approximately one fifth of the colonial population that remained loyal to the empire during the bitter civil war known as the American Revolution. If Country thought suffused late colonial America, why would so many people cling to the British Empire as the best protector of their property and liberty? Sensitive to that criticism, Bailyn responded with his finest work: a profound biography of a preeminent Loyalist, *The Ordeal of Thomas Hutchinson* (1974). The colonial-born royal governor of Massachusetts on the eve of the Revolution, Hutchinson has long been vilified in Patriot propaganda and historical writing as the archconspirator against American liberty. Bailyn hoped to transcend that American parochialism, which so neatly casts its Patriot heroes against British and Loyalist villains. He sought, instead, that "ultimate stage of maturity in historical interpretation where partisanship is left behind, where the historian can find equal humanity in all the participants, the winners and the losers."

Bailyn presents Hutchinson as a noble but tragic figure—as the Revolution's Hamlet. More rational and pragmatic than his Patriot foes, Hutchinson dispassionately understood the British as well-meaning imperialists. He worked to reconcile the colonists and Britons before they destroyed in blood the union of an empire that he, and so many other Americans, admired and cherished. But rationality and pragmatism ultimately proved to be liabilities, as Hutchinson underestimated the fear and loathing that drove the Patriots to revolt. His well-meant but naïve efforts at compromise only hastened the catastrophe that he had longed to avert.

*The Ordeal of Thomas Hutchinson* reaped far more than its fair share of academic criticism. Critics asserted psychological parallels between Hutchinson and Bailyn: both allegedly embattled by foes, sure of their superior reason, and self-pitying. Because Bailyn identified and sympathized with Hutchinson—they argued—he distorted history by vindicating a Loyalist. Such scholarly partisanship revealed that the moral polarities of Patriot history were too cherished to permit any dispassionate reassessment of a leading Loyalist.

In fact, Bailyn should have gone even farther toward understanding the Loyalists on their own terms. Instead, he remained fundamentally wedded to the Whiggish, teleological version of Patriot history, which holds that because the revolutionaries were destined to win, opposing the Revolution was foolish; and because the revolutionaries had a powerful ideology, opponents, by definition, lacked equally potent convictions. By negatively defining Hutchinson's thought as the absence of Patriot passion, Bailyn underestimated Loyalism, casting it as a pallid and ineffectual response to the irrational but invincible emotions of a revolutionary age.

In fact, the American Revolution was a hard-fought and close-run thing: the British and the Loyalists nearly won. Respect for the true contingency of the past would take them seriously as viable candidates for making the American future. If they had prevailed, a different victors' history would have rearranged the white and black hats awarded to the heroes and villains of that generation.

And the American Loyalists *did* have an ideology, did have their own symbolic and selective understanding of political reality that inspired their passionate defense of the union of the empire. Taking Catholic and absolutist France as their traditional foe, the American Loyalists understood the British Empire as the world's last best hope for the preservation of liberty, property, commerce, and Protestantism: values that they understood to be interdependent and fragile. They perceived the self-styled Patriots as power-hungry, self-serving hypocrites driven by avarice and ambition to conspire against the freedoms best protected by clinging to the union of the empire and to the constitutional balance of king, aristocracy, and commons. In the Patriots' brutal treatment of the Loyalists and their newspapers—and in the Patriot military alliance with Catholic France—the Loyalists found perverse vindication for their views.

Until we give the Loyalists their due as ideologically committed to a just cause (as they saw it), our history of the American Revolution will remain naïve and parochial. If Bailyn fell short in 1974, he at least tried to enlarge the sphere of historiographical empathy, which is more than can be said of his critics.

In the wake of *The Ordeal of Thomas Hutchinson,* Bailyn turned to an ambitious new project that returned to painstaking empirical and archival research. Pioneering an "Atlantic perspective," he examined the massive flow of European immigrants to British America during the eighteenth century. Appalled by the proliferation of specialized studies of early American places and peoples conducted from multiple disciplines and perspectives, Bailyn hoped that he could combine and tame them into one consummate master-interpretation. During the 1980s, he assured his former graduate students that his "Peopling of America" project would synthesize "the whole world of cultural-anthropological, social-structural, and demographic history which lies scattered in hundreds of books and articles written over the past quarter century by scholars in several disciplines pursuing separate paths of inquiry."

This megaambition resembles that of Morris Zapp, a literary scholar created by the satirical novelist David Lodge. Irritated by the proliferation of specialized studies of Jane Austen's novels, Zapp aspires to combine every theoretical approach in his own massive, master study—to have the last word and put a stop to all further scholarship on the subject. And like Zapp, Bailyn has found his grand design easier to announce than to consummate. So far, the Peopling of America project has yielded a single "exploratory study": a massive volume of 636 pages devoted to analyzing one detailed register of emigrants who departed Britain between 1773 and 1776. At this rate, completing the master interpretation of all the emigration data from throughout the Atlantic basin vanishes far over the horizon, a century into the future.

The project's first volume, ably assisted by Barbara DeWolfe, appeared in 1986 as *Voyagers to the West: A Passage in the Peopling of America on the Eve of the Revolution*—and in a more concise, popular edition entitled *The Peopling of America.* In the larger tome, Bailyn declined to settle on one unifying framework. Instead, he and DeWolfe stitched together four distinct approaches—"descriptive exposition," "quantitative analysis," "structural analysis," and "micro-narratives" (of particular emigrants to colonial America). Pursued in distinct and prolonged sequence, the parts read like four distinct drafts of similar books, each of manageable length until combined. Each segment offers dazzling interludes of analysis or storytelling, but the repetitive whole is something less than the sum of the parts.

*Voyagers to the West* opens with a lurid picture of a barbaric colonial

America and its denizens: "They lived in the outback, on the far marchlands, where constraints were loosened and where one had to struggle to maintain the forms of civilized existence." The colonial frontier attracted "a disoriented white population for whom murder, thievery, and brutality had become commonplace." Colonial slave-masters reduced blacks "to the condition of work animals," while evangelists conducted "bizarre cults." But in the end, Bailyn reaches for the comforting consolations of American exceptionalism: that brutal marchland paradoxically produces a great good by simplifying the European emigrants, stripping away their artificial civilization to re-create their characters as autonomous, creative Americans: "It was a risky world where one lived not in a dense and elaborately nuanced human environment that nourished and civilized but also limited one's activities, but in a loose, still-forming society where it was possible to proceed alone, free of encrusted burdens and ancient obligations, and to become, like the emigrant Yorkshireman Luke Harrison, 'independent.'" Harrison meant the "independence" of owning a family farm, but Bailyn implies that such a people would soon accept nothing less than national independence from bad old Britain. The problem with this neat and upbeat conclusion is that the colonial emigrants featured in *Voyagers*—Scots and other North Britons of the early 1770s—did not, in general, embrace the American Revolution. Instead, they tended to remain loyal to the empire, undercutting the case that the American marchland had so quickly worked its alchemy on emigrant minds.

In an even more profound way, the North Briton emigrants of the 1770s were atypical of the human flow across the Atlantic to British America. Contrary to the doctrine of exceptionalism, most eighteenth-century immigrants did not come to America of their own free will in search of liberty and opportunity. Nor were they white Europeans. Most were enslaved Africans forced across the Atlantic to work on American farms and plantations. During that century, the British colonies (including the West Indies) imported about 1.5 million slaves—more than three times the number of all free immigrants and more than ten times the number of North British emigrants.

In the peopling of late colonial America, the real headline story was the massive expansion of race slavery—rather than the more modest growth of opportunity for the white minority of immigrants. And that conspicuous expansion of slave numbers contributed, at least as much as Country thought, to the special terror that the term "slavery" had in Patriot discourse. Detecting their own impending "slavery" to British taxes made subconscious sense to leading colonists, anxious over their own increased slaveholding and fearful that human exploitation would become more universal, spreading across racial lines, in a nightmare American future.

By casting North British emigrants of 1773–76 as perfectly emblematic of the coming America, then, Bailyn commits what he criticizes in other scholars: a presentism that recasts the past to serve present concerns. The champions of American exceptionalism charge Progressive scholars with distorting the past to serve present concerns with social equality. But Progressives can, with at least equal justice, counter that exceptionalism skews and foreshortens the past by rendering it too white and too happy, by reading back into the colonial era the conformity and prosperity of the middle class in contemporary America.

American exceptionalism offers a nice and appealing story, one true enough for thousands of free, white families who did find more opportunity on this side of the Atlantic. Yet this interpretation drains American history of drama and conflict. Why fight the Revolution and the Civil War if the colonial era had already produced an egalitarian society of opportunity and justice? American exceptionalism also minimizes attention to the less fortunate: to Indians decimated by imported diseases and colonial warfare; to the Africans enslaved to work for the free; to the indentured servants and other working poor who procured less prosperity than they expected; and to the women who found that emigration and abundance hardly affected the constraints of patriarchy.

Add those people up and you find the great majority of colonial Americans, leaving exceptionalism as the story of a fortunate minority. Indeed, economic historians have shown that an abundant land of scarce labor creates new incentives for especially exploitative systems of servitude including slavery premised on race. If colonial America offered unprecedented opportunity to the free and the white, it also imposed racial slavery on a scale and in an intensity unknown in Britain. If colonial America was the land of freedom, it was also the land of slavery. Indeed, freedom and slavery were tragically and inseparably intertwined until more than 600,000 Americans died during the Civil War either to dissolve or to preserve their combination.

Since *Voyagers to the West* appeared in 1986, the grand Peopling of America project has lain fallow, producing no more volumes. Instead, Bailyn has concentrated on recycling in book form previously published essays. The most substantial reappeared in 1990 as *Faces of Revolution: Personalities and Themes in the Struggle for American Independence*. Now dipping deeper into his inventory, Bailyn offers a new book, *To Begin the World Anew: The Genius and Ambiguities of the American Founders*. At fewer than 150 pages, 40 of them dedicated to illustrations, this is a book by the barest of margins. A set of five easy pieces, this brief collection recycles lectures, most of them previously published in more obscure venues. The pieces have the charming qualities of the best public lectures: a candid, genial, and sprightly informality. But these lectures also suffer from that genre's limitations when thrust into print: they are generally light on evidence and documentation.

Bailyn gives his pieces a familiar theme: "That [the Founding Fathers] were provincials—marginal, borderland people—in the broad context of eighteenth-century Euro-American civilization profoundly conditioned their lives and, I believe, stimulated their imaginations, freed them from instinctive respect for traditional establishments, and encouraged them to create a new political world." Once again, we find a Revolution initiated and controlled at the top, by learned colonists writing on behalf of an apparently prosperous and homogeneous American people grateful that they no longer lived in Britain.

Readers familiar with Bailyn's past work will find few surprises here, no new inspiration, and no engagement with recent work conducted by other historians (except for legal scholars of *The Federalist Papers*). Yet this amiable collection may do much good by reaching new readers in a broader public. Intrigued by this keen sample, perhaps they will explore more widely, discovering the riches of Bailyn's earlier work. If so, they will encounter a historian of unmatched influence, topical range, research ambition, and writing style.

Many readers will take reassurance from Bailyn's remarkable continuity of interpretation, his many soothing returns to colonial origins as a middle-class triumph. Others—count me among them—fear that Bailyn's repetitive allegiance to American exceptionalism has borne diminishing returns in recent decades, constraining a creative mind within an increasingly stagnant and misleading formula. No one can doubt that the British colonies presented a new and challenging environment that did transform social relations and political possibilities. The problem is that American exceptionalism tells only the upbeat part of that story, for the colonial environment created as much misery as opportunity, and more individual dependence than independence. The Revolution roiled a society that mixed exploitation with opportunity, hierarchy with mobility, and slavery with freedom.

22

# Poor Richard, Rich Ben

*January 13, 2003*

At age eighty-six, the distinguished American historian Edmund S. Morgan reappears in print with *Benjamin Franklin,* a popular biography that may well be the last hurrah of an extraordinarily long and productive career. Trained at Harvard, first employed at Brown, and long a fixture at Yale, Morgan represents the best of the Ivy League tradition of magisterial historians who gave intellectual weight to American nationalism. He has shaped the academic field of early American history with his numerous and talented graduate students, as well as with a publishing career that began in the 1940s. Ramifying Morgan's influence into new generations, his many accomplished protégés include T. H. Breen, David D. Hall, Christine Heyrman, Robert Middlekauff, and John Murrin.

Reversing the chain of influence to its origins, we begin at Harvard during the early 1940s, where Morgan studied with two great historians of colonial America: Samuel Eliot Morison and Perry Miller. The consummate narrative historian, Morison taught Morgan to spin stories in taut yet evocative language, creating vivid images of place and personality without a wasted word. A profound intellectual historian, Miller conveyed his respect for ideas as coherent and powerful imperatives to human behavior—an approach that challenged the era's Progressive historians, who built careers on debunking ideas as gloss to the self-interest that drove the past's social and economic conflicts.

Miller and Morison conveyed their dual (and interdependent) interests in seventeenth-century New England and the later American Revolution, in the Puritan founders and the Founding Fathers. In the Brahmin tradition of Harvard, they regarded New England's origins as essential to the subsequent founding of the United States: yoked together as the two great generations of early American history. For all their differences, the Calvinist leaders of New England and the republican ideologues of the Revolution were the great minds worth knowing to discern the essence of American history.

*Benjamin Franklin,* by Edmund S. Morgan (Yale University Press, 2003)

The Harvard formula focused on elites, favoring religious and intellectual history for the early seventeenth century and political and intellectual history for the later eighteenth century. That formula neglected the intervening century and the vast reaches of colonial America beyond New England, treating both as stagnant backwaters. It also tended to dismiss social history—the conditions and the patterns of common life—as best left to the occasional woman who infiltrated academia. And only less ambitious scholars should attend to Virginia (before the Revolution) or to the middle colonies (at any time), for there lay only infertile minds: the mules of American origins. Initially committed to that framework, Morgan emulated his mentors by studying and narrating New England Puritans and American revolutionaries.

During his first three decades as a publishing scholar, Morgan balanced academic tradition with cautious experiments in newer approaches. He was modest rather than flamboyant, careful instead of bold, measured rather than passionate, accessible instead of demanding, and ironic rather than ideological: the consummate historical craftsman of his generation. He mastered tight and clear writing, precise and consistent argument, and a rational tone in pursuing conventional subjects and in reaching reassuring conclusions. For thirty years, Morgan gently stretched the framework that he had learned at Harvard, determined to improve rather than to shatter its priorities and conclusions. Until 1975, that is, when he published his provocative masterpiece, *American Slavery, American Freedom.*

Thirty years earlier, Morgan began his publishing career with the Puritans, humanizing them with a measure of social history in *The Puritan Family: Essays on Religion and Domestic Relations in Seventeenth-Century New England.* As befit its origins as a doctoral dissertation, the book extended a theme dear to his mentor by exploring how Puritan families applied the covenant theology that Perry Miller had so brilliantly systematized. But while Miller depicted the Puritans as powerful minds confronting terrible existential truths, Morgan found loving men and women living within a daunting faith. He would return to such reasonable Puritans in 1958 in *The Puritan Dilemma: The Story of John Winthrop,* a biography of the preeminent founder of colonial Massachusetts, and again in 1963 in *Visible Saints: The History of a Puritan Idea,* a study of the Puritan attempts to balance religious passion with the structures of church and family needed to replicate their culture through the generations. In both books, Morgan challenged the popular stereotype of the Puritans as repressed and repressive, as dark-clad and dark-spirited killers of witches, oppressors of Quakers, and persecutors of Hester Prynne. Instead, his Puritans appeared much like Morgan: reasonable and moderate in all things.

At the same time, Morgan proved his mettle as a historian of the American Revolution, beginning with *The Stamp Act Crisis: Prologue to Revolution,* which appeared in 1953 and was written with his wife, Helen M. Morgan. Joining the winning side in a historiographical debate, Morgan espoused the "consensus interpretation" of American history, which belabored the fading "Progressive interpretation." To explain the coming of the Revolution, the Progressive stalwarts Carl Becker and Charles Beard had emphasized the clash of economic and political interests between the common working people and the monied and privileged elite of colonial America. Democratic and egalitarian aspirations drove the common people to challenge both the British overlords and their minions in the colonial elite. That pressure split the elite into Loyalists, who opposed the challenge, and moderate Whigs, who were determined to control it. In Becker's famous formula, the Revolution was fought over who would rule at home as much as for home rule. Impatient with political rhetoric, the Progressives sought reality behind the lofty words of revolutionary leaders by exposing their opportunism and inconsistency in the debates with British officials in the run-up to the Revolution. Finally, the Progressive historians regarded the federal Constitution of 1787 as a conservative reaction against the democratic movement expressed in 1776 by the Declaration of Independence.

Framed earlier in the century, the Progressive interpretation seemed unsettling to the cold war culture of the 1950s, which sought a more reassuring and unifying past in which Americans shared core values that protected property, cherished stability, and avoided conflict. Morgan and his fellow "consensus historians" celebrated the ideas of the revolutionaries and smoothed over their internal conflicts and intellectual contradictions, finding a continuum from resisting Britain to the Declaration of Independence, and from the Revolution to the Constitution. Reexamining the Stamp Act debates of the mid-1760s, Morgan concluded that the colonial leaders espoused consistent principles in opposing British taxation. In particular, they spoke of their right to pay no tax unless levied by their own representatives. When the empire refused to compromise, revolution became inevitable, unifying, and limited. Morgan extended that argument to the entire era in a concise and elegant synthesis, *The Birth of the Republic* (1956), which celebrated the Constitution as the fulfillment of the cautious and principled revolution begun in the 1760s.

As a consensus historian, Morgan risked trapping himself in a past of humane Puritans and cautious revolutionaries during the late 1960s and the early 1970s, when historical fashion changed. Younger radical scholars hoped to revitalize the Progressive approach, because consensus history seemed willfully myopic and unable to explain the sources of American inequality, racism, and militarism. In 1975, however, Morgan surprised many of his own generation by embracing the new history to produce its boldest and most profound work on colonial America. Where Progressives had focused on class conflict among whites, Morgan emphasized the critical importance of racial exploitation to the murky construction of class in America. Nothing in his preceding work anticipated the passionate engagement and simmering moral outrage manifest in *American Slavery, American Freedom.*

Transcending his conventional engagement with New England, Morgan turned to relatively neglected colonial Virginia. There he found the searing crucible of America's paradoxical political culture, where liberty for whites depended on slavery for African Americans and on the dispossession of native peoples. Morgan argued that the leaders of the American Revolution "had inherited both their slaves and their attachment to freedom from an earlier generation, and they knew that the two were not unconnected. The rise of liberty and equality in America had been accompanied by the rise of slavery."

In seventeenth-century Virginia, colonists and their reluctant Indian hosts died by the thousands of hunger, disease, and genocidal war. The colonial victors created a ruthless tobacco economy that imported and exploited thousands of English laborers as indentured servants. After four to seven years of hard labor in the tobacco fields, the survivors obtained freedom, some tools, and a small farm. But social mobility proved elusive, as the former servants (known as freedmen) felt oppressed by heavy taxes and restricted to marginal lands, where they competed violently with the Indians. Malcontents blamed the colony's corrupt and arbitrary governor, William Berkeley, who profited from the taxes, from large land grants to his cronies, and from a monopoly over the profitable fur trade with the Indians. In 1676, the frustrated freedmen rallied around an ambitious opportunist, Nathaniel Bacon, to exterminate Indians and to oust the governor and burn Jamestown, his capital.

Bacon's sudden death from disease invited Berkeley's triumphant and vindictive return, in which he executed twenty-three rebels as he restored order. But sobered by the rebellion, the colony's planter elite reevaluated its exploitation of the white freedmen, lowering their taxes, enhancing their political voice, and increasing their access to good farmland at the Indians' expense. To maintain their political ascendancy, the great planters needed to lead, rather than to obstruct, the wars to dispossess and destroy frontier Indians. Such wars united the free whites by providing convenient, external, and alien scapegoats for internal frustrations and inequalities. In 1720, Gov. Alexander Spotswood explained: "A Governour of Virginia has to steer between Scylla and Charybdis, either an Indian or a Civil War. . . . Bacon's Rebellion was occasioned purely by the Governour and Council refusing to let the People go out against the Indians who at that time annoyed the Frontier."

At the end of the seventeenth century, the planter elite also benefited from a transition in the labor system away from indentured servants to enslaved Africans, imported by the thousands. From a mere 300 in 1650, the number of slaves surged to 150,000 (40 percent of the colony's total population) by 1750. The planters shifted from servants to slaves for economic reasons, but that change incidentally improved their security against another freedmen's rebellion. More slaves meant fewer servants, which meant fewer new freedmen who might stew in their frustration and rally to another rebel demagogue. Bacon's Rebellion did not cause the switch from servants to slaves, but the shift did discourage poor whites from rebelling again.

Indeed, by shifting to African slaves, the great planters found yet another reason to cultivate the common man. Instead of a threat to social order, the armed whites of common status became essential to its defense against slave rebellion. Morgan concludes, "Thus by the second quarter of the eighteenth century, Virginians had established the conditions for the mixture of slavery and freedom that was to prevail for at least another century: a slave labor force isolated from the rest of society by race and racism; a body of large planters . . . who had become practiced in politics and political maneuvering; and a larger body of small planters who had been persuaded that their interests were well served by the leadership of their big neighbors." Comfortable in their popularity with common whites, the great slaveholders of Virginia—Jefferson, Madison, and Washington—led the American Revolution to secure national independence and republican government. At our national origins, freedom for whites depended on a system of slavery for blacks.

Other historians had linked American freedom to American slavery, but none had established this connection with such thorough research and careful attention to nuance over three centuries from Elizabethan England to the Jeffersonian republic. Morgan also perfectly balanced rhetorical restraint with moral purpose, producing the twentieth century's best historical work on American origins.

A dozen years of minor projects and revised editions elapsed before Morgan produced his next substantial and original book, *Inventing the People: The Rise of Popular Sovereignty in England and America* (1988). Written during the disenchanting Reagan presidency, *Inventing the People* expresses an ironic detachment toward American democracy—a descent from the passionate engagement manifest in *American Slavery, American Freedom.* The presidency of a movie star seems to inform Morgan's fundamental premise that "government requires make believe." All systems of effective government, even purported democracies, are fundamentally oligarchies that employ collective "fictions" to secure credulity and allegiance from the voting masses. "In a sense," Morgan argues, "representation had always been a fiction designed to secure popular consent to a governing aristocracy." Jefferson taught us to say that "all men are created equal," as a "self-evident truth" beyond challenge—despite the yawning gap with our reality of great and growing economic inequality in a corrupt polity where only multimillionaires and their friends can afford national office. But Morgan finds a silver lining: "a fiction must bear some resemblance to fact." Occasionally and conspicuously, the fiction of democracy does "restrain the few for the benefit of the many."

*Inventing the People* painstakingly documents the gradual creation of our dominant fiction—popular sovereignty—from the ruins of its predecessor: the divine right of English kings. Lacking the vivid personalities and episodes that humanize and dramatize Morgan's previous books, *Inventing the People* leaves readers cold: impressed by the author's expertise but unmoved by his interpretation, which more clearly reveals how democratic fiction perpetuates the ruling few than how it benefits the ruled many.

Now Morgan returns with an original book written in a more accessible and popular vein, a celebratory biography of Benjamin Franklin, the most avuncular and versatile of the men who led the American Revolution. Given the commercial success of Joseph Ellis's *Founding Brothers* and David McCullough's *John Adams,* Morgan can count on the revived cult of the Founding Fathers: the eagerness of many readers (mostly men) to find founts of original wisdom that might redeem our own political culture. Rarely has such an accomplished historian had such a golden opportunity to reach such a large audience. Unfortunately, Morgan has surprisingly little to say about Franklin that is new or challenging.

In Franklin, Morgan has a truly great subject. A self-educated polymath endowed with formidable charm and genius, Franklin became the leading figure in colonial politics, literature, science, and social reform. Born in 1706 into the modest circumstances of a candle-maker's family in the stagnating seaport of Boston, Franklin early bolted from his indenture as apprentice to his brother's newspaper. With impeccable timing, Franklin moved south to Philadelphia, just then becoming the most dynamic seaport city in the colonies. By hard work, formidable ability, and useful friends, Franklin developed a lucrative newspaper and an almanac. His almanac's witty aphorisms included the characteristic "He's a Fool that cannot conceal his Wisdom." Above all, Franklin became the first self-made man as public celebrity—a still-powerful and pivotal type in our culture.

Once enriched, Franklin gradually retired from business, entrusting his press to a junior partner. Freed from daily commerce, he remade himself as a public-spirited gentleman. He accumulated wealth to pursue fame, status, and influence—while doing good deeds for his common neighbors. During the 1730s and the 1740s, Franklin helped found and lead an array of cultural and philanthropic institutions, including the Library Company and the American Philosophical Society. He also conducted scientific experiments, primarily with electricity, demonstrating that it composed lightning. Published in London and Paris, his scientific reports dazzled European intellectuals, rendering Franklin more famous than any other British colonist. A utilitarian at heart, he also applied science to craft inventions meant to improve common life: a lightning rod to protect buildings and a stove to heat them. "Franklin took pleasure," Morgan explains, "in making daily life better for himself and everyone around him."

As a public-spirited gentleman, Franklin plunged into politics, becoming Pennsylvania's pre-eminent politician. By energizing the Pennsylvania assembly, he antagonized Thomas Penn, the colony's English proprietor. Determined to preserve his vast landholdings from assembly taxation, Penn directed his appointed governor to veto tax bills that funded frontier defenses. The assembly sent Franklin to London to lobby Penn. When that failed, Franklin lingered, pressing the imperial bureaucracy to convert Pennsylvania into a royal colony with a Crown-appointed governor. Foiled a second time, Franklin stayed on to represent the assemblies of Pennsylvania, Georgia, and Massachusetts in arguing against the new British program of colonial taxes and stricter regulations.

Frustrated again, Franklin headed back to Philadelphia, arriving in early 1775, ready to assist the armed revolution against British rule. In 1777, he left America for Paris to seek French military assistance. Persistent, tactful, and engaging, Franklin dazzled the French and won the alliance that proved essential to the Americans' military victory. Morgan remarks that "the experience was a little intoxicating, or would have been for a lesser man." In 1782 and 1783, Franklin led the American commission that negotiated an extraordinarily favorable peace treaty with the British.

In 1785, Franklin returned home in triumph and promptly won election and then reelection as the "president" of Pennsylvania's Executive Council. In 1787, he also represented his state in the convention that met in Philadelphia to draft a new, more national constitution for the American union. Slowed by age, Franklin played only a minimal role in the convention. Retiring from politics in 1788, he died two years later, at the age of eighty-four.

To narrate this rich but often contentious life, Morgan relies almost exclusively on the materials that Franklin wrote or received, currently available on a CD-ROM produced by the Packard Humanities Institute and in the forty-six edited volumes of papers published by Yale University

Press. *Benjamin Franklin* is, Morgan acknowledges, "the result of reading everything on the disk and in the volumes but not much else, and therefore pretty one-sided, a letter of introduction to a man worth knowing, worth spending time with." Morgan neglected the works of other historians and avoided visiting the archival collections of Franklin's contemporaries, who often radically dissented from his perspective. Consequently, Morgan can tell only half the story, for the one-sided sources skew his interpretation, denying fair play to Franklin's opponents and lacking sufficient complexity to explain his personality. Justifying a half effort as an introduction will not do, for in these pages we meet the preposterous: a bland and superficial Franklin. "Through his papers we can perhaps know him more thoroughly and comprehensively than his contemporaries could," Morgan insists. In fact, by depending almost exclusively on Franklin's friends and Franklin's own carefully crafted paper trail, Morgan misses darker dimensions too well known to his rivals.

Franklin shrewdly cultivated a charming, genial persona that dazzled his friends and now enamors his biographer. "We may be permitted a small regret of our own for having been born too late to enjoy his company," Morgan elegiacally observes. "We can never catch the warmth of his smile, the tone of his voice, the little gestures, the radiant presence that drew people to him wherever he went." Sometimes Morgan indulges his regret in the present tense, a voice of I-am-there-with-Benjamin-Franklin, who "likes to be in the open air, walking the city streets, walking the countryside, walking the deck of a ship. Indoors, he likes to be with people, sipping tea with young women, raising a glass with other men, playing chess, telling jokes, singing songs." Presenting the Founding Father as boon companion, Morgan concludes: "Wherever Franklin went, people loved him. Wherever he lived, he made friends, close friends, loyal friends, adoring friends." Franklin was "a man with a wisdom about himself that comes only to the great of heart."

Occasionally, Morgan considers that there might be more to Franklin than his sunny public persona revealed: "By now it must be apparent that Franklin is not so easy to know as he sometimes seems to be." After all, Franklin advised: "Let all Men know thee, but no man know thee thoroughly." Yet Morgan quickly reassures us that Franklin modestly masked only the depths of his commitment to the well-being of others, which ran to the very core of his being: "He is so hard to know because it is so hard to distinguish his natural impulses from his principles." But Morgan is not fooled, for, "if Franklin holds something back, he does not deceive us."

And so Morgan cannot easily account for the many enemies who considered Franklin especially devious. Morgan's first strategy is to minimize their number and to attribute their spite to politics: "True, in the course of a long life, especially after he entered politics, he made enemies and sometimes returned their enmity. But he made far more friends."

In fact, the young Franklin made his share of enemies before his midlife venture into politics. Ambitious and opportunistic, he could turn his charm off as well as on. His youthful departure from the service of his brother James was abrupt, acrimonious, and illegal. In Philadelphia, he quarreled violently with his former friend John Collins; with his initial employer Samuel Keimer; with an early partner, Hugh Meredith; and with the rival almanac writer Titan Leeds. None of these five early conflicts finds a place in Morgan's relentlessly sunny picture of Franklin.

Franklin made many more enemies once he plunged into politics, but Morgan dismisses them all as vicious or crazy. In England, Franklin tangled acrimoniously with Thomas Penn and with Lord Hillsborough, the Crown's Secretary of State for colonial affairs. After one especially contentious interview with Penn, Franklin exploded with rage, which leads Morgan to find only a variant of his bright side: "His anger even adds a little spice to a personality that would be almost too lovable without it." Reading only Franklin's side of the dispute with Hillsborough, Morgan dismisses the latter as "a prime example of the heedless aristocrat whom British politics could drop into positions of authority." True enough, Hillsborough was a stickler for imperial authority, but he was also a dedicated, efficient, and principled administrator.

Wedded to Franklin's perspective, Morgan contrasts the corruption of British politics (of which there was plenty) with American virtue (which was scarcer than legend insists). This moral polarity obscures Franklin's eager ability to play the British game for personal gain—and Hillsborough's capacity for self-sacrifice. Seeking wealth and power, Franklin assembled a cartel of colonial and English grandees with political clout to lobby the Crown to grant them a new colony of twenty million acres of fertile land in the Illinois country, then an Indian domain. The partners would profit from the colony's patronage and by selling the Indians' lands to colonial settlers. Hillsborough recognized that the ill-conceived colony would cost a fortune to administer; would provoke a costly new war with the Indians, and would increase, rather than reduce, colonial insubordination. Stubbornly principled, he committed political suicide by blocking the grant, thereby offending powerful politicians who were in on Franklin's land scheme. They forced Hillsborough's resignation in 1772. Morgan barely mentions this episode, so revealing of the character of both Franklin and Hillsborough, and so important to the building crisis between America and Britain. Preferring that Franklin represent American virtue, Morgan attributes the wheeling and dealing to bribe British politicos entirely to Franklin's English partner, Thomas Walpole.

During the Revolution, Franklin reaped a new set of American rivals, who did not consider him a paragon of virtue. In 1777–78, Congress saddled Franklin in Paris with two fellow commissioners, one the notoriously corrupt Silas Deane, whom Franklin defended, and the other, the congenitally suspicious Arthur Lee, whom Franklin despised. Franklin abruptly dismissed Lee's suspicions that their secretary, Edward Bancroft, was a British spy. In fact, Bancroft was on the British payroll. Sometimes, paranoids do have enemies. Morgan does not mention Bancroft, the better to share Franklin's insistence that Lee was simply insane.

In 1778, Congress replaced Lee with another commissioner, John Adams, who soon shared most of Lee's suspicions and added a few of his own. Adams regarded Franklin as lazy, dissipated, devious, and too accommodating to French interests. He also blamed Franklin for the many disputes in the American delegation: "Franklin's cunning will be to divide us. To this end, he will provoke, he will insinuate, he will intrigue, he will maneuvre." Siding with Franklin, Morgan dismisses "Adams's ravings" as "paranoid delusions of persecution and treachery." To vindicate Franklin, Morgan contradicts the celebration of Adams in David McCullough's biography. In the recent spate of popular biographies of Founders, readers find one placed on a pedestal at the expense of foolish others.

In addition to taking Franklin's rivals more seriously, a thorough biographer would have examined his family life more closely and critically. Before marrying, he fathered a child out of wedlock, perhaps with a servant. He later rather ungallantly praised his marriage to Deborah Read as necessary to satisfy the physical cravings that had previously led him into the dangerous embraces of prostitutes. Poorly educated, Deborah did not serve Franklin's ambition to move in learned and high society. He left her behind in Philadelphia for years as he pursued his career and other women in London. His letters to her are surprisingly dull and formulaic. He lavished his wit instead on letters flirting with a growing array of other women, increasingly of an age to be his daughters. But Morgan sees no marital evil, insisting that "Franklin's marriage to Deborah was loving and happy." Morgan concludes: "Deborah never faltered in her love and trust; and he never lost a deep affection for her, though we will never know whether he remained sexually faithful during his long absences." Certain that Franklin never deceives him, Morgan invokes uncertainty only to deny the bad news.

Franklin's troubled relationship with his son William also warrants more careful probing before we conclude that the father's affability ran to his very core. Initially devoted to William, Franklin secured his appointment in 1762 as royal governor of New Jersey. In 1775, when William chose loyalty to empire over deference to his father, Franklin abruptly, angrily, and permanently broke with his son. Despite having defied his own father (in leaving Boston), Franklin demanded political obedience from his own son: "There are natural duties which precede political ones, and cannot be extinguished by them." Franklin did nothing when his fellow revolutionaries imprisoned his son. Instead, he took in William's son—William Temple Franklin—and taught him to despise his father. After the war, Franklin coldly rebuffed William's earnest attempts at reconciliation. Morgan reports these events in passing as if they reveal nothing fundamental about Franklin's character.

Morgan's basic premise, that Franklin was a lovable, ingenuous, and talented man with lots of friends, cannot illuminate his political misjudgments, which reveal a man far too proud of his subtlety and a bit too sure of his superiority. Especially frequent during his stint in London as a colonial agent, Franklin's mistakes exacerbated the imperial crisis that he longed to alleviate. He foolishly and stubbornly worked to make Pennsylvania a royal colony, despite abundant evidence that the Crown had no interest in challenging Thomas Penn and that the empire would prove a more powerful and demanding master than the proprietor. Underestimating colonial resentment of the Stamp Tax, Franklin secured an appointment as tax collector in Pennsylvania for a friend, who soon rued the day, when mob intimidation compelled his resignation. To relieve the violent crisis provoked by that tax, Franklin pitched to British authorities a specious distinction between internal taxes (such as the Stamp Tax), which Americans would never accept, and external taxes (such as customs duties), which they long had accepted. In fact, they opposed both. Franklin's facile distinction enabled Parliament to lift one crisis, by repealing the Stamp Tax, only to substitute another by levying increased duties on colonial imports. Morgan clearly reveals these missteps, but treats each as an exception to the rule of Franklin's superior insight, failing thereby to recognize the damning picture that emerges as the "exceptions" accumulate.

In 1773, Franklin procured stolen letters, which he promptly sent to the radical leaders in Massachusetts. The letters revealed that the colony's royal governor, Thomas Hutchinson, had urged tighter British restrictions on American liberties. Incredibly, Franklin believed that the letters would relieve the imperial crisis by persuading Americans that they should blame only Hutchinson, in particular, and not the British administration, in general, for the tensions. Franklin expected his correspondent to show the letters only to trusted associates and, by all means, to keep them out of the press. Instead, the radicals published the letters, creating an uproar in Massachusetts against Hutchinson—and in Britain against Franklin. By dealing in purloined letters, Franklin had violated the code of honor expected of gentlemen. The royal Privy Council summoned Franklin to a hearing at which the acerbic prosecutor, Alexander Wedderburn, subjected him to an hour of diatribe, to the great applause and amusement of the aristocratic spectators. The government then summarily dismissed Franklin from his office as postmaster general for the colonies.

With some cause, British officials considered Franklin a cunning intriguer who sowed misunderstandings, but they mistook his miscalculations for a conscious and cunning plot to destroy the empire—which, in fact, he wanted to save (on colonial terms). To absolve Franklin, Morgan fully blames the British; his Franklin spent "year after year trying to patch up the empire, trying to undo the mistakes of a heedless ministry, trying to guide colonial protests in constructive ways, trying to interpret them constructively to an uncomprehending English public." True enough, Franklin tried to do all of those things, but he did them badly. Overconfident in his powers of reason and manipulation, he made mistakes that deepened the distrust between Britons and Americans, hastening a civil war between kindred peoples. Franklin's tragedy is that no one had better appreciated the potential of the united empire, and no one had been better situated to speak frankly to both peoples, to clarify their dispute before it proved fatal to thousands.

*23*

# Threads of History

*March 11, 2002*

Trained to seek and interpret written documents, American historians usually are flummoxed when confronted with the past's household objects. What is a historian to make of a spinning wheel or a linen tablecloth? Long abstracted from their original context and deposited in the display cases or dusty drawers of museums, such things seem mute about social meaning—and best left to antiquarians and fine-art curators, who can doggedly trace the stylistic connections and developments that matter so much to collectors but so little to historians.

But perhaps these objects can help historians who operate where the paper trail peters out. Such is the plight of scholars who study the colonial era; doubly so, when they seek the traces of common people rather than the well-documented elite; and triply so, when their subjects are women rather than men. Historians of women must struggle to extract meaning from a paucity of surviving writing by colonial women. Even for New England, the most literate region of colonial America, the texts by women are preciously rare: some letters and a handful of diaries or account books.

Necessity being the mother of inventive scholars, women's historians have proved especially ingenious at teasing evidence from stray references in the records of civil, criminal, and probate courts. Among these adepts, Laurel Thatcher Ulrich stands out as exceptionally accomplished and insightful. She reached scholarly leadership by an unorthodox route. Raising a family first, in midlife she began to pursue graduate study at a public university, where she devoted her dissertation to a topic doubly damned by the then-conventional wisdom as insignificant: colonial women in northern New England. Surely only someone resigned to academic marginality would investigate marginal people dwelling in marginal places—rather than, say, men in Massachusetts or Virginia.

But sheer ability prevailed. Published in 1982, *Good Wives: Image and*

*The Age of Homespun: Objects and Stories in the Creation of an American Myth,* by Laurel Thatcher Ulrich (Alfred A. Knopf, 2001)

*Reality in the Lives of Women in Northern New England, 1650–1750* introduced a distinctive new voice in historical scholarship. A social historian, Ulrich dutifully plunged into the court cases and probate inventories of local records to document the lives of common women. But she broke with the social science model that turned statistical averages into bland types, an approach that she characterizes as "freezing people into a collective anonymity that denies either agency or the capacity to change."

Instead, in obscure records she found vivid stories that illuminated the dramatic lives led by so-called common people. Determined to evoke the past as well as to analyze it, Ulrich offered "an extended description constructed from a series of vignettes." And she found drama where no one else had bothered to look, presenting "much about housekeeping, childbearing, and ordinary churchgoing, about small conflicts experienced by forgotten women, and about little triumphs that history has not recorded." Although attentive to scholarly questions—such as whether colonial women were losing or gaining in status—Ulrich primarily sought to recover what mattered to past women: "the magnification of motherhood, the idealization of conjugal love, and the elevation of female religiosity." With a humane imagination and a keen eye for telling details, she brought into focus a surprisingly coherent and compelling picture of women's importance in colonial life.

Eight years later, Ulrich published a still more eloquent, moving, and important book: *A Midwife's Tale: The Life of Martha Ballard Based on Her Diary, 1785–1812.* Once again, she took on a risky subject that had been rejected by more conventional historians: the life of an obscure woman from central Maine who left a long but repetitive and cryptic diary. Full of daily chores and transactions but thin on observation, the diary seemed dry, dull, and trivial to the few historians who bothered to examine its cramped handwriting. Through innovative and exhaustive research in local records, Ulrich reconstituted Martha Ballard's familial, social, and economic relationships with hundreds of neighbors—children, women, and men—to restore the rich meanings implicit in the diary's terse entries. Recast as an "earnest, steady, gentle, and courageous record," the diary revealed the lost world of a country village in the early republic. Ballard's diary helped Ulrich to reveal the vibrant female networks for making and exchanging labor and household produce, including homespun cloth. Eighteenth-century women reappeared as earthy, vibrant, and essential—rather than as the passive dependents of stereotype. In a vivid and telling metaphor, Ulrich likens the social interplay of men and women to cloth: "Think of the white threads as women's activities, the blue as men's, then imagine the resulting social web. Clearly, some activities in an eighteenth-century town brought men and women together. Others defined their separateness." No historian has done more to recover a detailed sense of the past from so many disparate scraps of apparently opaque evidence.

Striking as literature as well as research, *A Midwife's Tale* presents Ulrich's findings in a lyrical prose attentive to a reader's imagination. By focusing each chapter on a particularly difficult but implicitly rich passage, she draws her readers into the challenges and the rewards of historical research as detective work. She then constructs tight and compelling descriptions of action and place in a setting distant in time and culture, rendering tangible the differentness of the early republic. And yet Ulrich also treats her subjects with empathy, rendering them comprehensible as fellow humans in their abilities and limits, their joys and sorrow. While sensing the alienation of time, her readers also feel a sense of kinship with the people who lived there. No book in recent memory has better combined the respect of fellow scholars with the affection of general readers.

What could Ulrich do for an encore? In her new book, *The Age of Homespun,* she takes on the especially daunting challenge of finding meaning in the woven things of New England's museums: "sheets, pillowcases, tablecloths, napkins, towels, quilts, blankets, grain bags, handkerchiefs, aprons, coverlets" and Indian baskets. "This is a book," Ulrich explains, "about the objects nineteenth-century Americans saved, the stories they told, and the stories that got away." For small things, she makes large claims: domestic objects reveal "the flow of common life" that generates "the electricity of history," providing the context for more famous political events like the coming of the American Revolution. And who better to make history from mute objects than the historian who moved a Maine midwife and her diary into the center of historical scholarship?

Once again, Ulrich must convert a dense obstacle into a crystalline prism for viewing the past. Between us and the eighteenth century there looms a formidable nineteenth-century mythology that romanticized the colonial era as an "Age of Homespun." In that allegedly simpler, happier, and more authentic time, virtuous living and hard work by self-sufficient households produced an almost universal prosperity, without extremes of wealth and poverty, power and exploitation. The myth emerged during the 1840s and the 1850s as compensation for a new and troubling time of factory-made and store-bought goods. As household production withered, Yankee antiquarians avidly collected and displayed the old tools, furnishings, and clothing of their newly sanctified forbears. Ulrich observes: "The mythology of household production gave something to everyone. For sentimentalists, spinning and weaving represented the centrality of home and family, for evolutionists the triumph of civilization over savagery, for craft revivalists the harmony of labor and art, for feminists women's untapped productive power, and for antimodernists the virtues of a bygone age."

Yet those mythic and protean qualities tend to distance the objects from contemporary historians. Attentive to the ideological distortions of nineteenth-century "memory," historians cannot see beyond to find colonial meaning in the old things. Surely, a display of spinning wheels reveals more about nineteenth-century collectors than about eighteenth-century users. Ulrich, however, wishes to proceed beyond debunking the mythmakers. Indeed, she thanks them for saving so many objects made and used by women who left so few documents.

Ulrich does attend to the sort of big social transformation that historians ordinarily seek: in this case, to the rise and fall of a female-conducted household mode of production. During the early seventeenth century, in New England as in Britain, male artisans wove cloth as a specialized and centralized craft. But at the end of that century and the beginning of the next, cloth making in New England became decentralized and feminized, conducted in most households by women and their daughters—rather than by men.

In an era when cloth and clothing were relatively precious and rare, linen tablecloths were more valuable than the tables they covered. As the producers of critical goods, New England's women enjoyed considerable importance and authority within their households. During the mid-nineteenth century, however, they lost productive clout at home as the market and new technologies centralized cloth making in factories. Lower-class women had to seek wage work in the factories while middle-class women struggled to transcend new roles that threatened to be merely ornamental or admonitory.

Ulrich also corrects the nineteenth-century mythology that sanitized New England's colonial past. She detects "the dark underside of New England history" in beautiful embroideries that others read only for their fine workmanship and exquisite taste. Noting the wealth and leisure that allowed Eunice Bourne to make fine needlework in 1753, Ulrich concludes: "The economic development that elevated the Bournes . . . to the provincial elite left urban poverty and economic unrest in its wake." The Bournes derived their wealth by exploiting their trustee power over the Mashpee Indians to accumulate valuable lands on Cape Cod.

Throughout *The Age of Homespun,* Ulrich restores the Indian presence formerly erased by a mythic history that downplayed their violent dispossession and that suggested their consent to marginalization and disappearance. The bucolic myth of the Age of Homespun implies that Indians had vanished, giving way to an improved landscape tended by a happier people favored by divine providence. Ulrich, however, will not absolve domestic life and colonial women from the public violence of colonial men. Instead, she concludes: "cloth literally transformed the landscape as Algonkian beaver passed into the hands of English felt-makers and English sheep began to graze on American meadows."

While noting the colonists' grim effectiveness as conquerors, Ulrich denies their descendants' claims to total victory, their mythic insistence that New England's Indians had vanished. She closely analyzes the nineteenth-century Indian baskets collected by the myth-makers, who remained oblivious to their testimony that the natives had adapted and persisted long after their supposed disappearance. Ulrich also corrects the museums that have long defined Indians as a timeless, primeval essence that could experience change only as a form of decay.

The Maine State Museum, for example, displays a pocketbook made by an Abenaki (or Pigwacket) Indian woman named Molly Ocket. Treated by the museum as a vestige of ancient tradition, the displayed object loses its richest meaning: as a syncretic piece made in 1785 by a native woman particularly savvy in Yankee ways and for a Yankee consumer. Although woven in a traditional manner, the pocketbook is a European form, and Molly Ocket combined settler wool with native materials: hemp and moose hair. Ulrich notes: "The pocketbook is both an Abenaki and a colonial artifact." Through this syncretic pocketbook, Ulrich redefines the essence of "Indian-ness" away from an impossible purity to, instead, an adaptability that consistently interwove tradition with innovation in a struggle for cultural survival in a transformed land. So recast, New England's Indians reappear as a continuous presence, putting the lie to the mocking label applied to the pocketbook by a nineteenth-century curator:

Old Mollocket<br>
Made this Pocket<br>
She was a Pequawket<br>
And last on the Docket

Although attentive to big questions, Ulrich is once again primarily interested in the details, in the textures and the relationships of daily life: in "the unseen technologies, interconnections, and contradictions that lie beneath audible events." She delights in explaining the cultivation of flax, the operation of spinning wheels, the variety of stitches used in fine linens, and the diverse weaves employed in baskets. Above all, she loves to find and tell stories generated by supposedly ordinary people. Setting aside her larger argument for long stretches, she narrates "the stories of individual people—makers, collectors, and users of ordinary household goods."

Although individually fascinating, the stories are, ultimately, too many and too diffuse to preserve a clear sense of direction—which marks *The*

*Age of Homespun* as even more daring, but less cohesive, than *A Midwife's Tale.* Thanks to a central focus on one woman dwelling in a single town, *A Midwife's Tale* perfectly balances the details with a clear story: Martha Ballard's struggle to adapt to a society transformed by the American Revolution and to a life cycle that diminished her power over her children. In her new book, however, Ulrich ranges among dozens of capsule biographies and distinct episodes scattered over three centuries and six states, to produce a knotted texture that ultimately defies her creative ability to highlight a central thread.

Ulrich names, begins, and frames each chapter with a particular object or two crisply illustrated in beautiful black-and-white photographs. The featured fourteen include Indian baskets, spinning wheels, a cupboard, a chimneypiece, a niddy noddy, a bed rug, silk embroideries, a pocketbook, a tablecloth, a counterpane, a blanket, and a stocking. As opening gambits, the objects catch the eye and intrigue the imagination. Arranged in a chronological sequence from 1676 to 1837, the things and their chapters generally draw the reader forward through time—but with many digressions backward and anticipations forward. After discussing the object's apparent provenance and the story (if any) provided by the donor, Ulrich sets to work in the local records to correct or complete the original account, thereby illuminating the piece's social and cultural context.

This innovative framework sometimes works brilliantly. The best chapter features the largest and most striking piece, a cupboard made about 1715 in Hadley, Massachusetts. Its bright blue columns frame a bold array of inscribed flowers, vines, roman letters, and the owner's maiden name: Hannah Barnard. By boldly asserting a woman's identity and power of possession, the cupboard refutes the notion that colonial women were passive, anonymous, and powerless. True enough, the legal system awarded men a monopoly over family identity, real property, and most of the documents that survive for historians to use, but the cupboard attests that the written documents do not tell the whole story.

Through Hannah Barnard's cupboard, Ulrich recovers the informal and customary power that colonial women exercised within their families and through the generations. They inherited and controlled the dispensation of "movables"—cloth, clothing, furniture, and some livestock. Although usually neglected by probate inventories, these objects were as essential to a farm family as the land owned by the men. With ingenious research, Ulrich demonstrates the recurrence over the generations of the name "Hannah Barnard," whose possessor, in turn, inherited the precious cupboard. Ulrich observes: "The cupboard helped to preserve the name, but the name also transformed the cupboard. Marked with the first owner's name, it became . . . an inalienable possession." She concludes: "The cupboard teaches us that in a world where most forms of wealth were controlled by male heads of household, certain objects were informally owned by women." Through the transmission of names and objects, women created a sense of lineage that sometimes paralleled, but often crosscut, the more conspicuous and official patrilineal system. In this particular chapter, the featured object proves eloquent and central to the analysis, from beginning to end.

In other chapters, however, the featured objects prove far less revealing. Once introduced, they quickly recede as Ulrich, instead, pursues an eclectic set of stories loosely connected to the things or to her larger subject. Thus the fifth chapter begins with an intriguing niddy noddy—a cross reel for winding and measuring yarn—from Newburyport in 1769. The chapter, however, soon abandons this particular object and races far beyond that town and year. Ulrich discusses the widespread patriotic spinning bees that supported the boycotts to protest British taxation; then she turns to a detailed recounting of the diverse stories within a succession of eighteenth-century diaries kept by five disparate and far-flung New Englanders. Two New Hampshire men, Samuel Lane and Mathew Patten, noted the importance of their daughters in the production of cloth. Young Deborah Sylvester of Massachusetts linked cloth making to religion and marriage. Mary Cooper of Long Island vividly lamented her hard work and callous husband. Wealthy Elizabeth Porter Phelps mused about courtship, slavery, and religion in western Massachusetts. Ulrich asserts: "Household manufacturing is the thread that binds these stories together." Often it is a slender thread. Drawing on Phelps's diary, Ulrich reports that a servant named Sarah Bartlet burned down a tavern in 1767; her apparent tie to the larger story is that Bartlet began the fire in some flaxen yarn. Perhaps, Ulrich muses, Sarah felt cheated by her master's accounting of her spinning. Given Ulrich's talents as researcher and narrator, the twisting and turning stories are all fascinating—but they do not hang together.

And, in contrast to Hannah Barnard's eloquent cupboard, the opening niddy noddy provides scant information. The object's cameo appearance is merely symbolic: a convenient visual image. In the rest of the chapter, Ulrich applies her distinctive talents to interpreting the sort of written documents—diaries, letters, genealogies, and inventories—that are the stock-in-trade of social historians. She doesn't really need the niddy noddy, which fails to deliver on the apparent promise that things can serve as powerful sources in their own right.

The last chapter begins with a stocking from 1837, unfinished and still attached to two needles and balls of linen. What does it mean? "No one knows who began it or why it was saved," she laments. After catching the reader's eye, the linen stocking vanishes from the chapter as

Ulrich turns instead to an entertaining ramble through the various new forms of cloth making introduced by market incentives during the 1830s. She describes the brief, colorful, but futile boom in silk making; the development of textile factories with new forms of time and labor discipline—which led to strikes by young women workers; and to the outwork production of straw and palm leaf hats in country towns. Along the way, Ulrich details the lives and the cloth making of Sarah Weeks Sheldon of Vermont and Persis Sibley Andrews of Maine, as revealed by their letters and diaries. Finally, she narrates the experiences of two other Yankee women (Patty Sessions and Lucy Meserve Smith), who converted to Mormonism, emigrated to Utah, and continued to make cloth to the end of their lives.

Despite its geographic range, the final chapter seems incomplete. For balance, the book would benefit from a concluding counterpart to the opening attention afforded to the creation of New England's domestic mode of cloth production. In the early chapters, Ulrich presents detailed research in probate records to specify with quantitative precision the dissemination of spinning wheels and weaving looms at the start of the eighteenth century. But she offers nothing comparable for the 1830s and the 1840s to quantify and define the pace at which those objects left New England's households. Ulrich demonstrates the emergence of domestic cloth-making with precision, but she merely asserts the system's decline. Rather than concluding with Patty Sessions and Lucy Meserve Smith, who remained lifelong cloth makers to the end of the nineteenth-century, Ulrich might have provided examples of women gradually forsaking the spinning and weaving of their earlier lives. For want of that closure, the suggestive but unfinished stocking proves an apt symbol for the last chapter—and more generally for the difficult task of reading objects as texts.

24

# Transformer

*June 21, 2004*

During a long and accomplished career, Alfred F. Young has made a remarkable professional journey from the margins to the celebrated center of his chosen field, the study of the American Revolution. In decades past, the keepers of the scholarly mainstream delimited Young's work as "radical," a label which he wore as a badge of honor as he encouraged and defended like-minded historians. "What," he asks "is a 'radical historian'—a historian of radicalism, [or] a radical who is a historian?" Of course, Young remains both, studying the relatively weak and the poor in the past to shed light on persistent inequality and injustice in the present. This perspective has been deeply personal, driven by a sense of standing outside of true respectability in his profession.*

In recent years, however, Young has achieved a surprising degree of professional success. Seventy-eight years old, and some thirteen years after retiring from an academic post, he is at the peak of his productivity, influence, and professional standing. This shift is less a pilgrim's tale of his progress than a decisive, if belated, shift in the center of scholarly gravity toward the principles of inclusion that Young has championed for decades. Once deemed radical, his scholarly priorities have now become almost conventional. These include a focus on the history of protest movements by common people; the detailed biographical reconstruction of hitherto obscure lives; an exhaustive and innovative archival hunt for original documents to illuminate that obscurity; and a drive to communicate history to a broader audience through partnerships with museums and public historians.

Young began his career in the 1950s as a self-conscious outsider in a world of now largely forgotten constraints. An urban Jew determined to study colonial and revolutionary America, Young ventured into an

* The biographical information and quotations in this essay derive from Alfred F. Young, "An Outsider and the Progress of a Career in History," *The William and Mary Quarterly*, 3d ser. 70 (July 1995): 499–512

*Masquerade: The Life and Times of Deborah Sampson, Continental Soldier*, by Alfred F. Young (Alfred A. Knopf, 2004) especially conservative field dominated by cultural conservatives ruling from a handful of Ivy League institutions. In a notorious presidential address to the American Historical Association in 1962, the distinguished historian Carl Bridenbaugh wondered whether the "urban-bred . . . products of lower middle-class or foreign origins" could understand, or should study, colonial and revolutionary America, which he imagined as overwhelmingly English. The address understandably outraged the growing numbers of young Jewish scholars entering that field without a New England pedigree. They included Alfred F. Young, the son of an immigrant from Poland via London's East End to New York.

Although raised in a middle-class family, Young felt the pervasive anti-Semitism of leading institutions with quotas for "Hebrews." Denied admission to Harvard (despite graduating third in a high school class of four hundred), he instead attended nearby Queens College, where he wrote for the school newspaper and admired Vera Shlakman, a radical scholar of American radicalism and the urban working class. A few years later, she fell prey to McCarthyism, and was fired for refusing to confess her political beliefs and associations to a congressional committee—a formative moment in the progress of Young's alienation. Graduating from Queens in 1946, Young pursued graduate study in American history at Columbia and Northwestern, where he developed his identification "with the outsiders in early America, ignored, marginalized, or patronized by insider historians." Seeking an academic position, he found his niche "at nonelite schools," the University of Connecticut, Paterson State Teachers College, and Northern Illinois University.

From the beginning, Young's scholarly radicalism has been more sensibility than system, more populist than Marxist. Drawn to stories of popular protest, he balked at any comprehensive theory forced on the diverse evidence: "I was attracted very little to the laws of history but very much to the side that stressed movements." As a student, he voraciously read the Marxist historians and novelists of the Old Left, including Louis Hacker and Howard Fast. Although inspired by their subjects—rebellious slaves, Sons of Liberty, Jewish militants, and labor unions—Young resisted their formulaic approach. Imposing a "sterile economic determinism" while "ransacking the past for progressive forerunners[,] they showed little sense of critical inquiry." Ever questioning and probing, Young could never uncritically accept any orthodoxy, even from the Left.

Rather than apply any historical theory rigorously, he relentlessly pursued new evidence in primary documents meant "to give voice to ordinary people." Uneasy with facile generalizations, he found that "diaries, letters, memoirs, and oral history [were] more mind opening." During the 1960s, his "unending infatuation with original sources" led Young and two co-editors to collect and publish fifty volumes of primary sources, many on subjects long considered devoid of evidence: African American history, women's history, and popular protest movements. Although radical in his interests, Young tenaciously adhered to a conventional reliance on empirical evidence. "I am cautious about proof and conservative with my sources," he explains. With dogged determination, he reversed the conservative charge that radicals impose their politics on the past. On the contrary, he asserts, the documented truth shall set us free. This principled empiricism also preserved his work from the relativism that too often characterizes the cultural Left.

Fifteen years in the making, his first book, *The Democratic Republicans of New York: The Origins, 1763–1797,* is a massive tome, six hundred pages dense with particulars. Young found and tapped dozens of little-known collections from far-flung archives, all reached in a 1937 Ford, decades before microfilm and the Internet smoothed a scholar's way. Such painstaking attention to detail compelled readers to consider a novel interpretation of a classic issue: how the Jeffersonians had defeated the Federalists, vindicating a democratic understanding of the American Revolution. Challenging the conventional accounts, which paradoxically credited democracy to elite leaders such as Thomas Jefferson, Young advanced a political history "from the bottom up" by recovering the role of common voters and populist agitators such as Jedediah Peck. A small farmer who combined evangelical preaching with political mobilization, Peck helped to secure the electoral revolution of 1800–1801, which toppled the Federalist grandees from both state and national power.

A critical success, *Democratic Republicans* established Young in a paradoxical position within the profession: as "the dean of radical historians," he was an outsider become a variety of insider. He applied his improved standing in academia to promote and defend a new generation of radical historians who espoused the New Left during the late 1960s and the early 1970s. They examined the American past to expose the foundations of racial inequality and overseas militarism. Bitterly critical of their own academic institutions for various complicities, these scholars sometimes paid with their jobs. Taking up their cause, Young defended academic freedom by gathering nationwide evidence of abuses and by helping to lead a committee that produced a "Bill of Rights" for historians that was adopted by the American Historical Association in 1974, a dozen years after Bridenbaugh's dyspeptic address to that same group.

From 1968 to 1993, Young also promoted a younger generation of scholars by collecting original essays into three influential collections on the history of American radicalism in general and the American Revolution in particular. Challenging the prior emphasis on the American Revolution as a consensual movement led by an elite, the essays attended to urban mobs, agrarian rebellions, evangelical religion, the cultural role of gender, and radical experiments in democracy. In retrospect, they also registered a shift in tone, from the assertive optimism of the 1960s to the measured sobriety of the 1990s. The first collection finds inspiration in the mobilization for the American Revolution, while the last collection focuses more on the often-disappointing aftermath of the struggle, finding as much to mourn as to celebrate. Rather than entirely blame the usual elite suspects, the last volume also attends to the contradictions and limitations within the radicalism of the revolutionary generation.

During the 1980s, Young also pursued his collaborative talents in public history, making a double set of discoveries. First, he mastered the material culture of eighteenth-century America—prints, broadsides, clothing, crafts, and tools—as another means of understanding the common men and women of the revolutionary generation. Second, he recognized the potential of local historical societies and museums as partners who could help academic historians reach a broader audience. In particular, Young helped to develop a permanent exhibit on the revolutionary generation at the Chicago Historical Society, along with a vivid book (coauthored with Terry J. Fife and Mary E. Janzen), *We the People: Voices and Images of the New Nation* (1993).

Preoccupied by these collaborative projects in academic freedom, edited collections, material culture, and public history, Young struggled for the time to write another book, his study of Boston's working people in the making of the American Revolution. From an immense mass of notes and draft chapters, he did cull and polish several essays for publication in scattered venues. The best of the strong lot, "George Robert Twelves Hewes (1742–1840): A Boston Shoemaker and the Memory of the American Revolution," first appeared in 1981 in the scholarly journal *The William and Mary Quarterly* and was republished in 1999 as the core of a book, *The Shoemaker and the Tea Party: Memory and the American Revolution.*

A laboring man active in the street politics of the Revolution, Hewes lived for nearly a century, long enough to become celebrated as the oldest survivor of the Boston Tea Party. In two late-life interviews published by interlocutors, Hewes recalled casting the tea overboard side-by-side with John Hancock, the celebrated gentleman and Patriot. In fact, Hancock was not present. That contradiction would lead a lesser historian simply to dismiss Hewes's doddering memory, but in the discrepancy Young finds powerful and pivotal meaning. The elderly Hewes understood the Revolution as a symbolic moment of equality, when Hancock and other Patriot gentlemen needed, and worked beside, the common mechanics to resist British rule and to create a new republic.

The Hewes essay crystallizes the biographical method central to Young's scholarship. Uneasy with abstractions in isolation, he always grounds them in particular human lives recovered by painstaking and imaginative research in new or recondite sources bypassed by others. This approach refutes the double trap set by critics of the study of common people. On the one hand, they allege that too few documents survive. On the other hand, when sources do persist, such as Hewes's interviews, they disqualify the subject as unrepresentative, as exceptional. In this view, only the typical will do, and only the undocumented were typical. Young counters that common people often led extraordinary lives that defy our attempts to keep them anonymous and homogeneous. "Time and again, I was amazed at what you could find—if you only looked," he observes.

Young's long pursuit of common biography now finds consummation in his most daring book, *Masquerade: The Life and Times of Deborah Sampson, Continental Soldier.* This title will jar readers who assume that only men fought in the ranks during the War of the American Revolution. Dressed as a man and called "Robert Shurtliff," Deborah Sampson passed for seventeen months as a soldier in George Washington's army, seeing and surviving combat with the wounds to show for it. Nor was Sampson the only woman to attempt that feat—at least four others did so for brief periods, although American society considered it sinful and criminal to don the attire and pretend to the identity of the other gender. Not only did Sampson escape punishment, but she became a postwar celebrity: the featured speaker on a lecture tour; the subject of a popular memoir; and the belated beneficiary of a congressional pension for her war service.

Given this sensational story, why has Sampson's life so long eluded a full and scholarly biography? A part of the answer is that so few documents by or about her have survived and reached a public archive—a common difficulty for anyone researching an eighteenth-century woman from an obscure family. Despite a century of avid investigation by antiquarians and genealogists, followed now by Young's relentless energy and ingenuity as a researcher, we still possess only a few scraps directly by or about her. We have her diary from one revealing year, 1802–3; two letters to creditors; and several petitions to the Massachusetts state legislature or to Congress. No letter written to Sampson apparently survives, and only a handful of contemporary observations about her remain. There is a brief published address from her lecture tour and a much longer printed memoir, but close examination reveals that they are full of garish fictions and conventional stereotypes. Distorting like the mirror at a fun house, such sources can seem worse than nothing. On the one hand, they seduce the literal into believing that Sampson once sojourned among Indians, barely escaping cannibalism, and that she rescued a female prisoner by marrying her. Or they can lead the unimaginative scholar to despair, to dismiss such texts as too thoroughly soiled by deception to warrant close investigation for biographical fact. "What does a biographer do," Young asks, "when his subject speaks so rarely in her own voice and her voice is strained through an author who blurs fact and fiction?"

To peel away the layers of fiction in search of something like truth, who better than Alfred Young, given his masterly decoding of George Robert Twelves Hewes's tricky yet revealing memory? By extending his quest to women and the cultural operation of gender, Young seeks "to reconstruct a kind of life in the era of the American Revolution that has never been recovered." Indeed, here is the perfect case for Young's long-standing crusade to find the past of ordinary people and to rescue it from "the enormous condescension of posterity." Given Sampson's extremity as a documented cross-dressing soldier, critics would dismiss her as unrepresentative of anything common; but Young finds in her sensational story an illumination of the norms that she struggled against by making herself extraordinary.

If previous biographers noted the distortions in her memoir and address, they blamed them entirely on the editor, Herman Mann, cast as her exploiter seeking sensational effect. This interpretation reduces Sampson to his passive victim, in print as in life. Young applies a shrewder perspective, depicting Sampson as Mann's collaborator in crafting fictions meant to preserve her secrets. Indeed, she often misled Mann. "I could see where she was leading him around by the nose," Young observes. "Very skilled at deception," Sampson "spent a good part of her life guarding a persona that obscured herself." Far more than mere obstacles to finding the veracious Sampson, those deceptions became the very fabric of her life and are now the essence of her biography by Young. Possessed of a powerful personality, but constrained by a patriarchal society, Sampson expressed her agency by manipulating and deceiving others.

To glean facts from Mann's fictions, Young mines collateral sources about the context of Sampson's life: records kept by the towns where she lived, by the church she attended, and by the army she joined. Young also examines the objects she once touched, the houses she lived in, and the memories nurtured by her descendants. By "building up a body of independent evidence," he "constructed a template on which I might lay the flimsy pieces of evidence about her and weigh what was likely, possible, or improbable." He frankly admits: "Which is which, where to draw the line, is sometimes vexing, and I am not sure I always get it right." Inviting the reader into the process of evaluation, he explores the weaknesses as well as the strengths of his case, carefully distinguishing his speculations from his convictions.

Mann aptly characterized Sampson as a "young female of low birth and station" who rebelled against "a contracted female sphere." Although her maternal great-great-grandfather was Gov. William Bradford of the Plymouth Colony, the Bradfords and the Samsons (as her father spelled his name) had experienced a "downward mobility Americans have pushed out of their national myths." Sampson's father was a peripatetic farm laborer who abandoned the family in 1765, when she was five. Her indigent mother placed her in another household to labor as an indentured servant for room and board until age eighteen. Although denied access to schooling by her master, a conservative farmer, Sampson taught herself with borrowed books, developing her mind and enhancing her aspirations. Freed in 1778, in the midst of a revolution, she supported herself as a spinner of thread and a weaver of cloth, boarding in a succession of neighbors' houses in Middleborough, Massachusetts. "A woman without a master," Sampson was an exception in a society that expected females to live with either father or husband. A robust five-foot-seven, she was as tall and strong as most men, which, along with her impoverished means and her forceful personality, diminished her prospects for marriage.

She later explained her enlistment as an escape from a marriage arranged by her parents—a sure fiction. In fact, she ran away from a stultifying small town in search of the wider options enjoyed by young men with mobility. In general, the Revolution inspired obscure people to imagine and to pursue new possibilities, which alarmed the gentlemen who dominated legislatures and commanded the army. Her halfway house to personal revolution was a local Baptist church, which she joined in late 1780, shortly before her twentieth birthday. Baptists rejected the dominant and orthodox Congregational Church, which offered "an exquisite weekly instruction in the social ordering of the community by class, gender, age, and race." By comparison, the Baptists promoted a more spontaneous worship by egalitarian "brothers and sisters" within a plain meeting house without special, honored seating for an elite. While offering "a close-knit fellowship" of common men and women, the Middleborough Baptists also imposed a moral "discipline more severe than any she had known." She ran afoul of that discipline when she tried to enlist as a man in the spring of 1782. Quickly discovered, threatened with legal prosecution, and censured by her church, Deborah Sampson felt compelled to leave town.

In an age when women could not travel alone without sacrificing their respectability, Sampson redoubled her determination to pass as a man to escape Middleborough. Adopting the name Robert Shurtliff and walking to central Massachusetts, where she was a stranger, she enlisted in the Continental army on May 20, 1782. Desperate for soldiers, recruiting officers asked few questions and demanded no physical examination. Instead, they provided a uniform and a cash bonus (paid by local men to avoid conscription). She told none of this to Mann, obliging Young to recover it from church and military records. "She was," he concludes, "a person with enough of a sense of herself to become someone else."

But how did she sustain her deception for seventeen months of active service, often in the close quarters of military huts or under the physical and psychological duress of long marches and occasional firefights? Young argues that Sampson "accomplished her deception by becoming an outstanding soldier in the light infantry. . . . She hid herself as a woman . . . by standing out as a man." Despite Washington's great victory at Yorktown in October 1781, the British army persisted in occupying New York City into 1783, pending the negotiation of a peace treaty. In the interim, small-scale patrols and skirmishes persisted in the notorious "neutral ground" north of the city but south of Washington's lines in upper Westchester County. Most of the patrols and fighting fell to elite units, the light-infantry companies. On reaching Washington's army, Sampson immediately qualified for the light infantry because of her uncommon alertness, manifest intelligence, and physical strength.

Eager to please, she became a military paragon: responsive to orders, too self-disciplined to drink or swear, active under fire. "Ironically," Young notes, "the attributes needed to maintain her deception—to be alert, quick, and street smart—were the very ones that made her an ideal choice for the light infantry." She deflected scrutiny by winning the applause of her officers, who never expected that a model soldier could be a woman. It also helped her deception that so many of her fellow soldiers were "undersized, beardless boys" accepted by desperate recruiting officers. Far from standing out as weaker and smaller, she was conspicuous for her height, strength, and good conduct. And the slack sanitary standards of an eighteenth-century army spared Sampson from close attention to her body—even, apparently, when she suffered wounds.

During the winter of 1782–83, Sampson became an orderly attached to Gen. John Paterson, an appointment that reflected her officers' respect. In the spring of 1783, she accompanied Paterson to Philadelphia, where she became gravely ill with a crippling fever. In a military hospital, a doctor discovered her secret and informed Paterson, who proved surprisingly sympathetic, permitting Sampson to remain in uniform until her honorable discharge with the rest of her regiment in October 1783.

Why did she escape the punishment and humiliation visited on previous women discovered in uniform? Her timing was fortunate and her service, exemplary. With the war over and won, officers felt magnanimous, particularly toward a soldier who had served so well. "A rebel against the constraints of gender, as a soldier she was a conservative who sided with authority," Young observes. Overcompensating for her deception, she passed in a potentially hostile world—rather like a radical historian exceeding conservative dons in his attention to research detail.

On discharge, Sampson walked to eastern Massachusetts, still wearing men's clothing. She could hardly return to Middleborough, where neighbors and Baptists awaited with pent-up determination to punish and humiliate. Instead, she proceeded to Sharon, in an adjoining county, where she stayed with a sympathetic aunt. At some point in 1784, Sampson reverted to women's clothing. In the spring of 1785, she married, bearing her first child seven months later—at a time and in a region where premarital pregnancy was common.

At first glance, she seemed extraordinarily fortunate in her husband, Benjamin Gannett Jr., the eldest son of an especially prosperous farmer and town leader. Apparently, her disreputable past did not preclude an advantageous marriage by the standards of her culture. "If, however, she anticipated life as the wife of a prosperous yeoman, she must have been deeply disappointed," Young notes. Although the patriarch's firstborn and namesake, Benjamin Gannett Jr. hardly basked in paternal favor. Apparently of limited intellect, the younger Benjamin procured very little property from his disappointed and grudging father, who favored his other sons. A tax list from 1798 reveals that the couple possessed only forty-nine acres of hardscrabble land—barely enough to sustain a farm. In 1804, Paul Revere visited and reported: "They have a few acres of poor land, which they cultivate, but they are really poor." He added that Gannett Jr. was "of small force in business." Envious and mean in spirit, Benjamin Jr. brought even less joy to the marriage. Her later diary dwelled on her love for their three children, but did not even mention her husband. After 1790, at the age of thirty, she stopped bearing children, inspiring local gossip that she would no longer sleep with her husband.

Deeply frustrated, Deborah Sampson Gannett reached within her own formidable resources to rescue her material aspirations. Herman Mann explained that she possessed an "ambitious disposition" and a "taste for a more elevated stile of life" than Benjamin could provide. Rather than hide her military service in conventional shame, during the 1790s, she began to highlight it for financial gain. In 1792, she boldly petitioned the Massachusetts state legislature for her back pay as a soldier. Far from dismissing her request, the legislators awarded the money, accompanied by their praise for her courage and virtue.

She then enlisted Herman Mann, an ambitious and impressionable young schoolteacher, to write her life story, which he published in 1797. Although an English woman, Hannah Snell, had published an account of military service in 1750, nothing like it had appeared in America, where the rare biographies of women dwelled on their passivity and piety as exemplars. Women were supposed to avoid calling attention to themselves, but Deborah Sampson Gannett pushed into print, accompanied by an engraving of her likeness commissioned by Mann. Feminine in attire, she bravely gazes directly back at the reader within a frame of musket, sword, battle flags, and American eagle. Although filled with absurdities and badly composed, the book sold its entire run of fifteen hundred copies, lifting "her from local notoriety to the status of a regional celebrity."

Proudly bearing copies of the book, she traveled to New York City, brazenly to introduce herself to the poet Philip Freneau, who had excellent political connections. Something of a radical, Freneau warmed to her bold self-promotion. No fool and no shrinking violet, Sampson sought nothing less than a literary lion and political activist to craft her petition to Congress for a pension. But very few veterans got pensions unless they could prove both a dependence on charity and a crippling disability as a consequence of war wounds or hardships. Despite her eloquent petition, Sampson had a rather weak case—given that her husband owned a farm and she could travel to New York without evident difficulty. Still, Young sees her petition as "an assertion of the right of a woman to equal treatment regardless of her marital status." Ill-prepared for such an assertion, Congress rejected her request.

Undaunted, persistent, and ingenious, she took her cause on the road, organizing a speaking tour that, in 1802–3, traversed New England and eastern New York. She covered about a thousand miles and delivered at least twenty lectures to paying audiences (admission cost twenty-five cents). Never before had an American woman staged a public lecture tour, defying the convention that women should remain at home away from a viewing public if they meant to enjoy respectability. "As America's first itinerant woman orator," Young explains, "Deborah Sampson Gannett was even more of a pioneer than she was as a woman soldier." Not only did she tour alone and speak publicly, but she also donned her military uniform and occasionally dazzled audiences with her dexterity at handling a musket through the complicated maneuvers of the manual of arms. A shrewd manager and promoter, she posted notices in local newspapers and disseminated handbills presenting "Mrs. Gannett (Late Deborah Sampson), The American Heroine." Her masterly address began with a modest apology that her military service was "a breach in the decorum of my sex unquestionably," but then asserted vindication on the grounds of an overwhelming, irresistible patriotism.

For this tour we have, at last, a detailed source in her own hand: a diary detailing her expenditures and offering observations. She effused at the acceptance she won from audiences of genteel people. Relieved at escaping catcalls, she basked in her greatest coup: enhancing her respectability while performing as a woman who had dressed as a man. She even won warm welcomes from former officers, including General Paterson, who hosted her for a happy month. Above all, Young observes, "the diary reveals a physical stamina, a willingness to take risks, a capacity to be on her own, a perseverance, a resourcefulness, and an attention to minute detail, as well as her social skills, befriending and charming strangers."

By promoting her celebrity, the tour strengthened her renewed bid, in late 1803, for a congressional pension. This time she succeeded, securing $4 a month, apparently thanks to critical support from Paterson, who had won election to Congress from New York. In 1809, she boldly asked for more, seeking a retroactive pension to begin from her discharge in 1783, a lump sum (including interest) of $960—enough to buy a farm. To support that extraordinary claim, she insisted that she had been crippled by wounds during the war and was unable to work. Congress refused that bid, but in 1821, she sought, and secured, a larger pension, raising her monthly pay to $8—a large cash income for a woman. Admiring her persistence, Young concludes that, if her husband was "'of small force in business,' she was of large force."

Of Herman Mann, Young writes: "He clearly was taken by her, and at times, as we have seen, he was taken in." Young is also clearly taken by Sampson, an assertive woman and war veteran who refused to accept the constraints of gender and poverty. Is he also taken in by her? For most of the book, he subjects her claims to a careful, and critical scrutiny. But in the end he, too, succumbs to her charm. In seeking a $960 payment, Sampson asked for far more than Congress customarily granted to other veterans who were truly crippled. Far from being disabled, as she claimed, Sampson could travel a thousand miles to deliver twenty lectures. In petitioning Congress, she also deceived by claiming to have fought at the celebrated battle of Yorktown (fought six months before she enlisted). Yet Young treats the congressional rejection as a great injustice.

He also accepts her special pleading in pension applications of persistent poverty in her later years. In fact, her pension combined with an inheritance from Benjamin Gannett Sr., who died in 1813, to improve her material circumstances substantially. When the patriarch died, he bestowed most of his land on his grandson, Earl Bradford Gannett. As the son of Deborah and Benjamin Gannett Jr., Earl shared the benefits of the property with his parents, who moved into a new and much larger house on the premises. That house permitted the display of middle-class gentility: a parlor with tea set and landscaping with willow trees. An 1813 tax list valued Earl's new property at $1,013 and his father's share at $781—assessments that placed both men near the median property holding in Sharon. But Young seems determined to keep Deborah poor to the very end by mustering Earl's own probate inventory from 1845 (eighteen years after she died) to reveal "how little wealth two generations of Gannetts had accumulated since 1813." On the contrary, the inventory reveals a farm of 121 acres valued at $2,585 plus $220 in household property. For Sharon in 1845, that farm must have been above average in both size and value. And it certainly represented more than a doubling over the value recorded on the 1813 tax list.

Sampson achieved her dreams of middle-class gentility, thanks to her own abilities, her persistence, and her guile. Transcending skeptical neighbors and an inept husband, she wrested more from Congress than did other veterans. Her secret was her bravura performance as the impoverished and disabled soldier. With consummate skill, she charmed and manipulated genteel patrons, including Paul Revere, who attested to her poverty and lent her money. By recognizing her persistent manipulation of appearances, Young would have strengthened his fundamental case that she was no victim. Then again, by captivating her historian—and a new generation of readers—Deborah Sampson renews her extraordinary ability to escape from the constraints of her gender and her class. To do so, she had to deceive—not once, but throughout her life and beyond.

# Index

# Acknowledgments

In addition to Marvin Meyers, I dedicate this collection to Harold B. Raymond, my undergraduate teacher at Colby College. Quiet and reflective in personal conversation, Hal could light up a classroom with his wry wit, keen intelligence, humane sensibility, and uncanny dramatic timing. It was my great good fortune to enjoy dozens of hours of his personal attention as I pursued an individual tutorial and a senior thesis: experiences that developed and deepened my love for historical research and for crafting narratives. Without his encouragement and counsel, I could never have become a historian. As a teacher, I think every day of Hal and hope someday to match his generosity of spirit and his ability to nurture students.

I am especially grateful to Leon Wieseltier for the opportunity to write for *The New Republic,* for his patience with my early reviews, and for the careful editing that has taught me a great deal about writing. At that magazine, Ruth Franklin, Erin Leib, and Deborah Friedell have also given generously of their time and assistance, smoothing the process of publication in innumerable ways.

Many friends have provided generous moral support, but I especially wish to thank Rachel Klein, Jan Lewis (and Barry), Michael Meranze, and, of course, His Majesty Clarence Walker. By writing a thoughtful foreword for this collection, Chris Clark has compounded the many debts I already owe for his generosity and scholarly example.

At the University of Pennsylvania Press, Peter Agree conceived of this project and carefully shepherded the collection to fruition. The Associate Managing Editor, Erica Ginsburg, patiently and ably improved the final revision. And I am indebted to the sage and efficient literary representation of Andrew Wylie, assisted by Elena Schneider.

And all thanks go to Emily Albu, who daily strives to leaven my Maine edge with her boundless Ohio kindness and good cheer.

Lightning Source UK Ltd.
Milton Keynes UK
UKHW010920280922
409568UK00001B/67

9 780812 219104